THE SOVEREIGN STATES
BY
ZETH KRAUSE

Part 1
The Sovereign States

1. The Beginnings
2. The State
3. The Articles of Confederation
4. "We the People"
5. The States in the Constitution
6. The Prophetic Mr. Henry
7. The States Ratify

Part 2
The Right to Interpose

1. A Cast of Characters
2. The Chisholm Case
3. Debt Assumption
4. The Kentucky and Virginia Resolutions
5. Mr. Madison's Report of 1799

Part 3
The States Fight Back

1. The Olmstead Case
2. The Case of the Lands of Lord Fairfax
3. The Embargo Crisis
4. Matters of the Militia
5. Events of 1814
6. The Hartford Convention
7. The Bank of the United States
8. Internal Improvements
9. Kentucky vs. the Court
10. Georgia vs. the Court
11. Calhoun and Nullification
12. The Case for Nullification

13. **The Personal Liberty Laws**
14. **The Obligation of Contracts**
15. **After the War**
16. **The Reconstruction Cases**
17. **The Commerce Clause (Commenced)**
18. **Interlude in a Speakeasy**
19. **The Commerce Clause (Continued)**

Part 4
The States Today

1. **The Southern States**
2. **Some Notes on the Fourteenth Amendment**
3. **Some Notes on Police Power**
4. **The Transcendent Issue**

> The States within the limitations of their powers not granted, or, in the language of the Tenth Amendment, "reserved," are as independent of the general government as the general government, within its sphere, is independent of the States.
>
> —JUSTICE SAMUEL NELSON
> *Collector vs. Day* (1871)

1

The Beginnings

"THE TRUE DISTINCTION," said Mr. Pendleton, with some irritation, "is that the two governments are established for different purposes, and act on different objects."[1]

This was on the sunny afternoon of Thursday, June 13, 1788, in the New Academy on Shockoe Hill in Richmond. The Virginia Convention had been grappling for ten days with the new Constitution, and Edmund Pendleton, aging and crippled, had been sitting in dignified silence for as long as he could stand it. Patrick Henry, who was a hard man to live with at any time, was being especially difficult. Once before, on the 5th, Pendleton had attempted to sooth him, but Henry was not to be soothed.

The State and Federal governments would be at war with one another, Henry had predicted, and the State governments ultimately would be destroyed and consolidated into the general government. One by one their powers would be snatched from them. A rapacious Federal authority, ever seeking to expand its grasp, could not be confined by the States.

"Notwithstanding what the worthy gentleman said," remarked Mr. Pendleton with some warmth, for there were times when he regarded Mr. Henry as neither worthy nor a gentleman. "I believe I am still correct, and insist that, if each power is confined within its proper bounds, and to its proper objects, an interference can never happen. Being for two different purposes, as long as they are limited to the different objects, they can no more clash than two parallel lines can meet. . . ."

They were big ifs that Edmund Pendleton, a judicious man, here used as qualifications. If the State and Federal governments were each confined within its proper bounds, he said, the clash could never come. But the Federal government could not be kept confined, even as Henry feared, and the clash did come. It continues to this day. Mr. Pendleton's geometry was fine, but his powers of prophecy (for he believed that each government could be kept in check) were sadly in error.

To understand how the parallel lines of State and Federal powers have turned awry, it is necessary to look back at the period before these lines were drawn. The acts of ratification by Virginia and her neighbors were acts of sovereign States. At stake was their consent to a written constitution. How, it may be inquired, did they come to be "sovereign States"? What is this concept of State sovereignty?

It would be possible, in any such review, to go back to the great roots of Runnymede, but it will suffice to begin much later, in the turbulent summer of 1776. The startling commitments of Lexington and Concord were behind us then; the bitter trials of White Plains, Vincennes, Camden, and Yorktown still lay ahead. March and April and May had passed—a time of bringing forth, of newness, of fresh hope#151;and great human events had run their course. Now, in June, a resurgent people made the solemn decision *to dissolve the political bands which had connected them with another.* Thus Jefferson's draft began, thus the Continental Congress adopted it at Philadelphia; from this moment Americans unborn were to date the years of their independence.

The eloquent beginning of the <u>Declaration</u>—the assertion of truths self-evident and rights beyond alienation—is well known: It is a towering irony that Jefferson, whose convictions were cemented in the *in*equality of man, should have his precise phrase corrupted by the levellers of a bulldozer society. The Declaration's beginning is too much recited and too little read.

What counts, for our present purpose, is not the first paragraph, but the last. Let us inquire, What, precisely, was it that we declared ourselves to be that Fourth of July? Hitherto there had been colonies subject to the King. That form of government would now be abolished. We would now solemnly publish and declare to a candid world—what? That the people of the colonies had formed a free and independent *nation?* By no means. Or that they were henceforth a free and independent *people?* Still no.

This was the declaration: "That these United Colonies are, and of Right ought to be, FREE AND INDEPENDENT STATES." Not one State, or one nation, but in the plural—*States;* and again, in the next breath, so this multiple birth could not be misunderstood, "that as Free and Independent States, they have full Power to levy War, conclude Peace, contract Alliances, establish Commerce, and to do all other Acts and Things which Independent States may of right do."[2]

It had opened, this Declaration, as an enunciation of what often are termed the "human rights," but it concluded, in the plainest terms, as a pronouncement of political powers—the political powers of newly created States. And these powers of war and peace, these powers of alliance and commerce, were published not as the powers of a national government, but as powers henceforth asserted by thirteen free and independent States.

To be sure, the States were united. Their representatives styled themselves representatives of the united States of America, in Congress assembled, but it was not the spokesmen of a nation who gathered in parliament. These were States in Congress. "One out of many," it is said. In a sense, yes. But the many remained—separate States, individual entities, each possessed, from that moment, of sovereign rights and powers.

Certainly Jefferson so understood our creation. "The several States," he was to write much later, "were, from their first establishment, separate and distinct societies, dependent on no other society of men whatever."[3]

So Mr. Justice Samuel Chase comprehended it: He considered the Declaration of Independence, "as a declaration, not that the united colonies jointly, in a collective capacity, were independent States, etc., but that *each* of them was a sovereign and independent State, that is, that each of them had a right to govern itself by its own authority, and its own laws without any control from any other power on earth." From the Fourth of July, said Chase, "the American States were *de facto* as well as *de jure* in the possession and actual exercise of all the rights of independent governments. . . . I have ever considered it as the established doctrine of the United States, that their independence originated from, and commenced with, the declaration of Congress, on the Fourth of July, 1776; and that no other period can be fixed on for its commencement; and that all laws made by the legislatures of the several States, after the Declaration of Independence, were the laws of sovereign and independent governments."[4]

So, too, the sage and cool-minded Mr. Justice Cushing: "The several States which composed this Union . . . became entitled, from the time when they declared themselves independent, to all the rights and powers of sovereign States."[5]

Even Marshall himself had no doubts: In the beginning, "we were divided into independent States, united for some purposes, but in most respects sovereign."[6] The lines which separate the States, he later remarked, were too clear ever to be misunderstood.

And for a contemporary authority, it is necessary only to turn to Mr. Justice Frankfurter, who some years ago fell to discussing the dual powers of taxation preserved under the Constitution: "The States," he said, "after *they* formed the Union"—not the people, but the *States,* "continued to have the same range of taxing power which they had before, barring only duties affecting exports, imports, and on tonnage."[7] Regrettably, Mr. Justice Frankfurter appears in more recent times to have lost his concept of States forming a Union.

It is no matter. Evidence of the States' individual sovereignty is abundantly available. Consider, for example, the powers asserted on the part of each State in the Declaration "to levy War, conclude Peace, and contract Alliances." Surely these are sovereign powers. The States exercised them, as States, in the Revolutionary War. But it is of value to note that New York also very nearly exercised her war powers to enter into formal hostilities with the State of Vermont. Tensions reached so grave a point that Massachusetts, in 1784, felt compelled to adopt a formal resolution of neutrality, enjoining her citizens to give "no aid or assistance to either party," and to send "no provisions, arms, or ammunition or other necessities to a fortress or garrison" besieged by either belligerent. When New York adopted a resolution avowing her readiness to "recur to force," Vermont's Governor Chittenden (whose son was to be heard from thirty years later in another row) observed that Vermont "does not wish to enter into a war with the State of New York." But should this unhappy contingency result, Vermont "expects that Congress and the twelve States will observe a strict neutrality, and let the contending States settle their own controversy."

They did settle it, of course. New York and Vermont concluded a peace. The point is that no one saw anything especially remarkable in two separate sovereignties arraying themselves against each other. Vermont was then an individual political entity, as remote at law as any France or Italy. And New York, though a member of the Confederation, and hence technically required to obtain the consent of Congress before waging war, had every right to maintain a standing army for her own defense.

The status of the individual States as separate sovereign powers was recognized on higher authority than the proclamations of Vermont and Massachusetts. It is worth our while to keep in mind the first article of the treaty of September 3, 1783, by which the War of the Revolution came to an end:

His Britannic Majesty acknowledges the said United States, viz., New Hampshire, Massachusetts Bay, Rhode Island and Providence Plantations, Connecticut, New York, New Jersey, Pennsylvania, Delaware, Maryland, Virginia, North Carolina, South Carolina and Georgia to be free, sovereign and independent States; that he treats with them as such.

More than five years earlier, a treaty of amity and commerce with France had established the same sovereign status of the contracting parties. Louis XVI treated with the thirteen American States, but he recognized each of them as a separate power. And it is interesting to note that Virginia, feeling some action desirable to complete the treaty, prior to action by Congress, on June 4, 1779, undertook solemnly to ratify this treaty with France on her own. By appropriate resolution, transmitted by Governor Jefferson to the French minister at Philadelphia, the sovereign Commonwealth of Virginia declared herself individually bound by the French treaty.(8) In terms of international law, Virginia was a nation; in terms of domestic law, she was a sovereign State.

Notes

Go to top.

2

The State

TO REVIEW the process by which the colonies became States is not necessarily to answer the basic question, What is a *State?* It is a troublesome word. The standard definition is that a State is "a political body, or body politic; any body of people occupying a definite territory and politically organized under one government, especially one that is not subject to external control." Chief Justice Chase, in *Texas vs. White*,(9) put it this way: "A State, in the ordinary sense of the Constitution, is a political community of free citizens, occupying a territory of defined boundaries, and organized under a government sanctioned and limited by a written Constitution, and established by the consent of the governed." In the Cherokee case, John Marshall described a State as "a distinct political society, separated from others, capable of managing its own affairs and governing itself."(10)

Thus, variously, a State is defined as a body, a community, and a distinct society. Plainly, mere boundary lines are not enough; a tract of waste and uninhabited land cannot constitute a State. Nor are people, as such, sufficient to constitute a State. James Brown Scott once offered this clear and succinct definition:

The State is an artificial person, representing and controlled by its members, but not synonymous or identical with them. Created for a political purpose, it is a body politic. It is a distinct body, an artificial person; it has a will distinct from its members, although its exercise is controlled by them; it has rights and duties distinct from its members, but subject to being changed by them; it may hold property distinct from its members, but in trust for them; it may act separately and distinctly from them and bind them by its acts, but only insofar as it is authorized by the law of its creation, and subject to being changed by the source of that power.(11)

Thus the State is seen as a continuing political being, controlled by its citizens and yet controlling them. The State can be bound in ways that its own people cannot be bound; it can exercise powers that no citizen or group of citizens may exercise for themselves. The State may buy, sell, hold, grant, convey; it may tax and spend; it may sue, and if it consent, be sued; it exists to create law and to execute law, to punish crime, administer justice, regulate commerce, enter into compacts with other States. Yet there is no State until a community of human beings create a State; and no State may exist without the will and the power of human beings to preserve it.

It is this combination of will and power which lies at the essence of the State in being. This is sovereignty. In the crisp phrase of John Taylor of Caroline, sovereignty is "the will to enact, the power to execute."(12) Long books have been written on the nature of sovereignty, but they boil down to those necessities: The will to make, the power to unmake.(13)

It was this power, this will, that the people-as-States claimed for themselves in 1776. Henceforth, they said, we are sovereign: The State government is not sovereign, nor is any citizen by himself sovereign. By the "sovereign State" we mean we citizens, the State; we collectively, within our established boundaries; this community of people; we alone who are possessed of the power to create or to abandon.

God knows it was a great, a priceless, power these people-as-States claimed for themselves. True, not everyone saw it that way. Mr. Justice Story, for one, never grasped the concept of States. Nor did Jackson. Albert J. Beveridge, in his biography of Marshall, refers sneeringly to the States as "these pompous sovereignties," but in a way, Beveridge's is perhaps a high acknowledgment of the simple truth: These infant States *were* sovereignties, and the people within them were proudly jealous of the fact. They saw themselves, in Blackstone's phrase, "a supreme, irresistible, absolute, uncontrolled authority."(14) This, among other things, was the aim they had fought for. It cannot be imagined that they ever would have relinquished this high power of sovereignty except in the most explicit terms.

Notes

Go to top.

3

The Articles of Confederation

IN TIME, the Continental Congress gave way to the Articles of Confederation. The Articles merit examination with the utmost care; they are too little studied, and there is much to be learned from them.

First proposed in 1778, the Articles became binding upon all the States with Maryland's ratification in 1781. Throughout this period, as the war ran on, each of the States was individually sovereign, each *wholly* autonomous. Mr. Justice Iredell was to observe, in 1795, that had the individual States decided not to unite together, each would have gone its own way, because each "possessed all the powers of sovereignty, internal and external . . . as completely as any of the ancient kingdoms or republics of the world, which never yet had formed, or thought of forming, any sort of Federal union whatever."(15)

But they did form a Federal union—a "perpetual union between the States of New Hampshire, Massachusetts Bay, Rhode Island and Providence Plantations, Connecticut, New York, New Jersey, Pennsylvania, Delaware, Maryland, Virginia, North Carolina, South Carolina, and Georgia." They styled themselves, "The United States of America," and in the very second article of their compact, they put this down so no one might miss it:

Each State retains its sovereignty, freedom, and independence, and every power, jurisdiction, and right, which is not by this Confederation expressly delegated to the United States in Congress assembled.(16)

The third article is almost equally brief, and may be quoted in less space than would be required to summarize it:

The said States hereby severally enter into a firm league of friendship with each other, for their common defense, the security of their liberties, and their mutual and general welfare, binding themselves to assist each other against all force offered to, or attacks made upon them, or any of them, on account of religion, sovereignty, trade, or any other pretence whatever.

There will be seen, in these opening paragraphs, the genesis of Constitutional provisions that were to follow in less than a decade. Here is the forerunner of the Tenth Amendment, with its reservation of undelegated powers to the States or to the people; here are the aims set forth of "common defense" and the "general welfare."

The Fourth Article advanced other phrases that have come down to us: The free inhabitants of each State ("paupers, vagabonds and fugitives from justice excepted") were to be entitled to "all the privileges and immunities of free citizens in the several States." Here, too, one finds the provision, later to be inserted substantially verbatim in Article IV of the Constitution of 1787, providing for the extradition of fugitives. Here the States mutually agreed that "full faith and credit shall be given in each of these States to the records, acts, and judicial proceedings of the courts and magistrates of every other State."

The fifth Article provided for representation of the States in Congress. There were to be no less than two, no more than seven delegates from each State. They would assemble on the first Monday in November of every year. In this Congress, each State cast one vote; each State paid the salary and maintenance of its own delegates. These provisions, of course, were later abandoned; but we may note that the Fifth Article prohibited delegates to the Congress from "holding any office under the United States for which he or another for his benefit receives any salary, fees, or emolument of any kind," and also provided that "freedom of speech and debate in Congress shall not be impeached or questioned in any court or place out of Congress." Both provisions were to turn up later in Article I, Section 6, of the Constitution.

The Sixth and Seventh Articles dealt generally with limitations upon the States in terms of foreign affairs and the waging of war. Again, many a familiar phrase leaps from this much maligned compact of Confederation. No State, nor the Congress, was to grant a title of nobility; no two or more States were to enter into any treaty, confederation or alliance without the consent of the other States in Congress assembled; no State was to keep vessels of war in time of peace ("except such number as shall be deemed necessary by the United States in Congress assembled"), nor was any State to engage in war without the consent of Congress "unless such State be actually invaded by enemies, or . . . the danger is so imminent as not to admit of a delay. . . ."

The Eighth Article provided for defraying the expenses of war among the States "in proportion to the value of all land within each State," and the Ninth Article dealt with the powers of Congress. Once more, the origin of a dozen specific phrases in our present Constitution is evident. Congress was given the "sole and exclusive right and power of determining on peace and war." It was to enter into treaties and alliances, establish certain courts, fix standard weights and measures, and establish post offices.(17) But the Congress alone could do almost none of these things—it could exercise no important power—without the consent of nine of the member States.

The remaining four articles are of less interest and concern, though it may be noted that in three places, the framers of the Articles of Confederation provided that their union was a permanent union. The articles were to be inviolably observed by the States the delegates respectively represented, "and the Union shall be perpetual."

Notes

Go to top.

4

"We the People"

OF COURSE, it wasn't perpetual at all. Before six years had elapsed, the States came to recognize grave defects in the Articles of Confederation. And because they were sovereign States—because they had the will to enact and the power to execute, *because they who had made could unmake*—they set out to do the job again.

What they made, this time, was the Constitution of the United States. So much has been written of the deliberations that summer of 1787 in

Philadelphia—so many critics have examined every word of the great document which came forth—that probably no new light can be shed upon it here. Yet the Constitutions of most States command their citizens to recur frequently to fundamental principles, and the commandment is too valuable an admonition to be passed by. There is much of interest to be found if one examines the Constitution, the debates and the commentaries of the time, *in terms of the relationship there established between the States and the new Federal government they formed.*

It may be inquired, was sovereignty here surrendered in whole or in part? What powers were delegated, what powers retained? What were the functions to be performed by the States in the future? Was it ever intended that the States should be reduced to the weakling role thrust upon them in our own time? We must inquire whether this proud possession of State sovereignty, so eloquently proclaimed in 1776, so resolutely affirmed in the Articles of 1781, so clearly recognized in the events of the time, somehow vanished, died, turned to dust, totally ceased to exist in the period of the next six years.

Now, the argument here advanced is this—it is the argument of John Taylor of Caroline and John Randolph of Roanoke—that sovereignty, like chastity, cannot be surrendered "in part." This was the argument also of Calhoun: "I maintain that sovereignty is in its nature indivisible. It is the supreme power in a State, and we might just as well speak of half a square, or half a triangle, as of half a sovereignty."(18) This was the position, too, of the bellicose George Troup of Georgia, of Alexander H. Stephens, of Jefferson Davis. It is the position of plain common sense: Supreme and ultimate power must be precisely that. Finality knows no degrees. In law, as in mountain climbing, there comes a point at which the pinnacle is reached; nothing higher or greater remains. And so it is with the States of the American Union. In the last resort, it is *their* prerogative alone (not that of Congress, not that of the Supreme Court, not that of the "whole people") to make or unmake our fundamental law. The argument here is that the States, in forming a new perpetual union to replace their old perpetual union, remained in essence what they had been before: Separate, free, and independent States. They *surrendered* nothing to the Federal government they created. *Some of their powers they delegated; all of their sovereignty they retained.*

It is keenly important that this distinction be understood. There is a difference between "sovereignty" and "sovereign power." The power to coin money, or to levy taxes, is a sovereign power, but it is not sovereignty. Powers can be delegated, limited, expanded, or withdrawn, but it is through the exercise of sovereignty that these changes take place. Sovereignty is the moving river; sovereign powers the stone at the mill. Only while the river flows can the inanimate stone revolve. To be sure, sovereignty can be lost— it can be lost by conquest, as in war; the extent or character of sovereignty can be changed, as in the acquisition or relinquishment of territory or the annexation of new peoples; sovereignty can be divided, when two States are created of one. But properly viewed, sovereignty is cause; sovereign powers, the effect: The wind that blows; the branches that move. Sovereignty is the essence, the life spirit, the soul: And in this Republic, sovereignty remains today where it was vested in 1776, in the people. But in the people as a whole? No. In the *people-as-States*.

The delusion that sovereignty is vested in the whole people of the United States is one of the strangest misconceptions of our public life. This hallucination has been encouraged, if not directly espoused, by such eminent figures as Marshall, Story, and Andrew Jackson. It is still embraced by excessively literal and unthinking fellows who read "we the people" in the preamble to the Constitution, and cry triumphantly, "that means everybody!" It does not; it never did.

The preamble to the abandoned Articles of Confederation, it was noted, declared the articles "binding between the States of New Hampshire, Massachusetts Bay, Rhode Island and Providence Plantations, Connecticut, New York," and so forth. The preamble offered by the Convention of 1787, reads:

We the People of the United States, in Order to form a more perfect Union, establish Justice, insure domestic Tranquility, provide for the common defence, promote the general Welfare, and secure the Blessings of Liberty to ourselves and our Posterity, do ordain and establish this Constitution for the United States of America.

The opening few words were questioned repeatedly by Patrick Henry in the Virginia Convention of 1788. He kept asking, querulously, what was meant by "we the people," but he got no very satisfactory answer for his pains. (19) Governor Randolph ducked the question,(20)and Pendleton missed the point. Pendleton asked, rhetorically, "who but the people have a right to form government?" and the answer, obviously, in America, is "no one." Then Pendleton said this:

If the objection be, that the Union ought to be not of the people, but of the State governments, then I think the choice of the former very happy and proper. What have the State governments to do with it?(21)

Again, the obvious answer is, "the State governments have nothing to do with it," but *that was not the question Henry asked.* There is a plain distinction between "we the States" and "we the State governments," for States endure while governments fall. It was Madison who came closest to answering the insistent Henry. Who are the parties to the Constitution? The people, said Madison, to be sure, are the parties to it, but *"not the people as composing one great body."* Rather, it is *"the people as composing thirteen sovereignties."* And he added:

Were it . . . a consolidated government, the assent of a majority of the people would be sufficient for its establishment; and, as a majority have adopted it already, we remaining States would be bound by the act of the majority, even if they unanimously reprobated it.... But, sir, no State is bound by it, as it is, without its own consent.(22)

Colonel Henry Lee took the same point of view in responding to Patrick Henry. Light Horse Harry spoke as other proponents of the Constitution did, in irritation and perplexity. He could not comprehend why Henry's question should even be asked. Obviously, the "we the people" mentioned in the preamble—the "we the people" there and then engaged in ratifying the Constitution—were we "the people of Virginia." If the people of Virginia "do not adopt it, it will always be null and void as to us."(23)

Here Lee touched and tossed aside what doubtless was so clear to others that they could not understand what Henry was quibbling about. Of course, "we the people" meant what Madison and Lee found so obvious: It meant "we the people *of the States*." Why argue the point? "I take this," said Randolph testily, "to be one of the least and most trivial objections that will be made to the Constitution."(24)

The self-evident fact, as plain as the buttons on their coats, was that the *whole* people, the mass of people from Georgia to New Hampshire, obviously had nothing to do with the ratification of the Constitution. The basic charter of our Union never was submitted to popular referendum, taken simultaneously among the 3,000,000 inhabitants of the country on some Tuesday in 1788. Ratification was achieved by the people of the States, acting in their sovereign capacity not as "Americans," for there is no "State of America," but in their sovereign capacity as citizens of the States of Massachusetts, New York, Virginia, and Georgia.

This was the sovereign power that sired the new Union, breathed upon it, gave it life—the power of the people of the States, acting as States, binding themselves as States, seeking to form a more perfect union not of people but of States. And if it be inquired, as a matter of drafting, why the preamble of the Articles of Confederation spelled out thirteen States and the preamble of the Constitution referred only to "we the people," a simple, uncomplicated explanation may be advanced: The framers of the Constitution, in the Summer of 1787, *had no way of knowing how many States would assent to the compact.*

Suppose they had begun the preamble, as they thought of doing, "We the people of New Hampshire, Massachusetts Bay, Rhode Island," etc., and the State of Rhode Island had refused to ratify?

It very nearly did. It was not until May 29, 1790, by a vote of 34-32, that Rhode Island agreed to join a union that actually had been created with New Hampshire's ratification nearly two full years before. Given a switch of two votes, Rhode Island might have remained, to this day, as foreign to the

United States (in terms of international law) as any Luxembourg or Switzerland.

Some of these forebodings clearly passed through the minds of the delegates at Philadelphia. When the preamble first appears in the notes, on August 6, it reads: "We the people of the States of New Hampshire, Massachusetts," etc., "do ordain, declare and establish the following Constitution." In that form it was tentatively approved on August 7. But the preamble, in that form, never is mentioned again. When the document came back from the Committee on Style in early September, the preamble had been amended to eliminate the spelled-out names of States, and to make it read simply that "we the people" ordain and establish. The change was not haggled over. No significance was attached to it. Why arouse antagonism in New York or North Carolina (where there was opposition enough already) by presuming to speak, in the preamble, as if it were unnecessary for New York or North Carolina even to debate the matter? The tactful and prudent thing was to name no States. Only the people-as-States could create the Union; only the people in ratifying States would be bound, as States, by its provisions.

Notes

Go to top.

5

The States in the Constitution

IN THE end, that was the way the compact read. It bound States—"The ratification of the Conventions of nine States shall be sufficient for the establishment of this Constitution between"—between whom?—"*between the States so ratifying the same.*" Not among people; it was "between States." And this proposal was put forward "by the unanimous consent," not of delegates assembled or of people gathered, but by "the unanimous consent of the States present the 17th day of September in the year of our Lord 1787...."

On the plain evidence of the instrument itself, it is therefore clear: States consented to the drafting of the Constitution; States undertook to bind themselves by its provisions. If nine States ratified, the Constitution would bind those nine; if ten, those ten. Rhode Island had not even attended the convention; "poor, despised Rhode Island," as Patrick Henry later was to describe her, could stay aloof if she chose. There was no thought here of people in the mass. There was thought only of people-as-States, and while the new Constitution would of course act directly upon people—that was to be its revolutionary change—it would reach those people *only because they first were people-of-States.*

The one essential prerequisite was for the State, as a State, to ratify; then the people of the State would become themselves subject to the Constitution. No individual human being, in his own capacity, possibly could assent to the new compact or bind himself to its provisions. Only as a citizen of Virginia or Georgia or Massachusetts could he become a citizen also of the United States.

Madison recognized this. He acknowledged in his famed *Federalist 39* that ratification of the Constitution must come from the people "not as individuals composing one entire nation, but as composing the distinct and independent States to which they respectively belong." Each State, he said, in ratifying the Constitution, "is considered as a sovereign body, independent of all others, and only to be bound by its own voluntary act." This fact lay at the essence of the *Federal* union being formed. The States, and within them their local governments, were to be "no more subject, within their respective spheres, to the general authority, than the general authority is subject to them, within its own sphere." The jurisdiction of the Federal government was to extend "to certain enumerated objects only, and leaves to the several States a residuary and inviolable sovereignty over all other objects."(25) Even the most casual reading of the Constitution, it may be submitted, abundantly supports Madison's comment here.

But the Constitution ought not to be read casually. Viewed from the standpoint of State and Federal relations, what does the Constitution say and do? The rubrics do not demand, before an ordinary mortal may explore the question, that he be ordained a Constitutional lawyer or put on the chasuble of the bench. Our Constitution is not the property of a juridical clergy only. The laity may read it too, and with equal acuity and understanding. The terms are not ambiguous.

The first thing to note, perhaps, is that the words "State" or "States" appear no fewer than ninety-four times, either as proper nouns or pronominals, in the brief six thousand words of the original seven articles. The one theme that runs steadily through the whole of the instrument is the knitting together of States: It is a union that is being formed, and while the people are concerned for themselves and their posterity, the Constitution is to be established binding States.

Legislative powers, to begin at the beginning, are vested not in one national parliament of the people, but in a Congress of the United States. The word *Congress* was chosen with precision; it repeated and confirmed the political relationship of the preceding eleven years, when there had been first a Continental Congress and then a Congress under the Articles of Confederation.

This Congress is to consist of two houses. The first is the House of Representatives, whose members are to be chosen "by the people of the several States." And here, in the very second paragraph, the framers encountered an opportunity to choose between a "national" and a "federal" characteristic: They might have established uniform national qualifications for the franchise, but they did not. Electors qualified to vote for candidates for the House of Representatives are to have "the Qualifications requisite for Electors of the most numerous Branch of the State Legislature."

Representatives and direct taxes are to be apportioned—how? "Among the several States which may be included within this Union, according to their respective Numbers." How is this enumeration to be determined? The provision should be noted with care, for it is the first of four clauses that speaks eloquently of the plural nature of our Union: "The actual Enumeration shall be made within three Years after the first Meeting of the Congress of the United States, and within every subsequent Term of ten Years, in such Manner as *they* shall by Law direct." (Emphasis supplied.) Now, the antecedent of *they* is not "Congress," but "United States." Nowhere in the whole of the Constitution or in any of the subsequent amendments is the United States an "it." The singular never appears.

What else sheds light in the second section of Article I? We find that "each State shall have at Least one Representative," whereupon follows a roll call of the States themselves: "Until such enumeration shall be made, the State of New Hampshire shall be entitled to chuse three, Massachusetts eight," and so forth. And when vacancies happen "in the Representation from any State," the Governor thereof is to issue a writ of election.

The dignity and sovereignty of States are made still more evident in the composition of the Senate. It is to be composed "of two Senators from each State," and whereas Representatives are required to be inhabitants of the States "in which" they shall be chosen, Senators must be inhabitants of the States "for which" they shall be chosen.(26)

It is in section four that the first grant of authority to the Federal government appears: "The Times, Places and Manner of holding Elections for Senators and Representatives, shall be prescribed in each State by the Legislature thereof; but"—and here the qualified concession—"the Congress may at any time by Law make or alter such Regulations, except as to the Places of chusing Senators."

The delegations of power to a Federal government appear most fully, of course, in Section 8, but it is worth noting that not all the powers delegated to Congress are exclusive and unqualified powers. Thus, the Congress may raise and support armies, "but no Appropriation of Money to that Use shall be for a longer Term than two Years." Thus, the Congress may provide for organizing, arming, and disciplining the militia, and for governing such part of the militia as may be employed in the service of the United States, but there is reserved "to the States respectively" the appointment of officers and the authority to train their militia according to regulations established by Congress. Thus, too, Congress may exercise Federal authority over Federally-owned property within the States, but how is such property to be acquired? The authority of the Congress extends only to those places "purchased by the Consent of the Legislature of the State in which the Same shall be," and this applies not only to military and naval installations but also to "other needful Buildings."

Several provisions in Section 9 merit attention. As a concession to the slave trade—one of the essential compromises without which the Constitution never would have come into being at all—it was provided that "the Migration or Importation of such Persons as any of the States now existing shall think proper to admit," shall not be prohibited prior to 1808. Then follow seven paragraphs of specific restrictions upon the powers of Congress. The privilege of the writ of habeas corpus shall not be suspended; no bill of attainder or ex post facto law shall be passed; no direct tax shall be levied except according to the census of the people as a whole; no tax or duty shall be laid on articles exported "from any State"; and—again emphasizing the separateness of the member States forming the union—"No Preference shall be given by any Regulation of Commerce or Revenue to the Ports of one State over those of another: nor shall Vessels bound to, or from, one State, be obliged to enter, clear, or pay Duties in another."

In Section 10, the States undertook to restrict themselves. No State shall enter into any treaty, alliance, or confederation; no State shall coin money or make anything but gold and silver legal tender; no State shall make any law impairing the obligation of contracts. Yet even here, the prohibitions are not without qualification. Thus, the States reserved to themselves the right to levy tariffs on imports or exports sufficient to execute their inspection laws; and though the fact is often forgotten, the States even reserved to themselves the solemn power they had claimed under the Articles of Confederation, to "engage in war," as States, if "actually invaded, or in such imminent Danger as will not admit of delay."

In the second Article of the Constitution, dealing with the Presidency, the framers again had an opportunity to choose between national and federal characteristics. At least twice during the convention of 1787, on July 17 and again on August 24, it was proposed that the President be chosen by popular, national election, but each time the proposal was overwhelmingly rejected. Instead, the framers agreed upon the plan of presidential electors which exists to this day: "Each State shall appoint, in such Manner as the Legislature thereof may direct, a Number of Electors, equal to the whole Number of Senators and Representatives to which the State may be entitled in the Congress." These electors are to meet "in their respective States." If any person fail to obtain a majority of the electoral vote, the House of Representatives is to elect a President, but how is this to be done? "In chusing the President, the Votes shall be taken by States, the Representation from each State having one Vote." Other protective clauses follow, still further emphasizing the role and the importance of the States: "A quorum for this Purpose shall consist of a Member or Members from two thirds of the

States, and a Majority of all the States shall be necessary to a Choice."

Article III, defining the judicial power of the United States, contains several provisions of interest in this review. We may note, for example, two further uses of the plural: First, the judicial power is to extend "to all Cases, in Law and Equity, arising under this Constitution, the Laws of the United States, and Treaties made, or which shall be made, under *their* authority." Second, treason against the United States is to consist "only in levying War against *them,* or in adhering to *their* Enemies." Because the authority of the Court will be considered at length in a later chapter, it will suffice here merely to point out that nowhere in Article III is the Court given jurisdiction over controversies *between a State and the United States.* That proposal was specifically advanced during the convention, *and specifically rejected.*

Every section—indeed, every paragraph—of Article IV touches upon the federal nature of the Union. Full faith and credit are to be given "in each State" to the acts and judicial proceedings "of every other State." If this were not a federal union, the provision would be nonsense. Beyond this, "the Citizens of each State" shall be entitled to all privileges and immunities of citizens "in the several States." A person charged "in any State" with crime, who shall flee from justice "and be found in another State," shall be delivered up on demand "to be removed to the State having Jurisdiction of the Crime."

Then comes the provision that Northern States were to flout over a period of thirty years: "No Person held to Service or Labour in one State, under the laws thereof, escaping into another, shall, in Consequence of any Law or Regulation therein, be discharged from such Service or Labour, but shall be delivered up on Claim of the Party to whom such Service or Labour may be due."

Finally, we may note in Article IV the provision for admitting new States "into this Union" (not this Nation, but this Union): "No new State shall be formed or erected within the Jurisdiction of any other State; nor any State be formed by the Junction of two or more States, or Parts of States, without the Consent of the Legislatures of the States concerned as well as of the Congress."

Article V had best be quoted in full. It has not been changed by so much as an apostrophe in the years since it came from Philadelphia in September of 1787. It still fixes and defines the sovereign power:

The Congress, whenever two thirds of both Houses shall deem it necessary, shall propose Amendments to this Constitution, or, *on the Application of the Legislatures of two thirds of the several States,* shall call a Convention for proposing Amendments, which, in either Case, shall be valid to all Intents and Purposes, as Part of this Constitution, *when ratified by the Legislatures of three fourths of the several States,* or by Conventions in three fourths thereof, as the one or the other Mode of Ratification may be proposed by the Congress; Provided that no Amendment which may be made prior to the Year One thousand eight hundred and eight shall in any Manner affect the first and fourth Clauses in the Ninth Section of the first Article; *and that no State, without its Consent, shall be deprived of it's equal Suffrage in the Senate.* [Emphasis supplied.]

Pause for a moment over this article of the Constitution. We are dealing here with Taylor's "will to enact" and "power to execute" we are dealing with Marshall's "power to make and unmake." It was plainly envisioned by the framers that their work would require amendment through the years. "That useful alterations will be suggested by experience, could not but be foreseen," Madison was to write.[27] There was a double aim in the provision, even a triple aim. Article V, Madison tells us, was intended, first, to guard equally against too-easy amendment on the one hand and too-difficult amendment on the other. It was drafted, secondly, to permit amendments to originate both with the Federal and with the State governments. But it was intended, finally, to leave the ultimate decision upon changing the Constitution to the sovereign States themselves—not to the people as a mass, nor even to a bare majority of the States as such. It was recognized that the great, overriding principle of protection for minorities should apply here as bindingly as it was to apply elsewhere. If one-fourth-of-the-States-plus-one should object to a change in the Constitution—even if that change were desired by three-fourths-minus-one (and even if this larger fraction should include the great bulk of the total population)—the change could not be engrafted to the Constitution.

Article VI is brief. Its first provision covers debts and engagements entered into under the Articles of Confederation and continues these obligations under the proposed new Constitution; its third provision prohibits any religious test as a qualification for public office and requires an oath to support the Constitution of all public officers, both State and Federal.

It is the second provision that merits brief attention in this summary review:

This Constitution, and the Laws of the United States which shall be made in Pursuance thereof; and all Treaties made, or which shall be made, under the Authority of the United States, shall be the supreme Law of the Land; and the Judges in every State shall be bound thereby, any Thing in the Constitution or Laws of any State to the Contrary notwithstanding.

Let us go back: What is to be supreme? Three things. First, "this Constitution." Secondly, "laws of the United States which shall be made in pursuance thereof." Third, treaties made "under the authority of the United States." That is all. Not executive orders of the President. Not even judgments of the Supreme Court. The Constitution, the laws made in pursuance thereof, the treaties.

In passing, note the phrase "law of the land." It stems originally from the Magna Charta; but as it appears in the Constitution, "law of the land" was merely a substitution, proposed by the committee on style, for "law of the several States and their citizens and inhabitants." The object was to extend this new supreme law to territories as well as to the States.(28) And this phrase, "law of the land," is as close as the Constitution ever comes to suggesting a "nation." Actually the word "nation" or the word "national" never appears in the Constitution.(29)

The aim, we will recall, was to form "a more perfect Union." Representatives and taxes were to be apportioned among the several States which may be included "within this Union." The militia may be called forth to execute "the Laws of the Union." The President is to provide Congress with information on the "State of the Union." New States are to be admitted "into this Union." The guarantee of a republican form of government goes "to every State in this Union." But never, at any point, are the United States described, in the Constitution, as comprising a "nation."

This is not to contend, of course, that ours is not a nation, or that the Federal government does not operate "nationally." It is only to suggest that the deliberate terms of the Constitution speak for themselves, and should be heeded: Our country is, first and foremost, originally and still, *a union of States*. And when we speak of the "law of the land," it should be kept steadily in mind that "the land" is a federal union, in which each of the States stands co-equal with every other State. The Constitution is supreme not only in its *authority* over each State, but also in its *protection* over each State. And each State, each *respective* State, is entitled to rely upon the Constitution as embodying supreme law that all other States must adhere to with equal fidelity, like it or not, until the Constitution be changed by the States themselves.

Note, too, the careful qualification that defines laws enacted by the Congress. Just any laws of the United States are not enough: Laws, to be binding, must be laws made *in pursuance of the Constitution*. Any attempted statutes that invade the residuary authority of the States, Hamilton tells us, (30) "will be merely acts of usurpation, and will deserve to be treated as such." And he adds, at another point, that:

There is no position which depends on clearer principles, than that every act of a delegated authority, contrary to the tenor of the commission under which it is exercised, is void. No legislative act, therefore, contrary to the Constitution, can be valid. To deny this, would be to affirm, that the deputy is greater than his principal; that the servant is above his master; that the representatives of the people are superior to the people themselves; that men acting by virtue of powers, may do not only what their powers do not authorize, but what they forbid.(31)

Surely, it may be urged that precisely the same standard must be applied to other branches of the Federal government—the executive and judicial no less than the legislative. By extension, thus, judgments of the Court, to be supreme law of the land, must be made pursuant to the Constitution. A judgment of the Court, so violative of the clear terms and understandings of the Constitution as to invade the residuary authority of the States, must also be regarded as a usurpation, and should deserve to be treated as such. The argument will be pursued at greater length hereafter.

Finally, this brief examination of the Constitution from the standpoint of the States may be concluded with a second look at Article VII. It should be read carefully, for this is the clause that binds: "The Ratification of the Conventions of nine States"—not, again, the approval of a majority of the *people* in a popular referendum, but the ratification of nine *States* —"shall be sufficient for the Establishment of this Constitution between the States so ratifying the Same."

Thus, on September 17, the Convention concluded its work. George Washington, as president of the Convention, transmitted the document to the Congress. A prophetic sentence appeared in his letter, as he mentioned the compromises necessary for the surrender of sovereign powers: "It is at all times difficult to draw with precision the line between those rights which must be surrendered, and those which may be reserved." The States had done the best they could through their delegates. Eager to consolidate their Union, each State had been disposed "to be less rigid on points of inferior magnitude than might have been otherwise expected." They launched the ship.

"Well, Doctor," said the lady to Mr. Franklin, "what have we got, a republic or a monarchy?"

"A republic," replied the doctor, "if you can keep it."

Notes

Go to top.

6

The Prophetic Mr. Henry

FOR THE States' understanding of what the Constitution was to mean to them, as States, we can look not only to the internal evidence of the Constitution itself, but to the debates in the ratifying conventions and to some of the contemporary criticism, notably in the Federalist papers. We can look, also, to some of the pronouncements of the Supreme Court from time to time, and to the writings of scholars of our own day.

The evidence is overwhelming. By written compact, solemnly ratified, the

States agreed mutually to delegate certain of their sovereign powers to a federal government. They enumerated these powers. All other powers they reserved to themselves, and these reserved powers did not need to be enumerated: The reserved powers constituted *all* inherent powers of sovereign States, not specifically abridged.

So plain was this understanding that the feeling most frequently encountered, in reading comments of the period, is one of incredulity that anyone should doubt it.

"The proposed Constitution," said Hamilton, "so far from implying an abolition of the State governments, makes them constituent parts of the national sovereignty, by allowing them a direct representation in the Senate, and leaves in their possession certain exclusive and very important portions of sovereign power."(32)

So, too, said Madison:

It is to be remembered that the general government is not to be charged with the whole power of making and administering laws. Its jurisdiction is limited to certain enumerated objects, which concern all the members of the republic, but which are not to be attained by the separate provisions of any. The subordinate governments, which can extend their care to all other objects which can be separately provided for, will retain their due authority and activity.(33)

Neither Hamilton nor Madison could quite imagine the Federal government ever seriously encroaching upon the States.

"Allowing the utmost latitude to the love of power which any reasonable man can require," said Hamilton, "I confess I am at a loss to discover what temptation the persons intrusted with the administration of the general government could ever feel to divest the States of the authorities of that description. The regulation of the mere domestic police of a State appears to me to hold out slender allurements to ambition. Commerce, finance, negotiation, and war seem to comprehend all the objects which have charms for minds governed by that passion; and all the powers necessary to those objects ought, in the first instance, to be lodged in the national depository."(34)

Then he added, with a singular absence of prophecy:

The administration of private justice between the citizens of the same State, the supervision of agriculture and of other concerns of a similar nature, all those things, in short, which are proper to be provided for by local legislation, can never be desirable cares of a general jurisdiction. It is therefore improbable that there should exist a disposition in the Federal councils to usurp the powers with which they are connected. . . .

It will always be far more easy for the State governments to encroach upon the national authorities, than for the national government to encroach upon the State authorities.

Madison, also, imagined that the Federal government would "be disinclined to invade the rights of the individual States, or the prerogatives of their governments."(35) For his part, Hamilton thought it more probable that the States would encroach upon the Federal government, and he imagined that in such contests the State governments, because they "will commonly possess most influence" over the people, would dominate Federal agencies "to the disadvantage of the Union." However, all such conjectures Hamilton viewed as "extremely vague and fallible."(36) He preferred to assume that the people "will always take care to preserve the constitutional equilibrium between the general and the State governments."

In *Number 45*, Madison treated at considerable length the widespread apprehension that the States would be obliterated. Some of his comments have been outdated; what he has to say about the election of Senators, for example, unhappily has been superseded by the misfortune of the Seventeenth Amendment. Some of his other observations, dealing with functions of what was to become the Bureau of Internal Revenue, may occasion some wry reflection on the lengths by which even a Madison could miss his guess. But as contemporary evidence of the role guaranteed to the States, *Number 45* justifies quotation at some length:

The State governments will have the advantage of the Federal government, whether we compare them in respect to the immediate dependence of the one on the other; to the weight of personal influence which each side will possess; to the powers respectively vested in them to the predilection and probable support of the people; to the disposition and faculty of resisting and frustrating the measures of each other.

The State governments may be regarded as constituent and essential parts of the federal government; whilst the latter is nowise essential to the operation or organization of the former. Without the intervention of the State legislatures, the President of the United States cannot be elected at all. They must in all cases have a great share in his appointment, and will, perhaps, in most cases, of themselves determine it. The Senate will be elected absolutely and exclusively by the State legislatures. Even the House of Representatives, though drawn immediately from the people, will be chosen very much under the influence of that class of men, whose influence over the people obtains for themselves an election into the State legislatures. Thus, each of the principal branches of the federal government will owe its existence more or less to the favor of the State governments, and must consequently feel a dependence, which is much more likely to beget a disposition too obsequious than too overbearing towards them. On the other side, the component parts of the State governments will in no instance be indebted for their appointment to the direct agency of the federal government, and very little, if at all, to the local influence of its members.

The number of individuals employed under the Constitution of the United States will be much smaller than the number employed under the particular States. There will consequently be less of personal influence on the side of the former than of the latter. The members of the legislative, executive, and judiciary departments of thirteen and more States, the justices of peace, officers of militia, ministerial officers of justice, with all the county, corporation, and town officers, for three millions and more of people, intermixed, and having particular acquaintance with every class and circle of people, must exceed, beyond all proportion, both in number and influence, those of every description who will be employed in the administration of the federal system. Compare the members of the three great departments of the thirteen States, excluding from the judiciary department the justices of peace, with the members of the corresponding departments of the single government of the Union; compare the militia officers of three millions of people with the military and marine officers of any establishment which is within the compass of probability, or, I may add, of possibility, and in this view alone, we may pronounce the advantage of the States to be decisive.

If the federal government is to have collectors of revenue, the State governments will have theirs also. And as those of the former will be principally on the seacoast, and not very numerous, whilst those of the latter will be spread over the face of the country, and will be very numerous, the advantage in this view also lies on the same side. It is true, that the Confederacy is to possess, and may exercise, the power of collecting internal as well as external taxes throughout the States; but it is probable that this power will not be resorted to, except for supplemental purposes of revenue; that an option will then be given to the States to supply their quotas by previous collections of their own; and that the eventual collection, under the immediate authority of the Union, will generally be made by the officers, and according to the rules, appointed by the several States. . . .

The powers delegated by the proposed Constitution to the federal government are few and defined. Those which are to remain in the State governments are numerous and indefinite. The former will be exercised principally on external objects, as war, peace, negotiation, and foreign commerce; with which last the power of taxation will, for the most part, be connected. The powers reserved to the several States will extend to all the objects which, in the ordinary course of affairs, concern the lives, liberties, and properties of the people, and the internal order, improvement, and prosperity of the State.

The operations of the federal government will be most extensive and important in times of war and danger; those of the State governments in times of peace and security. As the former periods will probably bear a small proportion to the latter, the State governments will here enjoy another advantage over the federal government. The more adequate, indeed, the federal powers may be rendered to the national defence, the less frequent will be those scenes of danger which might favor their ascendancy over the governments of the particular States.

If the new Constitution be examined with accuracy and candor, it will be found that the change which it proposes consists much less in the addition of NEW POWERS to the Union, than in the invigoration of its ORIGINAL POWERS. The regulation of commerce, it is true, is a new power; but that seems to be an addition which few oppose, and from which no apprehensions are entertained. The powers relating to war and peace, armies and fleets, treaties and finance, with the other more considerable powers, are all vested in the existing Congress by the articles of Confederation. The proposed change does not enlarge these powers; it only substitutes a more effectual mode of administering them. . . .

Even John Marshall, who did more than any man in our history to aggrandize the Federal government and to weaken the States, never doubted the basic structure of divided powers. Consider, briefly, his comment in the famed case of _McCulloch vs. Maryland._(37) The case arose when Congress established the Bank of the United States, and Maryland undertook to levy a tax upon the bank's Baltimore branch; James McCulloch, the cashier, refused to pay the tax, and Maryland sued.

The legal questions were two: Did Congress have power to incorporate the bank, and secondly, did Maryland have power to tax it? Marshall answered the first one yes, the second, no. With the bulk of his reasoning, strict constructionists and apostles of States' rights will disagree: Marshall's sophisticated mind did not boggle at stretching "necessary" to mean "convenient." In considering the actual act of ratification by which the Union was formed, Marshall was not much impressed by the fact, which he could not escape, that the people met in State conventions. "Where else should they have assembled?" he asked. But even here, a couple of sentences merit quotation as evidence from the States' greatest detractor:

It is true, [the people] assembled in their several States—and where else should they have assembled? No political dreamer was ever wild enough to think of breaking down the lines which separate the States, and of compounding the American people into one common mass. Of consequence, when they act, they act in their States.

Marshall went on in his opinion to confuse "States" and "State governments," thus setting up a convenient straw man to batter down. No one ever had contended that the Constitution was ratified by State governments, but Marshall, with a glittering display of intellectual swordsmanship, neatly skewered the non-existent objection. Then he went on to say:

This government is acknowledged by all to be one of enumerated powers. The principle, that it can exercise only the powers granted to it, would seem too apparent to have required to be enforced by all those arguments which its enlightened friends, while it was depending before the people, found it necessary to urge. That principle is now universally admitted. But the question respecting the extent of the powers actually granted, is perpetually arising, and will probably continue to arise, as long as our system shall exist.

True enough, the question of "the extent of powers" does continue to arise to this day, though the doctrines of Marshall have so pervaded public thinking that it often is forgotten that the Federal government has any limitations whatever.(38) But the separateness of the States and the nature of their delegated powers were clearly recognized when the Constitution was created. The prophets who foresaw the trend toward consolidation—notably Patrick Henry and George Mason—were told they were old women, seeing ghosts.

Consider, if you will, the debate on ratification in Virginia. The transcript offers some absorbing reading. If the clash of a Henry and a Mason with a Pendleton and a Madison does not prompt reflection upon subsequent corruption of the Constitution, at the very least their battle must lead to regrets at the decline in the quality of today's legislative debates. There were giants in those days. This was, to paraphrase Marshall, a *Constitution* they were debating.(39) What was said of the relationship of the States and the Federal government?

Go back in time. This was a sultry summer in Richmond. At least twice the brief convention was interrupted by thunder storms so severe the delegates were forced to recess. Tempers flared sharply: At one point Edmund Randolph, infuriated with Patrick Henry, was prepared to let their friendship "fall like Lucifer, never to rise again." They began on Monday, June 2; they adjourned *sine die* on Friday, June 27. Into those four weeks, the Virginians of 1788 packed a world of profound reflection upon the meaning and intention of the Constitution.

Edmund Pendleton served as president of the Virginia Convention. He was a remarkable man: lawyer, scholar, statesman, thinker. In advocating ratification, Pendleton was joined by James Madison, John Marshall, Edmund Randolph, and Light Horse Harry Lee. They carried the day against Patrick Henry and George Mason, as leading opponents of the proposition.

The convention scarcely had begun before Henry established the broad spread of argument. He did not propose to abide by any parliamentary decision to debate one clause at a time. Before the convention in Philadelphia the previous summer, said Henry, a general peace and a universal tranquility had prevailed. Now he was "extremely uneasy at the proposed change of government." He swept the room with a cold eye: "Be extremely cautious, watchful, jealous of your liberty. Instead of securing your rights, you may lose them forever."(40)

George Mason came to his side. He charged that the new Constitution would create "a national government, and no longer a Confederation." He especially denounced the authority proposed in the general government to levy direct taxes. This power, being at the discretion of Congress and unconfined, "and without any kind of control, must carry everything before it." The idea of a consolidated government, he said, "is totally subversive of every principle which has hitherto governed us. This power is calculated to annihilate totally the State governments.. . . These two concurrent powers cannot exist long together; the one will destroy the other; the general government, being paramount to and in every respect more powerful than the State governments, the latter must give way to the former."(41)

Then Mason voiced the argument that is as applicable in the mid-twentieth century as it was toward the end of the eighteenth:

Is it to be supposed that one national government will suit so extensive a country, embracing so many climates, and containing inhabitants so very different in manners, habits, and customs? It is ascertained, by history, that there never was a government over a very extensive country without destroying the liberties of the people. . . . Popular governments can only exist in small territories.(42)

On Thursday, June 5, Pendleton undertook to respond to Henry and to Mason. Was the proposed government, he inquired, truly a consolidated government? Of course not. "If this be such a government, I will confess, with my worthy friend, that it is inadmissible. . . ." The proposed Federal government, he said, "extends to the general purposes of the Union. It does not intermeddle with the local, particular affairs of the States. . . . It is the interest of the Federal to preserve the State governments; upon the latter the existence of the former depends. . . . I wonder how any gentleman, reflecting on the subject, could have conceived an idea of the possibility of the latter. . . ."(43)

Henry conceived it. He conceived it very clearly. The proposed Constitution, he felt, was "extremely pernicious, impolitic and dangerous." He saw no jeopardy to the people in the Articles of Confederation; he saw great jeopardy in this new Constitution. And he had this to say:

We are descended from a people whose government was founded on liberty: Our glorious forefathers of Great Britain made liberty the foundation of every thing. That country is become a great, mighty and splendid nation; not because their government is strong and energetic, but, sir, because liberty is its direct end and foundation. We drew the spirit of liberty from our British ancestors: By that spirit we have triumphed over every difficulty. But now, sir, the American spirit, assisted by the ropes and chains of consolidation, is about to convert this country into a powerful and mighty empire. If you make the citizens of this country agree to become the subjects of one great consolidated empire of America, your government will not have sufficient energy to keep them together. Such a government is incompatible with the genius of Republicanism.(44)

And note this prophetic observation:

There will be no checks, no real balances, in this government. What can avail your specious, imaginary balances, your rope-dancing, chain-rattling, ridiculous ideal checks and contrivances?

What indeed? What have these ideal checks and balances availed the States in the twentieth century? Henry saw the empty prospect: "This Constitution is said to have beautiful features; but when I come to examine these features, sir, they appear to me horribly frightful. Among other deformities, it has an awful squinting; it squints toward monarchy; and does not this raise indignation in the breast of every true American?"

It was monarchy, *per se,* that Henry foresaw. And it was despotism at the hands of a general government that he feared.

"What are your checks in this government?" he kept asking.

No one ever answered him accurately, though half a dozen members of the convention undertook to refute Henry and to allay his apprehensions. Randolph, replying to the objection that the country soon would be too large for effective government from the capital, commented that "no extent on earth seems to me too great," but he added, "provided the laws be wisely made and executed." It has proved to be a large qualification.

Madison also responded to Henry's general objection that the liberty of the people was in danger: "Since the general civilization of mankind," he said, "I believe there are more instances of the abridgment of the freedom of the people by gradual and silent encroachments of those in power, than by violent and sudden usurpations."(45)

Follow closely what Madison had to say next. He is expounding the relationship of the State and Federal governments as he, above all men, understood it:

Give me leave to say something of the nature of the government. . . . There are a number of opinions; but the principal question is, whether it be a federal or consolidated government. In order to judge properly of the question before us, we must consider it minutely in its principal parts. I conceive myself that it is of a mixed nature; it is in a manner unprecedented; we cannot find one express example in the experience of the world. It stands by itself. In some respects it is a government of a federal nature; in others it is of a consolidated nature.... Who are parties to it?

Note this, especially; it was quoted earlier but it bears repetition:

The people—but not the people as composing one great body; but the people as composing thirteen sovereignties.(46)

Francis Corbin, one of the ablest political students of his time, then joined Madison in soothing the growing fear that the Federal government might one day absorb the State governments. "The powers of the general government," he said, "are only of a general nature, and their object is to protect, defend, and strengthen the United States; but the internal administration of government is left to the State legislatures, who exclusively retain such powers as will give the States the advantages of small republics, without the danger commonly attendant on the weakness of such governments."(47)

Henry, undaunted, straightened his red wig and returned to the debate. "That government is no more than a choice among evils," he remarked, "is acknowledged by the most intelligent among mankind, and has been a standing maxim for ages." He could not accept the idea that this new government would be "a mighty benefit to us."

Sir, I am made of so incredulous materials, that assertions and declarations do not satisfy me. I must be convinced, sir. I shall retain my infidelity on that subject till I see our liberties secured in a manner perfectly satisfactory to my understanding.(48)

This exchange occurred on Friday, June 16. The following Monday, Henry renewed his assault:

A number of characters, of the greatest eminence in this country, object to this government for its consolidating tendency. This is not imaginary. It is a formidable reality. If consolidation proves to be as mischievous to this country as it has been to other countries, what will the poor inhabitants of this country do? This government will operate like an ambuscade. It will destroy the State governments, and swallow the liberties of the people, without giving previous notice.(49)

Madison came back with fresh replies and new remonstrances. The States were safely protected, he assured the Virginia convention. And renewing the arguments he had advanced in the *Federalist,* "There will be an irresistible bias toward the State governments." It was utterly improbable—almost impossible—that the Federal government ever would encroach upon the States.

The means of influence consist in having the disposal of gifts and emoluments, and in the number of persons employed by and dependent upon a government. Will any gentleman compare the number of persons which will be employed in the general government with the number of those which will be in the State governments? The number of dependents upon the State governments will be infinitely greater than those on the general government. I may say, with truth, that there never was a more economical government in any age or country, nor which will require fewer hands, or give less influence.(50)

Pendleton again gained the floor to tackle Henry's objection. We are told, he said,

that there will be a war between the two bodies equally our representatives, and that the State government will be destroyed, and consolidated into the general government. I stated before, that this could not be so. The two governments act in different manners, and for different purposes—the general government in great national concerns, in which we are interested in common with other members of the Union; the State legislature in our mere local concerns. . . . Our dearest rights—life, liberty and property—as Virginians, are still in the hands of our State legislature. . . .(51)

Patrick Henry remained unconvinced. His opinion and Madison's were "diametrically opposite." The mild-mannered Madison said the States would prevail. Henry, a dramatic and eloquent speaker, feared the Federal government would prevail. Bring forth the Federal allurements, he cried,

and compare them with the poor, contemptible things that the State Legislatures can bring forth. . . . There are rich, fat, Federal emoluments. Your rich, smug, fine, fat, Federal officers—the number of collectors of taxes and excises—will outnumber anything from the States. Who can cope with the excise man and the taxmen?(52)

Henry did not imagine that the dual governments could be kept each within its proper orbit. "I assert that there is danger of interference," he remarked, "because no line is drawn between the powers of the two governments, in many instances; and where there is a line, there is no check to prevent the one from encroaching upon the powers of the other. I therefore contend that they must interfere, and that this interference must subvert the State government as being less powerful. Unless your government have checks, it must inevitably terminate in the destruction of your privileges."

William Grayson, burly veteran of the Revolution, was another member of the Virginia convention who clearly perceived the absence of effective checks and balances. "Power ought to have such checks and limitations," he said, "as to prevent bad men from abusing it. It ought to be granted on a supposition that men will be bad; for it may be eventually so."(53)

Grayson was here discussing his apprehensions toward the powers vested by Article III in the Supreme Court of the United States. "This court," he protested, "has more power than any court under heaven." The court's appellate jurisdiction, especially, aroused his alarm: "What has it in view, unless to subvert the State governments?"

But Grayson was not alone in foreseeing the possibilities of judicial corruption of the Constitution. Even so stout an advocate of ratification as Governor Randolph admitted strong doubts and reservations. The court's jurisdiction was to extend to "all cases in law and equity. . . arising under the Constitution." What did the phrase relate to?

I conceive this to be very ambiguous. If my interpretation be right, the word "arising" will be carried so far that it will be made use of to aid and extend the Federal jurisdiction.

Grayson agreed: "The jurisdiction of all cases arising under the Constitution and the laws of the Union is of stupendous magnitude. It is impossible for human nature to trace its extent. It is so vaguely and indefinitely expressed that its latitude cannot be ascertained."(54)

True, said Mason: The court's jurisdiction "may be said to be unlimited." He was profoundly disturbed by the prospect. The greater part of the powers given to the court, he felt, "are unnecessary, and dangerous, as tending to impair, and ultimately destroy the State judiciaries, and, by the same principle, the legislation of the State governments." Indeed, the court was "so constructed as to destroy the dearest rights of the community." Nothing would be left to the State courts: "Will any gentleman be pleased, candidly, fairly, and without sophistry, to show us what remains?"

He continued his criticism of the court's jurisdiction:

There is no limitation. It goes to everything. . . . All the laws of the United States are paramount to the laws and Constitution of any single State. "The judicial power shall extend to all cases in law and equity arising under this Constitution." What objects will not this expression extend to? . . . When we consider the nature of these courts, we must conclude that their effect and operation will be utterly to destroy the State governments; for they will be the judges how far their laws will operate. . . . To what disgraceful and dangerous length does the principle of this go! . . . The principle itself goes to the destruction of the legislation of the States, whether or not it was intended. . . . I think it will destroy the State governments. . . . There are many gentlemen in the United States who think it right that we should have one great, national, consolidated government, and that it was better to bring it about slowly and imperceptibly rather than all at once. This is no reflection on any man, for I mean none. To those who think that one national, consolidated government is best for America, this extensive judicial authority will be agreeable; but I hope there are many in this convention of a different opinion, and who see their political happiness resting on their State governments.(55)

It was John Marshall, who fifteen years later would do so much to justify Mason's apprehensions, who undertook to allay his fears now. The Federal government, he insisted, certainly would not have the power "to make laws on every subject." Could members of the Congress make laws affecting the transfer of property, or contracts, or claims, between citizens of the same State?

Can they go beyond the delegated powers? If they were to make a law not warranted by any of the powers enumerated, it would be considered by the judges as an infringement of the Constitution which they are to guard. They would not consider such a law as coming under their jurisdiction. They would declare it void.(56)

Marshall saw no danger to the States from decrees of the Supreme Court: "I hope that no gentleman will think that a State will be called at the bar of the Federal court. . . . It is not rational to suppose that the sovereign power should be dragged before a court."(57)

Madison, Monroe, and others joined Marshall in defending the Third Article. Their debate was long and detailed. Much of it was concerned with questions of pleading and practice. But after several days, they went on to other aspects of the Constitution: The prospect of judicial despotism was recognized by the few, and denied by the many.

Notes

Go to top.

7

The States Ratify

IN THE END, Virginia ratified. It was a close vote. A motion to postpone ratification until amendments, in the nature of a bill of rights, could be considered by "the other States in the American confederacy," failed by 88 to 80. Then the main question was put, and this was what Virginia agreed to. It merits careful reading:

We, the delegates of the people of Virginia, . . . having fully and freely investigated and discussed the proceedings of the Federal Convention, and being prepared, as well as the most mature deliberation hath enabled us, to decide thereon, Do, in the name and in behalf of the people of Virginia, declare and make known, that the powers granted under the Constitution, being derived from the people of the United States, be resumed by them whensoever the same shall be perverted to their injury or oppression, and that every power, *not granted thereby, remains with them, and at their will;* that, therefore, no right, of any denomination, can be cancelled, abridged, restrained, or modified, by the Congress, by the Senate or House of Representatives, acting in any capacity, by the President, or any department or officer of the United States, except in those instances in which power is given by the Constitution for those purposes; and that, among other essential rights, the liberty of conscience and of the press cannot be cancelled, abridged, restrained, or modified, by any authority of the United States. . . .

The vote on that main question was 89 to 79, but even that narrow margin of approval was predicated upon a gentlemen's agreement that the Virginia Convention would recommend a number of amendments, in the form of a Bill of Rights, to be presented to the first Congress. And the first of these recommended amendments reads: "That each State in the Union shall respectively retain every power, jurisdiction, and right, which is not by this Constitution delegated to the Congress of the United States, or to the departments of the Federal government."

By the time Virginia completed ratification, of course, her decision no longer carried compelling importance. The Virginia convention had opened on June 2, not quite two weeks after South Carolina, on May 23, had become the eighth State to ratify. But while the Virginians were debating the issue, New Hampshire, on June 21, had become Number Nine: The new Union had been formed, and the Constitution had become binding upon the nine States "ratifying the same." It has ever been Virginia's fate to make the right decisions, but to put off making them as long as possible.

In this consideration of State and Federal relationships, there is something to be learned from the other resolutions of ratification. The easy ones came first: Delaware came first, on December 7, 1787, "fully, freely and entirely" approving and assenting to the Constitution; and then, in quick succession, Pennsylvania on December 12, after a bitter fight; New Jersey on December 18, and Georgia—Georgians had not even read the Constitution—on January 2, 1788.(58) Connecticut followed a week later, with a comfortable vote of 128 to 40.

Then a month's hiatus set in. Massachusetts did not become Number Six until February 7, and her approval of this "explicit and solemn Compact" was not unqualified:

It is the opinion of this convention that certain amendments and alterations in the said Constitution would remove the fears and quiet the apprehensions of many of the good people of this Commonwealth, and more effectually guard against an undue administration of the Federal government. (59)

It will come as no surprise that the very first amendment recommended by Massachusetts was "that it be explicitly declared that all Powers not expressly delegated by the aforesaid Constitution are reserved to the several States to be by them exercised."

Two months later, on April 28, Maryland ratified. Then there was another lapse of nearly a month before South Carolina, on May 23, became Number Eight. South Carolina accompanied her resolution of ratification with a pointed statement that she considered it essential "to the preservation of the rights reserved to the several States" and for the freedom of the people, that the State's right to prescribe the manner, time, and places of Congressional elections "be forever inseparably annexed to the sovereignty of the several States." Then South Carolina added:

This Convention doth also declare that no Section or paragraph of the said Constitution warrants a Construction that the States do not retain every power not expressly relinquished by them and vested in the General Government of the Union.(60)

New Hampshire, in voting its approval on June 21, closely paralleled the action of Massachusetts, but New Hampshire's declaration as to reserved powers was even more explicit. The people of New Hampshire wanted it understood that all powers not "expressly and particularly delegated" were reserved.

So, too, with New York, which became Number Eleven on July 26. The convention at Poughkeepsie wished to make it known:

That every Power, Jurisdiction, and right, which is not by the said Constitution clearly delegated to the Congress of the United States, or the departments of the Government thereof, remains to the People of the several States, or to their respective State Governments to whom they may have granted the same; And that those Clauses in the said Constitution, which declare, that Congress shall not have or exercise certain Powers, do not imply that Congress is entitled to any Powers not given by the said Constitution; but such Clauses are to be construed either as exceptions to certain specified Powers, or as inserted merely for greater Caution.(61)

Interestingly enough, New York's convention also wanted certain things made known about the Supreme Court of the United States, to wit,

That the Jurisdiction of the Supreme Court of the United States, or of any other Court to be instituted by the Congress, is not in any case to be encreased enlarged or extended by any Fiction Collusion or mere suggestion; —And That no Treaty is to be construed as to alter the Constitution of any State.(62)

With New York's ratification, a quite extended period of inaction began. It was not until November 21, 1789, nearly a year and a half later, that North Carolina became Number Twelve in the Union. And North Carolina, for her part, inserted a declaration:

That each State in the Union shall, respectively, retain every power, jurisdiction and right, which is not by this Constitution delegated to the Congress of the United States or to the departments of the Federal government.(63)

Finally, after another lapse of half a year, Rhode Island completed the chain of member States. On May 29, 1790, Rhode Island, with great caution and reluctance, joined the Union. The margin of ratification, we have noted, was a bare 34 to 32. Clearly, the necessary votes would not have been obtained if the resolution of approval had not included eighteen detailed paragraphs of understandings, plus no fewer than twenty-one proposed amendments. The third of these "impressions" declared:

That the powers of government may be reassumed by the people, whensoever it shall become necessary to their happiness:—That the rights of the States respectively, to nominate and appoint all State Officers, and every other power, jurisdiction and right, which is not by the said Constitution clearly delegated to the Congress of the United States or to the departments of government thereof, remain to the people of the several States, or their respective State governments to whom they may have granted the same. . . . (64)

And the very first of Rhode Island's recommended amendments proposed that:

The United States shall guarantee to each State its sovereignty, freedom and independence, and every power, jurisdiction and right, which is not by this Constitution expressly delegated to the United States.(65)

All these various recommendations as to Constitutional amendment were grouped together by the First Congress in a resolution on March 4, 1789, submitting what is now the Bill of Rights to the member States. Twelve proposals in all were offered. Numbers One and Two failed of ratification; the first would have fixed representation in the House according to a precise guarantee by population; the second would have provided that no law changing the salaries of Congressmen could take effect "until an election of Representatives shall have intervened." The remaining ten amendments won a sufficient number of States; and the tenth of these, as it is now embedded in our Constitution, forever proclaims that:

The powers not delegated to the United States by the Constitution, nor prohibited by it to the States, are reserved to the States respectively, or to the people.

In recent years, the Supreme Court of the United States has undertaken to repeal the Tenth Amendment by treating it as a meaningless appendage to the

Constitution—mere surplusage, a tautological expression of self-evident facts. The Tenth Amendment "added nothing to the instrument as originally ratified," said the Supreme Court in 1931.(66) The Amendment "states but a truism," added Chief Justice Stone ten years later.(67) But the overwhelming preponderance of evidence proves that when the Tenth Amendment was nailed into the Constitution, the ratifying States regarded this statement of reserved powers as a vital, indeed an absolutely necessary addition to the Constitution.

The Supreme Court, it may be suggested, has no authority to repeal any provision of the Constitution. Mr. Justice Frankfurter, no less, is a recent authority on the point: "Nothing new can be put into the Constitution except through the amendatory process," he said recently for the court. "Nothing old can be taken out without the same process."(68) And so long as the Tenth Amendment remains a part of the Constitution, it is elementary that it must be given full meaning—that the intention of its framers must be acknowledged and respected. Plainly, the intention of the Tenth Amendment was to restrict the Federal government—to hold it within the strict boundaries of the delegated powers. To be sure, John Marshall, not long after the Union was formed, was to seize upon the fact that the restriction went only to the "powers not delegated," and not to the "powers not expressly delegated," as if this made some large difference. But by that time Marshall was at the helm, and the powers of the States already were being eaten away by slow judicial erosion. The process continues, at an accelerated pace, to this day.

> . . . this Assembly doth explicitly and peremptorily declare that it views the powers of the federal government as resulting from the compact, to which the States are parties, as limited by the plain sense and intention of the instrument constituting that compact; as no further valid than they are authorized by the grants enumerated in that compact; and that in case of a deliberate, palpable, and dangerous exercise of other powers not granted by the said compact, the States who are parties thereto, have the right, and are in duty bound, to interpose for arresting the progress of the evil, and for maintaining, within their respective limits, the authorities, rights, and liberties appertaining to them. . . .
>
> *The Virginia Resolution*
> December 21, 1798

1

A Cast of Characters

WE HAVE come this far in the argument: First, that the political entities created with the Declaration of Independence were free and independent States, even as the instrument proclaimed them to be; second, that the States asserted for themselves the powers of sovereignty, and exercised those powers for more than a decade thereafter; third, that it was the States, as States, which formed the new Union of 1788; fourth, that in binding themselves to the Constitution the States delegated—not surrendered, but *delegated*—only certain of their powers, retaining all others to themselves.

It was foreseen, we have noted, that conflicts would arise between the States and the Federal government which the States jointly had created, but the extent of these conflicts was minimized. It was assumed by those whose views prevailed—by Hamilton, Marshall, Madison, Pendleton, and Washington—that the State and Federal governments would confine their activities each to its allotted realm of authority. No one dreamed, then, of a massive Federal government, extending its authority into every phase of personal and public affairs; the functions of the Federal government, it was said, would be few and limited—those of the States, many and indefinite.

More mistaken prophecy never was made by men of vision. The Union barely had become complete, with Rhode Island's long-delayed ratification, before the States were shocked by a decision of the Supreme Court which challenged their sovereign authority and violated a clear Constitutional understanding. This was, of course, the Chisholm case. It marked the first major conflict in the continuing struggle of the States to preserve their rightful powers. It is here that a brief account of that struggle must begin.

First, let a stage be set. Time, 1790. It is a turbulent, tumultuous, exciting year. The assault upon the Bastille had come the preceding summer, only four months after Washington's inauguration in March. Now, in 1790, Louis XVI and Marie Antoinette have but three years left to them. Napoleon is twenty-one, a junior lieutenant in the artillery; his time is still ahead. In Prussia, Frederick II reigns; in England, George III is still on the throne. This was the year that Papa Joseph Haydn, passing through Bonn, heard a mass by a stormy, violent young man of twenty, and arranged to have young Beethoven come to Vienna to study under him. Mozart in 1790, ill and poverty-stricken, is thirty-four, at work on *The Magic Flute,* with *Don Giovanni* behind him; his brief candle is almost out. Wordsworth is twenty, Coleridge eighteen, Jane Austen a solemn little girl of fifteen.

In the United States, there is not much concern for the finer arts, though the new Republic boasts twenty-four colleges or universities, nine of them created in the preceding ten years. The country is too new, too raw, the hazards of the expanding frontier too much a reality. Linking the States—perhaps "linking" is too strong a word—is a primitive network of postroads and trails. One stage a day serves Boston and New York.[1] Of the 3,929,000 inhabitants enrolled in the census of 1790, all but 201,000 live in rural areas; and while communications are improving beyond the miserable level of the Revolution, news still filters with great slowness to remote places.

What is the news that carries the most absorbing meaning? Politics. Government. The novelty, and the passion, of a new union. "Never in American annals," Charles Warren once observed, "has there been a period when men 'took their politics so hard' as in the twenty-five years between the framing of the Constitution and the end of the War of 1812."[2]

They are hard men: Washington, loved but enigmatic, rides at the crest of his popularity; the bitterness of his last years has not begun. That thin-skinned and well-stuffed Federalist, John Adams, presides over the Senate. In Massachusetts, the pugnacious diarist of Dedham, Nathaniel Ames, is warring with his brilliant Federalist brother, Fisher. The Spring of 1790 brings the death of Benjamin Franklin, an old man, much honored—but we forget how young so many of the founding fathers were: Jefferson is forty-seven in 1790; Madison thirty-nine, John Marshall thirty-five, Hamilton only thirty-three. In Virginia, Spencer Roane, one of the most neglected jurists of our history, is twenty-eight. John Taylor of Caroline, farmer, soldier, profound political thinker, is thirty-seven.

Some of the players in the developing drama are not yet born—Upshur and Hayne will not appear until 1791—and some are only boys: Henry Clay in Virginia; Wilson Lumpkin in Georgia; John Randolph, a precocious seventeen, impatiently learning law and politics. And far apart, as the last decade of the 18th century opens, are two eight-year-olds: In New England, Daniel Webster; and in up-country South Carolina, a slender, dark-eyed, brooding boy, John C. Calhoun.

Notes

Go to top.

2

The Chisholm Case

IT WILL be recalled that Section 2 of Article III of the Constitution extended the Supreme Court's jurisdiction to "controversies . . . between a State and Citizens of another State." There was no question that a State could *bring* such an action. Georgia, in 1792, had brought an action against one Brailsford, a British subject, to confiscate payment of a debt that was owed him.(3) But it was equally clear, or so the States thought, that no citizen could sue a State without the State's consent. Hamilton, among other advocates of the Constitution, had declared this immunity to be "inherent in the nature of sovereignty."(4)

In the autumn of 1792, in Virginia, came rumblings of a storm ahead. Suit was filed in the Supreme Court of the United States against the Commonwealth of Virginia by the Indiana Company, seeking clear title to certain lands "between the Alleghany mountains and the river Ohio, above the mouth of the Little Kanawha Creek." The company contended that it held valid title as the result of a deed, in 1768, from the Six United Nations of Indians.

But Virginia did not agree to this at all. Thirteen years earlier, on June 12, 1779, the Virginia General Assembly had disposed of the claim: "All deeds which have been or shall be made," said the Assembly at the time, "by any Indians, or by any Indian nation or nations, for lands within the limits of the charter and territory of Virginia . . . to or for the use or benefit of any private person or persons, shall be, and the same are hereby declared utterly void, and of no effect."

Yet here, in a new Union, before a new court, was the Indiana Company again reviving its claim. On December 18, 1792, the Virginia Assembly adopted a brief resolution. Because it marks a significant step in the beginnings of State interposition, it merits quotation substantially in full. The resolution first recalled the Assembly's action of 1779, and continued:

From the foregoing resolutions it appears, that the claim of the Indiana Company, has been already decided on by the legislature of this Commonwealth: Your committee are therefore of opinion, that such decision having been made previous to the adoption of the present Constitution, and under the former instrument of confederation (which expressly guaranteed perfect and unimpaired sovereignty as to all matters of internal government to all the States leagued under it) cannot be again called in question, before any other tribunal than the General Assembly of this Commonwealth, without a dangerous and unconstitutional assumption of power, which, if exercised, would give birth to a series of pernicious and disgraceful consequences, the extent and duration of which it is hardly possible to measure or calculate.

Resolved therefore, That the jurisdiction of the Supreme Court of the United States, does not and cannot extend to this case, it having been already decided on before a tribunal fully competent to its decision.

Resolved, That the State cannot be made a defendant in the said court, at the suit of any individual or individuals.

Resolved, That the executive be requested, to pursue such measures in this case, as may to them seem most conducive to the interest, honor and dignity of this Commonwealth.(5)

Look back at that language for a moment. Here, in 1792, was Virginia saying bluntly that the court's jurisdiction "does not and cannot extend" to a certain case, and further, that Virginia "cannot be made a defendant in the said court." Here was Virginia instructing her Governor to take "such measures" as he deemed conducive with the "interest, honor and dignity" of the State. One hundred and sixty-four years later, it will be seen, Virginia was to echo the language.

Before the Indiana Company could perfect its suit against Virginia, however, Alexander Chisholm of South Carolina, in the fall of 1792 filed suit in the Supreme Court against the State of Georgia. Chisholm appeared as executor of one Robert Farquhar, seeking recovery of property confiscated during the Revolution. Chisholm appeared, but Georgia did not.

On December 14, 1792, a resolution was offered in the Georgia House of Representatives declaring that for the State of Georgia to respond to Chisholm's petition would not only involve the States in numberless lawsuits. Acquiescence before the Court, it was said, also

would effectually destroy the retained sovereignty of the States, and would actually tend in its operation to annihilate the very shadow of State government, and to render them but tributary corporations to the government of the United States.(6)

Therefore, Georgia would not appear. Georgia would not be bound by the court's decree, whatever it might be. The Court was acting in a fashion "unconstitutional and extra-judicial."

But the case came on to be heard the following February, and on February 18, 1793, in one of the milestone decisions of the Court, Pennsylvania's James Wilson had this to say:

This is a case of uncommon magnitude. One of the parties to it is a STATE; certainly respectable, claiming to be *sovereign.* The question to be determined is, whether this State, so respectable, and whose claim soars so high, is amenable to the jurisdiction of the Supreme Court of the *United States?* This question, important in itself, will depend on others, more important still; and may, perhaps, be ultimately resolved into one, no less radical than this—"do the people of the *United States* form a NATION"(7)

To the majority of the Court, there was no question of this. A nation had in fact been formed by "the People of the United States," among whom were the people of Georgia. And in this nation, judicial authority over all things, over even the State of Georgia, had been vested in the high Court. That had been the will of the people of Georgia. They had joined others in forming themselves "into a nation for *national purposes."* They had instituted, for such purposes, "a national government, complete in all its parts, with powers legislative, executive and judiciary; and in all those powers extending over the whole nation." No person, said Wilson, and no State, could claim exemption from the jurisdiction of the national government. And as for the action brought by Farquhar's executors? The action was validly filed.

It was a 4-1 decision by the Court, with Iredell dissenting. The Court ordered the plaintiff's suit to be served on the Governor of Georgia, and commanded the State to appear or suffer judgment in default. From argument to opinion, the whole thing had taken but fourteen days.

A sense of profound shock swept the country. Massachusetts adopted a resolution denouncing the court's opinion. Virginia's Assembly declared:

That a State cannot under the Constitution of the United States, be made a defendant at the suit of any individual or individuals, and that the decision of the supreme Federal court, that a State may be placed in that situation, is incompatible with, and dangerous to the sovereignty and independence of the individual States, as the same tends to a general consolidation of these confederated republics.

The outrage in Georgia can be well imagined. Wilson's opinion had come down in mid-February; the Georgia Legislature did not convene until the following November, but nine months provided no cooling-off period. Governor Edward Telfair advised the Legislature that he had refused to make an appearance, despite a process served upon him, because "this would have introduced a precedent replete with danger to the Republic, and would have involved this State in complicated difficulties abstracted from the infractions it would have made on her retained sovereignty."(8) On November 21, the Georgia House of Representatives passed a bill providing that any Federal marshal who attempted to levy upon the property of Georgia in executing the court's order "shall be . . . guilty of felony, and shall suffer death, without the benefit of clergy, by being hanged."(9)

Let us take careful note of what happened next. The Court had said one thing —that it had power to hear this suit against Georgia. And Georgia, interposing, had said another thing—that the Court had no such authority. How was this question of contested power to be resolved? Who was right, Georgia or the Court?

The issue went to the States themselves. On February 19, 1793, the day after the Court's opinion came down, a resolution was offered in Congress proposing an amendment to the Constitution. In January of 1794, this resolution was put in final form and in March it was submitted to the States. New Jersey and Pennsylvania, in effect, voted for the Court: they refused to ratify. But New York, Rhode Island, Connecticut, Massachusetts, New Hampshire, Vermont (which had joined the Union in March of 1791), Virginia, Kentucky, Maryland, Delaware, North Carolina—and of course, Georgia—held that the Court was wrong. They ratified what is now the Eleventh Amendment. They declared that:

The judicial power of the United States shall not be construed to extend to any suit in law or equity commenced or prosecuted against one of the United States, by citizens of another State, or by citizens or subjects of any foreign state.

The necessary number of ratifications could be counted by February of 1795, but the amendment was not formally proclaimed a part of the Constitution until 1798. What is important to note, in this regard, is that Georgia totally defied the Court from the very inception of the suit in 1792. *Georgia defied the Court, and Georgia remained in the Union.* There was no violence, no secession, no anarchy. There was simply a question of contested power, submitted to the States for decision. And when they had decided it, that was the end of it. The Court in 1798 struck the Chisholm case from its calendar, and with it went all other suits against States commenced prior to the effective date of the Eleventh Amendment.(10)

Notes

Go to top.

Debt Assumption

NOW, Georgia's drastic action in the Chisholm case was not the only instance of State interposition in the first half-dozen years of the republic; it was only the most spectacular, and the most decisive. It is the best place to begin.

Actually, however, the controversy over suits against a State was antedated by a warm dispute over Federal resumption of debts incurred by the individual States during the Revolutionary War. In Virginia, the people "by persevering and strenuous exertions" had redeemed a considerable portion of their debts through the collection of heavy taxes imposed by the Virginia Assembly. They could look forward to "the most certain prospect of extinguishing the whole at a period not very distant," and they were entirely unwilling to tax themselves further for the payment of debts contracted by other States "which either have not paid any part thereof themselves, or have reduced them but in a small proportion compared with the payments made by this State." When Congress approved an act providing for assumption of all State debts, Virginia vigorously objected; and her resolutions of November 3 and 4, 1790, provide what are perhaps the earliest instances of State protest against Federal action. The first of these resolved

That so much of the act intitled "An act making provision for the debt of the United States," as assumes the payment of the State debts is repugnant to the Constitution of the United States, as it goes to the exercise of a power not granted to the general government.

The second, on the following day, declared that the debt assumption act

is dangerous to the rights and subversive of the interest of the people, and demands the marked disapprobation of the General Assembly.

Again, on December 16, 1790, the Virginia Assembly continued its objections against an act that was warranted by "neither policy, justice, nor the Constitution." The assumption act gave preference to holders of the principal of the continental debt, over the holders of the principal of the State debts, which seemed to the Virginia Assembly unfair and discriminatory. But the Assembly then turned away "from the impolicy and injustice of the act," in order to view the law in another light "in which . . . it appears still more odious and deformed."

During the whole discussion of the Federal Constitution by the convention of Virginia, your memorialists were taught to believe "that every power not granted, was retained." Under this impression and upon this positive condition, declared in the instrument of ratification, the said government was adopted by the people of this Commonwealth; but your memorialists can find no clause in the Constitution, authorizing Congress to assume the debts of the States! As the guardians then of the rights and interests of their constituents, as sentinels placed by them over the ministers of the Federal Government, to shield it from their encroachments, or at least to sound the alarm when it is threatened with invasion, they can never reconcile it to their consciences, silently to acquiesce in a measure which violates that hallowed maxim: A maxim on the truth and sacredness of which the Federal Government depended for its adoption in this Commonwealth.(11)

May it be suggested, in passing, that the high duty of State legislators, thus defined by Virginia in 1790, merits revival in our own time? The members of State legislatures could perform a service of immense value by serving today "as sentinels placed by [their constituents] over the ministers of the Federal Government," to shield the people's freedom from Federal encroachments "or at least to sound the alarm when it is threatened with invasion." It is a pity to reflect that this obligation of State legislatures, as conceived by the Virginia Assemblymen of 1790, has been so neglected. Our sentinels have slept; and the few alarms they have sounded in recent years have come too late.

Two other instances of State interposition in this period may be noted.

One occurred late in 1790, in North Carolina, when a Federal circuit court attempted, by writ of certiorari, to transfer a case to its jurisdiction from the Supreme Court of North Carolina. The State judges, said Nathaniel Macon later, simply refused to obey the Federal command, and the marshal found himself unable to execute the order. North Carolina's General Assembly warmly approved the State judges' resistance.(12)

A second chapter of interposition against Federal courts was written in New Hampshire in 1793 and 1794. Here the grievance dated from the capture of the brig *Susannah* by the privateer *McClary* in October of 1777. The *McClary* was owned and manned by citizens of New Hampshire, but was acting under a commission of the Continental Congress. New Hampshire's courts condemned the *Susannah* as a lawful prize, and in the view of New Hampshire, that ended the matter: No appeal was permitted, by State laws, to the Congress. However, objectors did appeal, and in September, 1783, the newly created Court of Appeals in Cases of Capture undertook to reverse the Supreme Court of New Hampshire. But New Hampshire paid no attention to this edict, and there the matter rested until the new Union was formed in 1788, and the new Federal courts came into being.

Then, to the amazement and chagrin of the people of New Hampshire, the principal petitioner, Elisha Doane, successfully revived an action in 1793 which they thought had been disposed of in 1778—before there had been Articles of Confederation, let alone a Constitution for the United States. On February 20, 1794, the New Hampshire Legislature warmly protested that the action was unsettling all the proceedings of the State governments prior to the existence of the Constitution; and will inevitably involve the States, and this State in particular, in confusion, and will weaken, if not perhaps destroy, the National Government.(13)

When this accomplished nothing, the New Hampshire Legislature, in January, 1795, for a second time remonstrated "against a violation of State independence and an unwarrantable encroachment in the courts of the United States."(14)

"Can the rage for annihilating all the power of the States, and reducing this extensive and flourishing country to one domination, make the administrators blind to the danger of violating all the principles of our former Government?" asked the Legislature. For their part, the New Hampshiremen well remembered tyranny; they were aware of the meaning of the Confederation; they would remind Congress that under that Confederation, State powers not expressly delegated were reserved. What New Hampshire had done prior to formation of the Union was wholly the business of New Hampshire: Her legislature would not submit laws made before the Constitution "to the adjudication of any power on earth, while the freedom of the Federal government shall afford any constitutional means of redress."

The declaration was in vain. A month later, the Supreme Court handed down a decision upholding the power of the new Federal courts to carry into effect decrees of the old Prize Court.(15)

It was a bitter dose for the States to swallow. The new Union was scarcely six years old. Yet already a pattern was taking shape along the lines that Patrick Henry had feared and Pendleton, Marshall, Madison, and Hamilton had discounted. In the debt assumption act, Congress had taken an action deemed unconstitutional by Virginia. Federal courts in two States had attempted to arrogate powers unto themselves in orders angrily resented by the States themselves. Worse still, the Supreme Court of the United States had acted in the Chisholm case in a manner so palpably unconstitutional that the States had been compelled to amend their fundamental law to preserve their sovereign power.

All this was part of the background that figured in events of 1798 and 1799, when the right of the States to interpose against Federal encroachment took eloquent and emphatic form.

Notes

Go to top.

The Kentucky and Virginia Resolutions

THE EVENTS that were to lead to the Kentucky and Virginia Resolutions in the winter of 1798 had their genesis at least five years earlier, and in a sense, twenty years earlier. On the one hand were those patriots, among them some courageous officers in the Revolution, who maintained a warm affection for England even as they made war upon the tyranny of George III. On theother were the followers of Jefferson, grateful for the aid of Lafayette, who viewed the coming French Revolution as a further flowering of the independent man.

This loose division abruptly widened in 1793, with the beheading of Louis XVI and Marie Antoinette; many a New Englander, generally indifferent in the cause, suddenly awoke to the excesses of the French Revolution. Friendly salutations of "Citizen Banker" and "Citizen Farmer" seemed no longer so pleasant. As the conflict between France and England burst forth with new fury, the political cleavage in the United States widened still more with Washington's proclamation of neutrality. This was bitterly received by Republicans, and when Jay's Treaty of 1795 was added to it, their resentment knew no bounds. The French also were angered: By 1796, the number of raids by French corsairs on American shipping had reached a level just short of total humiliation to the United States. Diplomatic relations between France and the United States, severely strained, reached a breaking point as Ambassador Pinckney cooled his heels in Paris.

John Adams' first action, following his inauguration in March of 1797, was to send John Marshall and Elbridge Gerry to Paris to join Pinckney in negotiations with Talleyrand. The three accomplished no more than the one. Instead, the Americans were handed a contemptuous proposition: France would negotiate on two conditions—one, an American loan; and two, a bribe of $250,000 paid to the French Directory. When word of this outrage finally reached the Capital in March of 1798, Adams hastily asked defense measures of the Congress. Washington was recalled from Mount Vernon; General Hamilton was told to prepare for the field; an appropriation was passed to speed construction of three frigates. Congress established a Department of the Navy and re-established the Marine Corps. In the wave of anti-French sentiment that swept the country, France's help in the Revolution was wholly forgotten, and "Jacobins" were denounced at every hand.

The political situation that obtained then, in the spring of 1798, could not occur now: Adams, a stout Federalist, was President; Jefferson, an ardent Republican, was Vice-President. No ready comparisons come to mind, but it was almost as if a McKin-ley were in the White House and a Wilson were presiding over the Senate. When Jefferson and other Republicans demanded to know the basis on which Adams had requested his defense measures, the President made public (on April 3, 1798) the dispatches from abroad. The French go-betweens were identified only as X, Y, and Z. With publication of the insulting offer, a cry arose that has come down in history: *Millions for defense, but not a cent for tribute.* In Philadelphia and New York, French sympathizers were stoned or publicly ridiculed. There began what Jefferson later was to describe as "this reign of witches."

To say that political partisanship alone prompted the almost incredible events that followed is to oversimplify the story. The fight between Federalists and Republicans far transcended mere party labels. As James Morton Smith has emphasized,(16) the times reflected the growing division between the commercial North and the agrarian South, between creditors and debtors, and most significantly, between different views on the matter of how, and by whom, government should be administered. Adams and Hamilton saw control of government slipping from their hands into the hands of a rabble of wild Irishmen, Jacobins, and libertarians. They saw it happening, and in the fashion of distressed politicians from time immemorial, they undertook to meet the situation in the only manner that occurred to them: They undertook to pass a law.

Actually, in the period between June 18 and July 14, 1798, they passed four laws. The first of these was a tightened Naturalization Act, by which an alien's period of residence, prior to obtaining citizenship, was increased from five to fourteen years. The object here was to keep immigrants, and especially the Irish, out of the Republicans' clutches. A second law (though it was chronologically the third in the sequence) was an Alien Enemies Act, a permanent piece of wartime legislation, which was not too bad an enactment.

But on June 25, Adams signed the Alien Friends Act, and on July 14, he signed the Sedition Act.

These last two acts have a nightmare aspect as an American reads them today. It seems impossible that a Congress ever could have enacted them.

The first of them authorized the President, whenever he wished, "to order all such aliens as he shall judge dangerous to the peace and safety of the United States, or shall have reasonable grounds to suspect are concerned in any treasonable or secret machinations against the government thereof, to depart out of the territory of the United States." If an alien, placed under such a deportation order, could prove that no injury to the country would result from allowing him to remain, the President could license the alien to stay—under such bond as the President deemed proper, and until the bond might be revoked at the President's decree.

The second of the acts made it a crime, punishable by imprisonment of up to five years, for any persons to "conspire together" with intent "to oppose any measure or measures of the government of the United States, which are or shall be directed by proper authority." Further,

. . . if any person shall write, print, utter, or publish, or shall cause or procure to be written, printed, uttered or published, or shall knowingly and willingly assist or aid in writing, printing, uttering or publishing any false, scandalous and malicious writing or writings against the government of the United States, or either house of the Congress of the United States, or the President of the United States, with intent to defame the said government, or either house of the said Congress, or the said President, or to bring them, or either or any of them, into contempt or disrepute,

he could be punished by a fine of up to $2,000 or by imprisonment not to exceed two years. The Sedition Act made it a criminal offense "to excite the hatred of the good people of the United States" against Congress or the President. Still further, it was made unlawful for anyone to urge opposition or resistance to any law of the United States or any act of the President, "or to resist, oppose or defeat any such law or act."

Reasonably minded men might debate the constitutionality of the Alien Friends Act: Under the broad powers of the Congress to provide for the common defense and the national security, perhaps a case could be made for vesting such sweeping powers, even in peacetime, in a President—though the case would have to be made at the sacrifice of every tradition of Anglo-Saxon justice and right conduct.

It seems unbelievable, now, that anyone ever could have sustained the constitutionality of the Sedition Act. Its whole purpose was to stifle political opposition to Adams and the Federalist administration. The law crashed headlong into the Constitutional provision that "Congress shall make no law . . . abridging the freedom of speech or of the press." Yet the dismal truth is that every leading Federalist of the day approved the act; even John Marshall, though he thought it "useless," and "would have voted against it," never regarded the law as unconstitutional—indeed, he was to file a minority report in the Virginia General Assembly upholding its constitutionality. So, too, at least three justices of the Supreme Court—Paterson, Chase, and Bushrod Washington— repeatedly upheld the act. In time, the legislatures of half a dozen States also were to approve it.

The only virtue of the two acts was to be found in their early expiration dates. The Alien Friends Act was to expire June 25, 1800. the Sedition Act on the last day of Adams' term, March 3, 1801. But once they were passed, the country entered upon a period of persecution, suppression, censorship, and "McCarthyism" such as the junior Senator from Wisconsin, in our own time, never dreamed of. Mr. McCarthy was a piker. He should have known the Hon. Timothy Pickering, Secretary of State, and Mr. Justice Samuel Chase, perhaps the worst judge who ever sat on the highest court in the land.

The two years that elapsed after adoption of the Sedition Act merit our attention today for two reasons. One is to put in perspective the "dark night of oppression" that Mr. Elmer Davis is so fond of bewailing these days. The second is to comprehend the serious nature of the provocation that led to the

Kentucky and Virginia Resolutions, and to Madison's famed Report of 1799.

It would be unthinkable today to suppress a newspaper, to drive it out of existence, or to jail its editor, merely because the paper opposed acts of the administration in power. When a Senate committee in 1956 undertook merely to question a few copyreaders of the *New York Times,* who were suspected—with good reason—of Communist backgrounds, liberal journals across the country erupted with fulsome laments for freedom of the press.

Consider for a moment what happened in 1798 and 1799.

A contagion of "anti-Jacobinism," spread by some shrewd propagandists for the Federalist party, swept the land: "The eyes of the devouring monster are upon us."(17) Crowds of young Americans donned the black cockade, emblem of true Americanism, and roamed the streets of Philadelphia and New York searching for Jacobin sympathizers. It was the Federalists' contention that a "French faction" was at work under the sinister direction of Thomas Jefferson, a disloyal and subversive element engaged in infiltrating government, press, even textbooks and schools. French tutors were denounced as French spies. The entire Republican party, even then, was termed the party "of treason."(18) The only "true Americans" were Adams, Hamilton, and other leaders of the Federalist party.

The bulk of the press of that day supported the Federalist cause and fed the anti-Jacobin fires. But there were exceptions. One was Benjamin Bache's *Aurora,* in Philadelphia. Bache was a grandson of Benjamin Franklin, which surely might have provided him respectable auspices, but he was a stinging gadfly with a marvelous gift for the contemptuous phrase. A virulent, vindictive, scurrilous fellow, only twenty-nine the summer of the Sedition Act, he first traduced Washington and then turned on "the blind, bald, crippled, toothless, querulous ADAMS."

On June 27, 1798, two weeks before the Sedition Act was passed, Bache was arrested on a Federal warrant charging him with having libeled the President. Before Bache could be brought to trial, however, he died of yellow fever.

Bache was succeeded on the *Aurora* the following November by William Duane, another young journalist of Republican sympathies who also was a master of invective—so remarkable a master, indeed, that scarcely eight months passed before Pickering was demanding that he be prosecuted for pouring "an uninterrupted stream of slander on the American Government."(19) Duane was arrested in July, 1799, charged with seditious libel, and subjected to more than two years of vengeful harassment by Federalists before they abandoned their persecution.

Another influential editor of the day, who like Duane had an Irish background, was John Daly Burk, of the *Time Piece.* He had settled in Boston, then moved on to New York. He wrote, among other things, that

John Adams was responsible for the approaching war with France; that Adams had his heart set on becoming King; that Adams had deliberately falsified Gerry's dispatches from France. In a truculent impulse, Burk cried that he wished the French would come and put "every scoundrel in favor of the [Federalist] government . . . to the guillotine." On July 6, 1798, Burk was arrested for seditious libel, and bailed for trial in the autumn. While he waited trial, his newspaper collapsed.(20)

There also was Thomas Cooper, an Englishman who came to Northumberland County, Pennsylvania, in 1794, and in time became editor of the Northumberland *Gazette*. He, too, ran afoul of Pickering and Adams. On April 9, 1800, he was arrested for seditious libel. On April 24, he was found guilty, fined $400, and sent to prison for six months.

One of the most active Republican editors of the time was James Thompson Callender, of the Richmond *Examiner*. He was a despicable little man, usually filthy, most often dressed in a greasy jacket and a pair of stained and rumpled pants. One writer has described him as a "brilliant, drunken, fearless, mercenary product of Grubb Street, whose scurrilous pen was at the service of the highest bidder and whose libels were produced to order."(21) Callender had written a book, *The Prospect Before Us*, and a copy of this polemic, thoughtfully put in the hands of Justice Chase as he was out riding circuit, was sufficient to send Chase snarling after Callender's scalp. Callender's sin was that he had described Federal judges and ambassadors as "paper jobbers" and "poltroons." He had written that Adams "contrived pretenses to double the annual expense of government, by useless fleets, armies, sinecures and jobs of every possible description."(22) This was enough for Chase to see to it that Callender was indicted for sedition as "a person of wicked, depraved, evil-disposed, disquiet and turbulent mind and disposition," who falsely and maliciously had designed to defame the President and bring him into disrepute.

Thus Callender was tried, in the summer of 1800, before a justice of the Supreme Court determined to convict him at any price. Chase throttled defense counsel, and badgered attorneys until they retired in disgust. When William Wirt attempted to argue the constitutionality of the Sedition Act, Chase forced him to sit down, declared that no jury could pass on the point, and bellowed from the bench that to permit a petit jury to pass on the constitutionality of a law "would be extremely dangerous." "Hear my words," cried Chase, "I wish the world to know them—my opinion is the result of mature reflection." It was no surprise when Callender was found guilty, fined $200, and sentenced to nine months in prison.(23)

Bache, Duane, Burk, and Callender were not the only editors persecuted in this period; they were only the most influential. There was Thomas Adams, of the *Independent Chronicle* in Boston, who died before he could be brought to trial. There was Abijah Adams, his brother, sentenced to one month in jail; and Anthony Haswell, of the *Vermont Gazette*, a $200 fine and two months in jail; and Charles Holt, of the Bee in New Haven, tried before Bushrod Washington, six months and $200; and David Frothingham, of the New York *Argus,* driven to the wall by Alexander Hamilton, four months and $100.

Nor were editors the only victims. There was a Vermont Congressman, Matthew Lyon, a belligerent fellow who once tangled with a fellow Congressman on the floor of the House in a fight with canes and fire tongs. Because of articles he published in the Vermont *Journal* critical of Adams, Lyon was indicted for sedition, brought to trial before Paterson, and sentenced to four months in jail. While languishing in his cell at Vergennes, a martyr to the Republican cause, he proceeded to run for re-election and defeated his opponents by almost two to one.

There were still other prosecutions. In Newark, one July day in 1799, townsfolk turned out for a parade honoring Adams. As the cannons burst forth in presidential salute, a village drunk, one Luther Baldwin, came listing toward John Burnet's saloon. For what reason, inquired this bleary Republican, were the cannons firing? For Adams, he was told. To this Baldwin replied, perhaps with gestures, that for his own part, he did not care if the cannon ball went up the President's arse.(24) For this he was arrested for sedition, tried before Bushrod Washington and District Judge Robert Morris, found guilty, and fined $150.

There was also a crackerbox radical in Dedham, Massachusetts, David Brown, who made the mistake of refusing to tell Justice Chase the names of friends and associates who shared his Republican views: He was fined $450, and sent to jail for eighteen months.

The list could be much extended throughout the Eastern Seaboard. The whole period from mid-Summer of 1798 to Jefferson's inauguration in 1801 saw newspapers closed, Republican critics tarred and feathered, opposition Congressmen abused and vilified. Directing the whole ugly scene were the cool hands of Hamilton and Pickering. The hostile eyes of Judges Washington and Paterson gazed from the Federal bench, and everywhere there raged the burly, bustling, pig-eyed figure of Samuel Chase, a tyrant who held in his coarse hands the meaning of the Constitution.

Jefferson had almost clipped the wings of the Federalists' Naturalization Law of June 18, 1798. The fourteen-year requirement passed by one vote only. Presiding over the Senate, however, he was unable to block the Alien Act of June 25 or the Sedition Act that followed on July 14. Sick at heart, he watched the dominant Federalists make a mockery of individual liberties and press freedom. Barely ten years after a new Constitution had become the supreme law of the land, Jefferson witnessed its palpable violation.

He could not remain idle. Six years earlier, Kentucky had come into the Union, but six years had done little to quiet the frontier spirit of the

Kentucky wilderness. In Kentucky was his good friend John Breckinridge, who had studied law in Charlottesville, served in Congress from Virginia, and then returned to Lexington, to become first Attorney General of Kentucky and later a member of the Ken-tucky House of Representatives from Fayette County. So Jefferson arranged a meeting at Monticello one evening with Breckinridge and his fellow Kentuckian, Colonel W. C. Nicholas. "Happening to be together," he was to write Breckinridge's son in 1821, they consulted upon the dangers of the Alien and Sedition Acts. (25) "These gentlemen pressed me strongly to sketch a resolution," said Jefferson, but it may better be imagined that it was Jefferson himself who tactfully did the pressing. As Vice-President, he could not participate publicly in the move he had in mind; already, he was being denounced daily as a traitor and a Jacobin. But enjoining Breckinridge and Nicholas to secrecy, he did in fact draft a resolution for the Kentucky Assembly, and in early November of 1798, Breckinridge offered it in the Kentucky House.

Now, the Kentucky Resolution of November 16, 1798, is a fairly long document. It was composed of nine separate resolves. Numbers Two through Eight related to specific grievances under the Alien and Sedition Acts, and may be passed over here. But the first and the ninth resolves establish foundation stones for the whole concept of State sovereignty and States' rights. This was the first:

I. Resolved, that the several States composing the United States of America are not united on the principle of unlimited submission to their General Government; but that by compact under the style and title of a Constitution for the United States and of amendments thereto, they constituted a general government for special purposes, delegated to that government certain definite powers, reserving each State to itself, the residuary mass of right to their own self-government; and that whensoever the General Government assumes undelegated powers, its acts are unauthoritative, void, and of no force.

Let us pause there for a moment. Hamilton is handy authority (though not even the most ardent apostle of centralized government could deny it), that laws, to be lawful, must have proper weight behind them. "There is no position which depends on clearer principles," Hamilton had said, "than that every act of a delegated authority, contrary to the tenor of the commission under which it is exercised, is void. No legislative act, therefore, contrary to the Constitution [and, it may be interpolated, no judicial decree either] can be valid." That is exactly what Jefferson was saying here, in the opening sentence of the Kentucky Resolution, and it is as true today as it was in 1798. The resolution continued:

That to this compact each State acceded as a State, and is an integral party, its co-States forming, as to itself, the other party.

And then the essence of the right of interposition:

That the Government created by this compact was not made the exclusive or final judge of the extent of the powers delegated to itself, *since that would have made its discretion, and not the Constitution, the measure of its powers;* but that as in all other cases of compact among parties having no common judge, each party has an equal right to judge for itself, as well of infractions as of the mode and measure of redress. [Emphasis supplied.]

What Jefferson was saying here was that, yes, the *Constitution* is the supreme law of the land; and, yes, the *Constitution* is superior to anything in the laws and Constitutions of the States. But one ultimate power remains, superior to the instrument itself—the power that created the instrument, that made it and can unmake it, the power of the sovereign States themselves. By any other line of reasoning, a Frankenstein creature must be accepted, a creature more powerful than its creator—a general government with power to make "its discretion, *and not the Constitution,* the measure of its powers."

Kentucky's final resolve in 1798 began with a declaration of affection for the Union and faithfulness to "the plain intent and meaning" of the Constitution. But Kentucky profoundly believed

that to take from the States all the powers of self-government, and transfer them to a general and consolidated Government, without regard to the special delegations and reservations solemnly agreed to in that compact, is not for the peace, happiness, or prosperity of these States.

Then the resolve continued on a stronger and more ominous theme:

. . . Therefore, this Commonwealth is determined, as it doubts not its co-States are, tamely to submit to undelegated and consequently unlimited powers in no man or body of men on earth.

What were the "unlimited powers" here involved? Under the Alien and Sedition Acts, said the Kentucky Resolution,

the General Government may place any act they think proper on the list of crimes and punish it themselves, whether enumerated or not enumerated by the Constitution as cognizable by them; . . . they may transfer its cognizance to the President or any other person who may himself be the accuser, counsel, judge and jury, whose suspicions may be the evidence, his order the sentence, his officer the executioner, and his breast the sole record of the transaction. . . .

The "friendless alien" had been selected "as the safest subject of a first experiment" in the absolute dominion of one man, but the American citizen would soon follow. Indeed, the Sedition Act already had seized upon American citizens for its prey. Prosecutions under these offensive laws, unless halted, would furnish "new calumnies against Republican Governments, and new pretexts for those who wish it to be believed, that man cannot be governed but by a rod of iron."

Yet it had been urged that the Sedition Act was not intended to stifle honest criticism or reasonable opposition to the government; it was aimed only at libellers who would defame all government. Have confidence, the Federalists had urged, and all would be well.

Jefferson answered in hard and ringing words. Let it be resolved, said the Kentucky Resolution,

That it would be a dangerous delusion were a confidence in the men of our choice to silence our fears for the safety of our rights; that confidence is everywhere the parent of despotism; free government is founded in jealousy and not in confidence; it is jealousy and not confidence which prescribes limited Constitutions to bind down those whom we are obliged to trust with power; that our Constitution has accordingly fixed the limits to which and no further our confidence may go; and let the honest advocate of confidence read the Alien and Sedition Acts and say if the Constitution has not been wise in fixing the limits to the government it created, and whether we should be wise in destroying those limits. . . .In questions of power, then, let no more be heard of confidence in man, but bind him down from mischief by the chains of the Constitution.

Thus setting forth her views of the Alien and Sedition Acts, and of the nature of the Union, Kentucky asked in her resolution for co-States to resolve the question: Are these acts authorized, or are they not, by the Constitution? For Kentucky's own part, the Legislature viewed the acts

as so palpably against the Constitution as to amount to an undisguised declaration, that the compact is not meant to be the measure of the powers of the General Government, but that it will proceed in the exercise over these States of all powers whatsoever.

This would mean, said the Kentucky Resolution, that the States had surrendered the form of government they so recently had created—that they elected to live under a government "deriving its powers from its own will, and not from our authority." The Resolution prayed that the co-States, recurring to their natural right, would concur "in declaring these acts void and of no force," and would unite in demanding their repeal.

Speaking to this Resolution, Breckinridge made it plain in the Kentucky House that something more than a mere memorial was involved.

"When the government of the United States enact impolitic laws," he declared, "we can only say: We pray you to repeal them. As to matters of mere policy, they are, it is admitted, vested with a discretionary power.

"But when they pass laws beyond the limits of the Constitution —laws which they are no more authorized to pass than the Grand Turk—we do not ask a repeal, but ought to make a legislative declaration that, being unconstitutional, they are therefore void and of no effect."(26)

Breckinridge hoped that Congress would repeal the offending laws, without waiting for them to expire. Meanwhile, he prayed that honest judges would refuse to act upon them. But if the courts should nevertheless attempt to enforce the laws?

"I hesitate not to declare it as my opinion that it is then the right and duty of the several States to nullify those acts, and to protect their citizens from their operation."

It was objected that Paterson, Washington, Chase, and some lower Federal judges already had held the acts Constitutional. If the courts said the laws were Constitutional, who could say otherwise?

"Who are the judiciary?" demanded Breckinridge. "Who are they, but a part of the servants of the people created by the Federal compact? And if the servants of the people have a right, is it good reasoning to say that the people by whom and for whose benefit both they and the government were created, are destitute of that right?"

It was not to be supposed, he added, that the peoples' immediate representatives, serving in the government of a State, were to do nothing but "to behold in silence the most flagrant violations of their rights, and bow in silence to any power that may attempt to impress them." Certainly the States had a right "to remonstrate with men who may meditate their annihilation," and for the time being, only an expression, a remonstrance, and an appeal were proposed: "We do not pretend to set ourselves up as censors for the Union, but we will firmly express our own opinions and call upon the other States to examine their political situation."

Kentucky completed its action on November 16. Four weeks later, on Thursday, December 13, Virginia took up the cause. At the instance of James Madison, who was not himself a member of the General Assembly, John Taylor of Caroline offered in the House of Delegates what is now known simply as the "Virginia Resolution." Eight days later it won approval in the House by a party-line vote of 100-63; the Virginia Senate promptly concurred, 14-3, and on Christmas Eve, the Resolution went forth to sister States.

The Virginia Resolution(27) is considerably shorter than its counterpart in Kentucky. It opens with a conciliatory resolve that the Virginia General

Assembly doth unequivocally express a firm resolution to maintain and defend the Constitution of the United States, and the Constitution of this State, against every aggression either foreign or domestic, and that they will support the government of the United States in all measures warranted by the former.

The second resolve continues on a firmer note:

That this Assembly most solemnly declares a warm attachment to the Union of the States, to maintain which it pledges all its powers; and that for this end, it is their duty to watch over and oppose every infraction of those principles which constitute the only basis of that union, because a faithful observance of them, can alone secure its existence and the public happiness.

As Madison was to observe in his report the following year, "no unfavorable comment" could be directed toward the sentiments expressed to that point.

It is in the third paragraph that the Virginia Resolution gets to the heart of the State and Federal relationship under the Constitution:

That this Assembly doth explicitly and peremptorily declare, that it views the powers of the Federal Government, as resulting from the compact, to which the States are parties, as limited by the plain sense and intention of the instrument constituting that compact; as no further valid than they are authorized by the grants enumerated in that compact; and that in case of a deliberate, palpable, and dangerous exercise of other powers, not granted by the said compact, the States who are parties thereto, have the right, and are in duty bound, to interpose for arresting the progress of the evil, and for maintaining within their respective limits, the authorities, rights, and liberties appertaining to them.

One amendment was made in this paragraph by the House prior to approval of the Resolution. As Taylor introduced the resolution, the language would have recited that Federal powers result "from the compact to which the States *alone* are parties." With Taylor's consent, the word "alone" was dropped.

Because this third paragraph of the Virginia Resolution is so essential to the doctrine of States' rights which this essay undertakes to defend and to promote, it will be argued at some length hereafter. In the interests of an orderly presentation, it seems best at this point simply to proceed with the text of the Resolution as adopted in the Virginia Assembly that December.

The fourth resolve, except for its concluding reference to monarchy (which seems anachronistic now, but was a serious matter then), might have been drafted in our own time. It declares

That the General Assembly doth also express its deep regret, that a spirit has in sundry instances, been manifested by the Federal Government, to enlarge its powers by forced constructions of the Constitutional charter which defines them; and that indications have appeared of a design to expound certain general phrases (which having been copied from the very limited grant of powers in the former articles of confederation were the less liable to be misconstrued) so as to destroy the meaning and effect, of the particular enumeration which necessarily explains and limits the general phrases; and so as to consolidate the States by degrees, into one sovereignty, the obvious tendency and inevitable consequence of which would be, to transform the present republican system of the United States, into an absolute, or at best a mixed monarchy.

In the fifth and sixth paragraphs, the resolution takes up the immediate provocation of the Alien and Sedition Acts, and recalls the devotion to freedom of the press that was deeply held in Virginia then, and—it may be added, with a Virginia editor's pride in his State—is held as devotedly now. Here the Assembly resolved:

That the General Assembly doth particularly protest against the palpable and alarming infractions of the Constitution, in the two late cases of the "Alien and Sedition Acts" passed at the last session of Congress; the first of which exercises a power nowhere delegated to the Federal Government, and which by uniting legislative and judicial powers to those of executive, subverts the general principles of free government, as well as the particular organization, and positive provisions of the Federal Constitution; and the other of which acts, exercises in like manner, a power not delegated by the Constitution, but on the contrary, expressly and positively forbidden by one of the amendments thereto;—a power, which more than any other, ought to produce universal alarm, because it is levelled against that right of freely examining public characters and measures, and of free communication among the people thereon, which has ever been justly deemed, the only effectual guardian of every other right.

That this State having by its convention, which ratified the Federal Constitution, expressly declared, that among other essential rights, "the liberty of conscience and of the press cannot be cancelled, abridged, restrained, or modified by any authority of the United States," and from its extreme anxiety to guard these rights from every possible attack of sophistry or ambition, having with other States, recommended an amendment for that purpose, which amendment was, in due time, annexed to the Constitution, it would mark a reproachful inconsistency, and criminal degeneracy, if an indifference were now shewn, to the most palpable violation of one of the rights, thus declared and secured; and to the establishment of a precedent which may be fatal to the other.

In the seventh paragraph, the Virginia Resolution returns to the conciliatory note with which Madison and Taylor began. The people of Virginia express their sincere affection for their brethren in other States, acknowledge their anxiety for establishing and perpetuating the Union, and avow their "most scrupulous fidelity to that Constitution which is the pledge of mutual friendship and the instrument of mutual happiness." On this basis,

the General Assembly doth solemnly appeal to the like dispositions of the other States, in confidence that they will concur with this Commonwealth in declaring, as it does hereby declare, that the acts aforesaid, are unconstitutional;(28) and that the necessary and proper measures will be taken by each, for co-operating with this State, in maintaining the authorities, rights and liberties, reserved to the States respectively, or to the people.

The concluding, ninth, paragraph of the resolves directs that copies be sent to other States.

Now, that is the Virginia Resolution of 1798. It was thoroughly debated from December 13 through December 21 in the House of Delegates. To be sure, many of the most illustrious and best known Virginians of the Convention of 1788 were not present in the Hall: Mason was dead; Henry, dying by inches at Red Hill; Marshall, busily campaigning for Congress; Madison, on the sidelines—he had retired from Congress the year before, and was not to be elected to the Virginia Assembly until the following year. But no apologies are necessary for the quality of the debate. Led by John Taylor of Caroline in favor of the Resolution, and by George Keith Taylor of Prince George County, an ardent Federalist, against it, the argument profoundly explored the nature of the Federal Union.

Something should be said of John Taylor. He was born, probably in 1753, (29) in Orange County, Virginia; left an orphan at ten; raised by his uncle, Edmund Pendleton, in Caroline County. He had fought in the Revolution; as a major, he had commanded troops under Lafayette in the weeks before Yorktown. Twice he served in the Virginia Legislature, first from 1779 to 1785, again from 1796 to 1800. He was an active and successful lawyer, three times a member of the United States Senate, a resourceful farmer whose theories of soil conservation (set out in *Arator* in 1813) antedated many of the modern farm practices of today. Above all, Taylor was a student of politics and government. He set out, in *Construction Construed and Constitutions Vindicated* (1820) and again in *New Views of the Constitution* (1823) a veritable Summa Theologiae for the States' Righter. These works are not easy reading—John Randolph of Roanoke once complained that Taylor needed a translator for his books(30)—but they rank with Calhoun's great addresses of 1831 and 1832 in expounding the federal nature of the Union. Thomas H. Benton placed him high among "that constellation of great men which shone so brightly in Virginia in his day,"(31) and Beveridge much later was to describe him as "the bravest, most consistent, most unselfish, as well as one of the ablest of

Republicans."(32)

John Taylor of Caroline opened debate on the Virginia Resolution with a direct attack on the Alien and Sedition Acts, but shortly the issues broadened. And when Archibald Magill, a Federalist Delegate from Frederick County, declared it "clear and evident" that the Federal government had a right "at common law" to enact the Sedition Law,(33) the whole debate was enlarged to explore the State and Federal relationship. It was Taylor's position, of course, that the Federal government had no inherent powers of "common law." The truth was then (and is now), that the Congress draws its authority from the enumerated powers of the Constitution only, and beyond these limits Congress has no authority.

What if Congress palpably exceed its authority? What was the remedy, if, as in this case, Congress enacted a grossly unconstitutional law, the executive signed it, and the courts approved it? Were the States and the people helpless?

Taylor thought not. Almost six months earlier, on June 25, he had planted in Jefferson's fertile mind the seed of the Kentucky Resolution: "The right of the State governments to expound the Constitution," he had written, "might possibly be made the basis of a movement toward its amendment."(34) And beyond the State governments, said Taylor, anticipating South Carolina's action of November, 1832, were the people in State conventions—they are "incontrovertibly the contracting parties." But some step was imperative at once, and the asserted right of Virginia to interpose "for arresting the progress of the evil" provided a sound and Constitutional approach.

Now, William Cowan, a Federalist Delegate from Lunenburg County, had termed the Taylor-Madison Resolution a perfidious act, "because, by undertaking to declare one law of Congress unconstitutional, the Legislature would assume a power of declaring all their laws unconstitutional."(35)

Let us follow Taylor's response carefully, for he is replying here to the objection most frequently voiced against the doctrine of interposition—that it would breed constitutional chaos.

Let the proposition be reversed, said Taylor. Would it be said that the Legislature could not declare this act of Congress unconstitutional?

Admitting such a position, did not these consequences evidently follow, that the check meditated against Congress in the existence of the State governments, was demolished; that Congress might at its pleasure violate the Constitutional rights of these governments; that they must instantly become dependent, and be finally annihilated? Could it be perfidious to preserve the freedom of religion, of speech, of the press, and even the right of petitioning for a redress of grievances?(36)

Federalist speakers had insisted, Taylor observed, "that every government inherently possesses the powers necessary for its own preservation." Without conceding the point, in the case of a Federal government created by the States, was it not evident that the broad principle surely applied to the State governments themselves? It must follow "that the State governments have a right to withstand such unconstitutional laws of Congress [and, it may be interpolated, unconstitutional decrees of a Supreme Court] as may tend to their destruction, because 'such a power is necessary for their preservation.'"

Suppose, asked Taylor, Congress were to re-establish the plan of inheritance by primogeniture? Obviously, Congress had no Constitutional authority to enact such a law. Were the States to let their chancery courts fall into chaos, and all State laws of inheritance and descent be upset, while State legislatures merely remonstrated with the Congress or petitioned for repeal? By the time new Congressmen could be elected on a pledge to repeal the law, the mischief would be done; eggs once broken and scrambled could not be made whole again. Were the States to submit to such a clear invasion of their reserved powers, "all powers whatsoever would gradually be absorbed by, and consolidated in, the general government."

Turning to another argument, Taylor noted that Congress clearly had a procedure, under Article V, by which it could check and challenge encroachment by the States upon the Federal sphere: Two-thirds of each House of Congress could propose an amendment to the Constitution to resolve a question of contested power. Similarly, two-thirds of the States, perceiving an encroachment by Federal authority, could demand that a convention be called to propose an amendment for the same purpose. But in the end, *who was to decide such questions?* Obviously, *the States themselves*. Congress could propose; the States would dispose. Let it never be supposed, said Taylor emphatically, "that the States hold their constitutional rights by the courtesy of Congress."(37) No. "Congress is the creature of the States and of the people; but neither the States nor the people are the creatures of Congress. It would be evidently absurd, that the creature should exclusively construe the instrument of its own existence."

In a milder tone, Taylor then emphasized the intention of the Virginia Resolution. Was insurrection proposed? Or violent secession from the Union? Resort to arms? None of these. Are the Republicans, he asked, possessed of fleets and armies? If not, to what could they appeal for defense and support? To nothing save public opinion. If that should be against them, they must yield. Meanwhile, the resolution of interposition offered to Virginia "the only possible and ordinary mode of ascertaining the opinion of two-thirds of the States, by declaring its own, and asking theirs." The States, in the last resort, were the final referees.

It was objected that the Supreme Court was created to arbitrate such questions of contested power. This was Taylor's reply:

With respect, he said, to the remedy proposed in the talents and integrity of the continental judges, without regarding the prejudices which might probably exist in favour of the government, from which an appointment should flow, it might be remarked, that the judges by the Constitution are not made its exclusive guardians. That if continental judges were the proper referees as to the constitutionality of continental laws, State judges were the proper referees as to the constitutionality of State laws; that neither possessed a power over the other, whence a clashing of adjudication might ensue; and that if either had been a *superior,* the same consequences would result as would flow from a superiority of Congress, or of the States over the other, with this additional aggravation, that the people could not by their elections influence a constitutional question, to be decided by the judges, as they could to a certain extent, when it was to be decided by a general or State legislature. . . .(38)

Taylor's argument was long and tightly reasoned. Unlike Henry or Mason or Randolph, he had no gift for humor or for the digressions that relieve a major speech. His address of December 20 must have wearied the House, for late in the afternoon, when a Federalist Delegate from the Eastern Shore arose to reply, "such a noise prevailed, from the impatience of the committee to rise, that he could not be distinctly heard; he declined, and sat down."

Yet Taylor's arguments carried the day. On the next afternoon, despite an equally long and humorless address by George Keith Taylor, the Virginia Resolution came to a vote; and after three Federalist challenges had been beaten off; it passed and went to the Senate by a straight party-line division, 100-63. And on the 24th, as we have noted, the Senate sent it forth.

During the course of the debate, twenty-four-year-old James Barbour, who later was to have a brilliant career in Virginia, had freely predicted what would happen: Other States, under the domination of Federalist legislatures, would reject any resolutions from Kentucky or Virginia critical of the Adams administration.(39) Indeed they did: Delaware promptly declared the Virginia Resolution "an unjustifiable interference with the General Government . . . and of dangerous tendency." Rhode Island denounced "the very unwarrantable resolutions." Massachusetts said that "The people, in that solemn compact which is declared to be the supreme law of the land, have not constituted the State legislatures the judges of the acts or measures of the Federal governments." New York spurned these "inflammatory and pernicious sentiments and doctrines." Connecticut viewed the Resolution "with deep regret." New Hampshire, resolving that the Alien and Sedition Acts were "constitutional and expedient," declared that "State Legislatures are not proper tribunals to determine the constitutionality of the laws of the General Government." Vermont, which "highly disapproves," added that the power to decide on the constitutionality of laws made by Congress had been "exclusively vested in the judiciary courts of the Union."

And throughout the spring of 1799, the half-war with France brought new prosecutions of Republican sympathisers. Samuel Chase, his wig askew, continued on circuit. The Federalist party, bent on its own destruction, rushed headlong into the revolution of 1800 that swept Jefferson into the presidency.

The adverse replies of Federalist legislatures, as Barbour had noted, were clearly predictable; but predictable or not, they had to be answered:

Kentucky, acknowledging that further action would be "unavailing," nevertheless stood her ground in a second resolution, adopted unanimously on November 14, 1799. It is not long:

RiESOLVED, That this Commonwealth considers the Federal Union, upon the terms and for the purposes specified in the late compact, conducive to the liberty and happiness of the several States: That it does now unequivocally declare its attachment to the Union, and to that compact, agreeably to its obvious and real intention, and will be among the last to seek its dissolution: That, if those who administer the General Government be permitted to transgress the limits fixed by that compact, by a total disregard to the special delegations of power therein contained, an annihilation of the State Governments, and the creation upon their ruins, of a General Consolidated Government, will be the inevitable consequence: That the principle and construction contended for by sundry of the State legislatures, that the General Government is the exclusive judge of the extent of the powers delegated to it, stop nothing [short] of *despotism*—since the discretion of those who administer the government, and not the *Constitution,* would be the measure of their powers: That the several States who formed that instrument being sovereign and independent, have the unquestionable right to judge of the infraction; and, *That a Nullification by those sovereignties, of all unauthorized acts done under color of that instrument is the rightful remedy:* That this Commonwealth does, under the most deliberate reconsideration, declare, that the said Alien and Sedition Laws are, in their opinion, palpable violations of the said Constitution: and, however cheerfully it may be disposed to surrender its opinion to a majority of its sister States, in matters of ordinary or doubtful policy, yet, in momentous regulations like the present, which so vitally wound the best rights of the citizen, it would consider a silent acquiescence as highly criminal: That, although this commonwealth, as a party to the federal compact, will bow to the laws of the Union, yet, it does, at the same [time] declare, that it will not now, or ever hereafter, cease to oppose in a constitutional manner, every attempt at what quarter soever offered, to violate that compact. And, finally, in order that no pretext or arguments may be drawn from a supposed acquiescence, on the part of this Commonwealth in the constitutionality of those laws, and be thereby used as precedents for similar future violations of the Federal compact—this Commonwealth does now enter against them its solemn PROTEST.(40)

The most notable aspect of this Second Kentucky Resolution, and the one to which attention most frequently is drawn, is the use of the word "nullification"—that "a nullification by those sovereignties, of all unauthorized acts done under color of that instrument, is the rightful remedy." It is a mistake to read into Kentucky's protest of 1799 a Jeffersonian sanction for South Carolina's action of 1832. Considered as a whole, the resolution is what its concluding phrase declares it to be—a protest on the part of Kentuckians who "will bow to the laws of the Union," but "will not cease to oppose, in a Constitutional manner," laws which the State solemnly regards as palpably unconstitutional. This was an expression of opinion that the laws were void, and hence not laws at all; and it was a pledge to oppose them by every Constitutional means. When it is recalled that the hated enactments, at this point, had fewer than fifteen months to run before their statutory expiration, it may be submitted that neither Kentucky nor Virginia felt that more drastic action was required.

Notes

Go to top.

5

Mr. Madison's Report of 1799

THIS WAS Madison's view in Virginia. The month after Kentucky adopted her Second Resolution, Madison brought to the Virginia House of Delegates the long report of a special committee to which the replies of other States had been referred. His object was to re-examine the Resolution of 1798, "and to inquire whether there be any errors of fact, or principle, or of reasoning, which the candour of the General Assembly ought to acknowledge and correct." The committee gave special attention to the third resolve of the preceding year—they scanned it "not merely with a strict, but with a severe eye"—and confidently pronounced it, in its just and fair construction, to be "unexceptionally true in its several positions, as well as constitutional and conclusive in its inferences."

The third resolve had opened with an assertion that the powers of the Federal Government "result from the compact. . . ." Madison found it sufficient to remark that in all the debates and discussions when the Constitution was pending for ratification, "it was constantly justified and recommended, on the ground, that the powers not given to the government, were withheld from it." Indeed, he added, the subsequent Tenth Amendment should have removed all doubt in its reference to "the powers not delegated to the United States by the Constitution."

What of the declaration that it is a compact "to which the States are parties"? Admitting that the term "States" is sometimes used in a vague sense, Madison could find no objection to the language. The proper meaning of the term here was to be found in the sense of States as "the people composing . . . political societies, in their highest sovereign capacity." Thus employed, it could not be denied that

the Constitution was submitted to the "States"; in that sense, the "States" ratified it; and, in that sense of the term "States," they are consequently parties to the compact, from which the powers of the Federal government result.

The next assertion, in the controversial third resolve, was that Federal powers are limited "by the plain sense and intention of the instrument constituting that compact," and also, that Federal powers are "no farther valid than they are authorized by the grants therein enumerated." It does not seem possible, said Madison, that anyone could object to that statement. The Constitution meant what the participating parties to it intended it to mean; and as for the limit on Federal powers, this was clear: "If the powers granted be valid, it is solely because they are granted; and, if the granted powers are valid, because granted, all other powers not granted, must not be valid."

Then comes the key sentence: "That, in case of a deliberate, palpable, and dangerous exercise of other powers, not granted by the said compact, the States, who are parties thereto, have the right and are in duty bound, to interpose for arresting the progress of the evil, and for maintaining within their respective limits, the authorities, rights, and liberties appertaining to them."

This is the heart and soul of the "right to interpose." The language was to be re-affirmed, substantially verbatim, by the Hartford Convention in 1814; by the Wisconsin Legislature in 1859; and by the Virginia General Assembly in 1956. When men talk of the "Doctrine of '98," this is the paragraph they are talking of. Let Madison speak at length, and without interruption:

It appears to your committee to be a plain principle, founded in common sense, illustrated by common practice, and essential to the nature of compacts, that, where resort can be had to no tribunal, superior to the authority of the parties, the parties themselves must be the rightful judges in the last resort, whether the bargain made has been pursued or violated. The Constitution of the United States was formed by the sanction of the States, given by each in its sovereign capacity. It adds to the stability and dignity, as well as to the authority of the Constitution, that it rests on this legitimate and solid foundation. The States, then, being the parties to the constitutional compact, and in their sovereign capacity, it follows of necessity, that there can be no tribunal above their authority, to decide in the last resort, whether the compact made by them be violated; and, consequently, that, as the parties to it, they must themselves decide, in the last resort, such questions as may be of sufficient magnitude to require their interposition.

It does not follow, however, that because the States, as sovereign parties to their constitutional compact, must ultimately decide whether it has been violated, that such a decision ought to be interposed, either in a hasty manner, or on doubtful and inferior occasions. Even in the case of ordinary conventions between different nations, where, by the strict rule of interpretation, a breach of a part may be deemed a breach of the whole, every part being deemed a condition of every other part and of the whole, it is always laid down that the breach must be both wilful and material to justify an application of the rule. But in the case of an intimate and constitutional union, like that of the United States, it is evident that the interposition of the parties, in their sovereign capacity, can be called for by occasions only, deeply and essentially affecting the vital principles of their political system.

The resolution has accordingly guarded against any misapprehension of its object, by expressly requiring for such an interposition, the case of a *deliberate, palpable,* and *dangerous* breach of the Constitution, by the exercise of *powers not granted* by it. It must be a case, not of a light and transient nature, but of a nature *dangerous* to the great purposes for which the Constitution was established. It must be a case, moreover, not obscure or doubtful in its construction, but plain and *palpable*. Lastly, it must be a case not resulting from a partial consideration, or hasty determination; but a case stamped with a final consideration and *deliberate* adherence. It is not necessary, because the resolution does not require that the question should be discussed, how far the exercise of any particular power, ungranted by the Constitution, would justify the interposition of the parties to it. As cases might easily be stated, which none would contend ought to fall with- in that description, cases, on the other hand, might, with equal ease, be stated, so flagrant and so fatal, as to unite every opinion in placing them within that description.

But the resolution has done more than guard against misconstruction, by expressly referring to cases of a *deliberate, palpable,* and *dangerous* nature. It specifies the object of the interposition which it contemplates, to be solely that of arresting the progress of the *evil* of usurpation, and of maintaining the authorities, rights, and liberties appertaining to the States, as parties to the Constitution.

From this view of the resolution, it would seem inconceivable that it can incur any just disapprobation from those who, laying aside all momentary impressions, and recollecting the genuine source and object of the Federal Constitution, shall candidly and accurately interpret the meaning of the General Assembly. If the deliberate exercise of dangerous powers, palpably withheld by the Constitution, could not justify the parties to it, in interposing even so far as to arrest the progress of the evil, and thereby to preserve the Constitution itself, as well as to provide for the safety of the parties to it, there would be an end to all relief from usurped power, and a direct subversion of the rights specified or recognised under all the State constitutions, as well as a plain denial of the fundamental principle on which our independence itself was declared.

But it is objected that the judicial authority is to be regarded as the sole expositor of the Constitution, in the last resort; and it may be asked for what reason, the declaration by the General Assembly, supposing it to be theoretically true, could be required at the present day and in so solemn a manner.

On this objection it might be observed, *first,* that there may be instances of usurped power, which the forms of the Constitution would never draw within the control of the judicial department; *secondly,* that if the decision of the judiciary be raised above the authority of the sovereign parties to the Constitution, the decisions of the other departments, not carried by the forms of the Constitution before the judiciary, must be equally authoritative and final with the decisions of that department. But the proper answer to the objection is, that the resolution of the General Assembly relates to those great and extraordinary cases, in which all the forms of the Constitution may prove ineffectual against infractions dangerous to the essential rights of the parties to it. The resolution supposes that dangerous powers, not delegated, may not only be usurped and executed by the other departments, but that the judicial department also may exercise or sanction dangerous powers beyond the grant of the Constitution; and, consequently, that the ultimate right of the parties to the Constitution, to judge whether the compact has been dangerously violated, must extend to violations by one delegated authority, as well as byanother; by the judiciary, as well as by the executive, or the legislature.

However true, therefore, it may be, that the judicial department, is, in all questions submitted to it by the forms of the Constitution, to decide in the last resort, this resort must necessarily be deemed the last in relation to the authorities of the other departments of the government; not in relation to the rights of the parties to the constitutional compact, from which the judicial as well as the other departments hold their delegated trusts. On any other hypothesis, the delegation of judicial power would annul the authority delegating it; and the concurrence of this department with the others in usurped powers, might subvert forever, and beyond the possible reach of any rightful remedy, the very Constitution which all were instituted to preserve.

The truth declared in the resolution being established, the expediency of making the declaration at the present day, may safely be left to the temperate consideration and candid judgment of the American public. It will be remembered that a frequent recurrence to fundamental principles, is solemnly enjoined by most of the State constitutions, and particularly by our own, as a necessary safeguard against the danger of degeneracy to which republics are liable, as well as other governments, though in a less degree than others. And a fair comparison of the political doctrines not unfrequent at the present day, with those which characterized the epoch of our revolution, and which form the basis of our republican constitutions, will best determine whether the declaratory recurrence here made to those principles, ought to be viewed as unseasonable and improper, or as a vigilant discharge of an important duty. The authority of constitutions over governments, and of the sovereignty of the people over constitutions, are truths which are at all times necessary to be kept in mind; and at no time perhaps more necessary than at the present.

Special attention may be directed, perhaps, to the several paragraphs in which Madison dealt with the possibility of encroachment by the judiciary upon the reserved powers of the States. *In Federalist 39,* it will be recalled, he had described the Supreme Court as "the tribunal which is ultimately to decide" controversies between State and Federal authority. He had assumed, then, that such decisions would be "impartially made, according to the rules of the Constitution," and he had remarked that "some such tribunal is clearly essential to prevent an appeal to the sword and a dissolution of the compact." Some thirty years later, with two terms in the White House behind him, Madison again was to take the side of national authority.(41) He was to insist, then, that the States must submit to unconstitutional encroachments upon their authority or take the ultimate resort of armed rebellion and secession. Late in his life, the idea of action by the States "to arrest the progress of the evil" seemed to have escaped Madison's mind. The alternatives, to the Madison of 1830-31, were two: Submission, or war.

He was on the right track in 1799. As events in our own time have clearly demonstrated, it is indeed quite possible for the Federal judiciary, by arrogating unto itself the prerogatives of the Congress and the States, to usurp powers not granted to the general government by the Constitution nor prohibited by the Constitution to the States. In Madison's own phrase, it has been abundantly proven that "dangerous powers, not delegated" may be usurped not only by Congress, *"but that the judicial department also may exercise or sanction dangerous powers beyond the grant of the Constitution."* And what was Madison's remedy in 1799? Let it be repeated: The ultimate right of the parties to judge whether the compact has been dangerously violated "must extend to violations by one delegated authority as well as by another—by the judiciary, as well as by the executive, or the legislature."

What Madison here recognized—and what he later was to overlook—is that the Constitution had one major flaw: The Constitution had established an ingenious system of checks and balances by which every conceivable source of oppression, *with a single exception,* may effectively be held in bounds.

That single exception is the Supreme Court of the United States.

Consider the other weights and counterweights contrived by the founding fathers: The pressure of large blocks of population, as represented in the House, would be offset by the authority of the States, as represented in the Senate. The power of the Congress could be checked by Presidential veto.

The power of the President could again be balanced by the authority of Congress to over-ride a veto. The judicial branch, restraining Congress and the executive alike, was to provide a further barrier against usurpation of power. Beyond this, the people themselves, through their right of franchise, would serve as a direct check upon their Representatives in the House (and later in the Senate). The presidential electors, reflecting the will of the people, could refuse a second term to a President who overstepped his powers.

But in this whole remarkable machine, the founding fathers left one great power uncontrolled: The judiciary alone, of all agencies of government, was left with no effective restraint, save—as a learned justice was to comment much later—the judges' own sense of self-restraint.(42)

It was not planned that way. At the time the Constitution was formed, three misconceptions affected critical thought. The first was that judges named to the Supreme Court would be men of towering reputation at the bench or bar, learned, impartial, beyond political feeling. The second was that the judiciary, lacking control over both purse and sword, would ever be the weakest branch of government. The third was that, in the wholly improbable event that the Supreme Court should transgress its powers, Congress could invoke the weapon of impeachment against individual judges, or could control the Court's appellate jurisdiction by exercising its authority to fix "exceptions" and "regulations" under which cases could be heard on appeal.

In operation, these concepts swiftly proved faulty. Some of the early appointees to the Court were men of small stature; yet under Marshall, the Court was shaped into not the weakest, but in fact the strongest arm of the Federal government. Impeachment, as Jefferson scornfully remarked, (43) was no more than a scarecrow. As for making exceptions to the Court's appellate powers, Congress speedily saw the Pandora's box that would be opened by indiscriminate tinkering.(44)

But in the beginning, very little of this was foreseen; and those, like Henry, who perceived the dangers, were smoothly talked down. Little of the argument of 1787-88 went to the heart of the Court's powers; most of it groped around the edges.

"Whoever attentively considers the different departments of power," said Hamilton, "must perceive that in a government in which they are separated from each other, the judiciary, from the nature of its functions, will always be the least dangerous to the political rights of the Constitution; because it will be least in a capacity to annoy or injure them." He continued:

The Executive not only dispenses the honors, but holds the sword of the community. The legislature not only commands the purse, but prescribes the rules by which the duties and rights of every citizen are to be regulated. The judiciary, on the contrary, has no influence over either the sword or the purse; no direction either of the strength or of the wealth of the society; and can take no active resolution whatever. It may truly be said to have neither force nor will, but merely judgment; and must ultimately depend upon the aid of the executive arm even for the efficacy of its judgments.(45)

Beyond comparison, Hamilton went on to say, the judiciary "is the weakest of the three departments of power." He recalled a comment from Montesquieu—"Of the three powers above mentioned, the judiciary is next to nothing." The Court, Hamil-ton predicted, could never attack the executive or the legislative branch successfully. And while individual instances of judicial oppression might occur, "the general liberty of the people can never be endangered from that quarter." Hamilton's chief concern was for the judiciary itself: Considering its "natural feebleness," he thought it "in continual jeopardy of being overpowered, awed, or influenced by its coordinate branches."

To be sure, it was contemplated that the Supreme Court would have power to pronounce legislative acts contrary to the Constitution and hence void. This might imply a superiority on the part of the court over the Congress. Not so, said Hamilton. *It was the Constitution that would be supreme.* The Court was no more than its interpreter. And suppose the interpreter should err? Suppose that judges might substitute their will instead of their judgment in passing on laws? Hamilton gave no weight to this argument. It might as well happen, he said, that members of the legislative branch would err by adopting contradictory statutes. The caprice of lawmakers, the caprice of judges—he could see no difference; but what Hamilton here overlooked is that lawmakers are subject to a direct and recurring approval from the people at the polls. Judges serve for life, beyond the reach of the franchise.

Hamilton's point here was to emphasize that the Court and the Congress ranked as equals, but the power of the people, as declared in the Constitution, is superior to both. Ultimately, all authority must come back to the Constitution; here and here only is to be found the supreme law of the land.

The question that Hamilton was grappling with in the *Federalist* is the same question, basically, that troubles some of the States in the Union in mid-twentieth Century. How can the ultimate authority of the people declare itself effectively against encroachments by the Court? Is it to be argued that the judiciary, alone among all departments of government, is infallible—that it cannot commit an unconstitutional act? If that be the argument, then is it not true that a majority of five on a Court of nine have the power, subject to no immediate and effective check, to shape the Constitution as they please?

No such sweeping and authoritarian power, it may be submitted, ever was intended to be vested in the Supreme Court of the United States. To defend this proposition is to cancel out the entire philosophy of a federal union of States; to advance this argument is to make a mockery of the whole plan of checks and balances.

In logic, in reason, in history, in plain common sense, there must be, in the American plan, *some Constitutional check upon the Court*. It is to be found today where it has existed all along, in the right of the States to interpose their sovereign powers against judicial tyranny. And in 1799, Madison saw this to be true.

Now, it will be objected that it is nowhere spelled out in the Constitution, that the States have any right to raise a question of contested powers, and by such an appeal to seek to frustrate enforcement of an edict of the Court. For that matter, it is nowhere spelled out in the Constitution that the Court has any authority to declare an act of Congress, or of the executive, a void enactment. This power simply was asserted by the Court. It was a power that had to be asserted by the Court. Similarly, the power of the States to interpose against judicial tyranny is a power that must be asserted, simply in the nature of things, if the States are to survive. The alternative is a government in which the States-people are not supreme, but five men are supreme over them; it is a government in which the understood intention of the Constitution may be swept away by the caprice, or the sociology, of a majority of the Court.

In the 1830's, Madison himself was to object that the doctrine of interposition, effectively applied, is the doctrine of anarchy—that the right of a State to suspend one law, as to itself, is the right of a State to suspend all laws—or a right, vested in all of the States, to pick and choose those laws which they will obey, and those laws they will defy. But this objection is more theoretical than real. It presupposes, on the part of the States, a willingness to put State interests above national interests, which assumption scarcely can be defended in the light of a hundred years of submissive acceptance by the States of Federal expansion. It presupposes, also, that the States would interpose upon light or transient grounds. This is, at bottom, the assumption of those nationalists who aggrandize the Federal government as a power that can do no wrong (save only when it fails to reach as far as they would like), and treat the States as puny, self-interested bodies devoid of feeling or concern for those interests that truly are national in scope.

More than this, the objections to interposition by the States against "deliberate, palpable, and dangerous" encroachments upon their rights, are basically the weak and tremulous cries of spineless fellows who would rather bear the ills of despotism than risk the dangers of a transient anarchy. They are the docile, automaton voices repeating, in deadly unison, "we must obey, we must be slaves, we must comply." Opposed to them are the still vigorous voices, repeating, after Hamilton himself, "There is no position which depends on clearer principles, than that every act of a delegated authority, contrary to the tenor of the commission under which it is exercised, is void." No legislative act, no judgment of the Court, contrary to the Constitution, can be valid. To deny this would be to affirm that the deputy is greater than his principal, that the servant is above his master, that the judges, subject to the people's Constitution, are above the Constitution; that nine men named for life may exercise not only those powers of adjudication with which they are vested, but also those powers of effective Constitutional amendment which are denied them.

Quis custodiet custodies? Who will watch the watchdogs? The Madison Report of 1799 provided the only possible basis for answering the question; it set forth the missing check-and-balance; it suggested a means by which the progress of judicial tyranny may be arrested. The right of the States to interpose, he said, "must extend to violations by one delegated authority as well as by another—*by the judiciary, as well as by the executive or the legislature."*

But how is this right—not a privilege, but a *right*—to be exercised? Clearly, the first step is for an infraction of the compact to be charged. Who is to make such a charge? The answer must be, of course, the States. They are the parties to the compact, each standing equally with the others. Is it necessary that any particular number of States unite in charging an infraction? Obviously, no. A particular usurpation by the Federal government may affect only a single State, or no more than two or three, but the nature of the usurpation, to the affected States, may be such as to destroy their most cherished institutions. If the right to interpose could be exercised only by not fewer than one-fourth of the States, or one-third, acting in concert, the right would be meaningless; the federal nature of the compact, in which each *respective* State is an equal member, would thereby be subverted.

Now, the author of this essay is not here suggesting that in every case of grave usurpation of State prerogatives, the aggrieved State —or States— must exert the right to interpose in its most drastic form. Interposition, as the term is used herein, embraces the widest possible range of State protest, remonstrance, objection and intervention. The term covers what Madison himself described, in the *Federalist,* as means by which Federal encroachments could be resisted. Should an unwarrantable measure of the Federal government be unpopular in particular States, he said,

the means of opposition to it are powerful and at hand. The disquietude of the people; their repugnance and, perhaps, refusal to cooperate with the officers of the Union; the frowns of the executive magistracy of the State, the embarrassments created by legislative devices, which would often be added on such occasions, would oppose, in any State, very serious impediments; and where the sentiments of several adjoining States happened to be in unison, would present obstructions which the Federal government would hardly be willing to encounter.(46)

Yet if the right to interpose has any effective meaning, it must extend beyond the range of mere protest, as in the Kentucky and Virginia Resolutions; it must be more than remonstrance, as in Virginia's action on the debt assumption act. It must be more than a deferential memorial to the Congress. In practice, it must extend even beyond the "legislative devices" that Madison envisioned. In those rare and exceptional cases in which submission to usurped power would mean the destruction of a vital State institution, means must exist by which even one State may take action to suspend Federal encroachment pending an appeal to the ultimate sovereignty of all the States. In this last form, the right to interpose is the right of effective nullification; it is the right of appeal with supersedeas.

The States of the American Union, in their continuing conflict with Federal authority, have exercised this right many times, in varying forms and in different degrees of forcefulness. Not only State executives and legislatures, but State judges also have thus asserted State sovereignty. The right to interpose has been exercised by New England and Midwestern States no less than by Southern States, for the right is inherent in the existence of a State, apart from considerations of geography or commerce. In the next section, some of the applications of this right will be reviewed.

The Olmstead Case

THE UNION scarcely had been formed, we have noted, by the ratification of New Hampshire in June of 1788, before conflicts began between State and Federal authority. Such conflicts have continued, from that day to this, as the States have struggled to maintain the role promised them under the Constitution, and the centralists of passing generations have endeavored to wrest it from them.

The titans of American history have participated in this continuing combat. More often than not, it must be confessed, the centralists have won and the States' righters have lost. Over the whole span, the record unquestionably has been one of expanding power for the Federal authority and declining influence for the States.

Yet there is much to be learned, even in mid-twentieth century, from the conflict between State and Federal power over the years. Many of the questions propounded by a Spencer Roane, a John C. Calhoun, a Thomas McKean, cannot be answered satisfactorily by Federalist sympathisers to this day. These great conservatives of the American Constitutional union captured the essence of our fundamental law; they saw, with great prescience, the absolute necessity of preserving strong State and local governments if a despotism from Washington were not to replace the despotism of George III. They recognized, in a way that has escaped us now, that government is most responsive to the people when it is closest to the people; as government becomes more remote from the sovereign power, it becomes less responsible, less susceptible to check and control.

In the brief accounts that follow, it is proposed to review several of the more notable acts in this drama. The characters have all the color one could wish: An aging seafarer, Gideon Olmstead; an Indian murderer, Corn Tassels; a pair of New England missionaries, Samuel Worcester and Elizur Butler; an impulsive State auditor in Ohio, Ralph Osborn; and of course, a host of Governors, Senators, Judges, statesmen: Troup and Lumpkin in Georgia; Desha in Kentucky; in the Congress, Webster, Hayne, Calhoun, Randolph; and on the Court, Marshall, Taney, Chase, Fuller, Holmes, Brandeis, Stone. A more brilliant cast could not be assembled.

As the story unfolds this fact will become evident: At one time or another, every major section of the Republic has asserted the sovereignty of States, and has resisted Federal encroachment upon State prerogatives. *"States' rights" is not a doctrine peculiar to the South.* The essential rightness of the States' position has been acknowledged no less by New England than by Georgia; and the "Doctrine of '98" has been asserted as vigorously in Wisconsin as in Virginia and Kentucky.

Let us begin on a late summer night in 1778. It is September 6, and the war for American independence continues: Yorktown is still three years away, but the tide is turning—in June, the British have evacuated Philadelphia; the Battle of Monmouth is behind us. General Benedict Arnold, two years later a traitor, is now military governor of Philadelphia. But New York remains in British hands, and some miles off the coast of Pennsylvania a British sloop, *Active,* out of Jamaica, is pressing steadily toward her destination in Manhattan.

Aboard the *Active* on the night of September 6, 1778, were Gideon Olmstead, a middle-aged Connecticut sailor, and three other countrymen who earlier had been captured by the British and taken to Jamaica. They were being returned to New York to be put in a military prison there. But late at night, the four Americans fell upon Captain Underwood of the *Active.* "In pursuance of this bold and hazardous design," it was to be chronicled later, "they secured the captain and crew under deck, and contemplated running the sloop into Egg Harbor," but "a considerable contest then arose between those under, and those on deck, for the command of the vessel."(1) This contest continued throughout the day on September 7. On September 8, with the sloop only a few miles out of Egg Harbor, the brigantine *Convention,* Captain Thomas Houston, hove in sight and opened fire on the *Active.* Minutes later, Houston boarded the *Active* and took control. Meanwhile, the *Convention*'s consort, the privateer sloop *Le Gerard,* Captain James Josiah, had come in sight and joined the engagement.

Houston sent the captured sloop on to Philadelphia, where the vessel was libelled as a prize of war on September 14. The proceeding marked the beginning of thirty years of litigation and bitter conflict between Pennsylvania and the Federal government. To understand the position of the adversaries, it is necessary to look back briefly to November, 1775, when the Continental Congress, at the request of Washington, had recommended to the member States that they establish admiralty courts for handling prize cases. The act thus passed provided for appeal to the Congress from such State proceedings, but also requested the States "to provide that all trials in such case be had by a jury, under such qualifications as to the respective legislatures shall seem expedient."

Pursuant to this request, the Pennsylvania Legislature set about establishing a Court of Admiralty at Philadelphia; and on the very day after the *Convention* had seized the *Active,* before the sloop had reached port, the Legislature adopted an act providing for jury trials in prize cases, with this qualification—that from a jury's finding of fact, no appeal could be taken. It was most unusual for juries to be provided in prize proceedings; indeed, Pennsylvania's law, in this regard, was repealed in 1780. But it happened to be the fate of Gideon Olmstead that the *Active* was libelled before a new judge, in a new court, under a new and brief-lived system of jury trial; and that the jury, on November 5, rejected his claim for the whole of the prize. It was Olmstead's contention that he and his mates had wholly subdued Captain Underwood at the time the *Convention* came alongside; it was the position of the libellants that the struggle for command of the *Active* had not ceased when *Convention* and *Le Gerard* hove in view. On this issue, the case went to the jury; and the jury, after hearing the witnesses, gave one-fourth of the prize to Olmstead and his fellows, one-fourth to *Le Gerard,* and one-half to Houston and the *Convention.* A half of Houston's portion was to go to the Commonwealth of Pennsylvania, which had fitted and commissioned the brig for action.

Olmstead, disappointed, appealed to Congress. In December of 1778, a four-man committee of the Congress heard his petition and proceeded to reverse Judge Ross; the committee awarded the entire prize to Olmstead. Pennsylvania was outraged by the decision. Had not Pennsylvania done what the Congress had asked? Had not a State Court of Admirality been created? Had not juries been provided for? Did not Pennsylvania have the right to provide that from her juries' findings of fact, no appeal could be taken? With the warm support of State authorities, Judge Ross indignantly refused to respect the committee's decree. On December 28, he announced that the jury's verdict, so far as he was concerned, remained in full force. The following week, General Arnold, equally indignant, advised Congress that Judge Ross was "standing out obstinately against any orders that may be given."(2) Arnold predicted, with much truth, that before Olmstead were through with the case, "he will have the whole State to contend with," Judge Ross continued to hold firm; and when the Congressional committee, on January 4, issued an injunction to the marshal to detain the prize money, Judge Ross defied the committee, requisitioned the proceeds of the auction, and distributed the award.

That was how it began. Off and on through the rest of 1779, the Congressional commissioners negotiated with Pennsylvania, but got nowhere. In January of 1780, the Pennsylvania Legislature adopted a resolution declaring that further efforts by Congress to obtain "the money of this State" would be considered "as a high infringement on the honor and rights of the Commonwealth."(3) For quite some time, the case languished. Olmstead, growing older, continued to press his claim upon the Pennsylvania Legislature, and Pennsylvania continued to refuse him. Meanwhile, the Articles of Confederation gave way to the new Constitution; Judge Ross died; several hundred miles away, in New Hampshire, a wholly separate prize case, ultimately to be controlling, moved to a head(4); in Georgia, the Chisholm case arose, and led to the Eleventh Amendment.

Fourteen years after the capture of the *Active,* in 1792, the persistent Olmstead filed suit in the Court of Common Pleas of Lancaster County against Judge Ross's executors, still seeking his prize money. By this time, the sum had been deposited with David Rittenhouse, State Treasurer; and though Olmstead won by default in the trial court, he lost again on subsequent appeal: Chief Justice McKean, a jurist of towering reputation whose views of State and Federal relationships will be reviewed somewhat later in these notes, held that "the decree of the Committee of Appeals was contrary to the provisions of the act of Congress and of the General Assembly, extra judicial, erroneous and void."(5)

Three more years passed; but if the sequence of events in the Olmstead case is to be understood, it is desirable now to look briefly toward New Hampshire and the closely parallel case which arose there. In October of 1777, a controversy developed out of the capture of the brig *Susannah* by the privateer *McClary*. A prize suit followed, in which a New Hampshire State Court of Admiralty awarded the proceeds to one Penhallow, owner of the *McClary*, against the counter-claim of a group of Massachusetts seamen led by Elisha Doane. This judgment was sustained on appeal to the State Supreme Court, but just as Olmstead was to do, Doane appealed to Congress; and in September of 1783, the newly erected Court of Appeals in Cases of Capture undertook to reverse the New Hampshire court and restore the prize to Doane. Again, State authorities resentfully spurned the decision, and for ten years the case languished. But with a new Constitution, and new Federal courts, Doane revived his action before the United States Circuit Court for New Hampshire. He won an order in October, 1793 directing payment of the original proceeds with interest for sixteen years.

New Hampshire, even as Pennsylvania, was outraged. In February, 1794, the New Hampshire Legislature adopted a resolution denying emphatically that a Federal court created under the Constitution of 1788 could reverse the decree of a New Hampshire State court in 1777. During the Revolutionary period, it was insisted, "New Hampshire had a right to pass a law final in every way concerning the capture of vessels by this State, or citizens thereof, from the British."(6) After all, said the resolution, the States are forbidden by the new Constitution to make retrospective laws: "The Legislature conceived that Congress was under the same obligations; and that their courts could not re judge cases that were finally adjudged by courts existing prior to its adoption." In New Hampshire's view, the Congress that existed under the Articles of Confederation "was merely an advisory body." The States were separate and autonomous; and an effort to unsettle the proceedings of the States prior to the ratification of the Constitution "will inevitably involve the States . . . in confusion, and will weaken, if not perhaps destroy, the National Government." Terming the Federal Court's decree an "illegal act of power," New Hampshire protested strongly against it.

The protest was unavailing. In February, 1795, the United States Supreme Court held that Federal courts created under the new Constitution could, indeed, review decisions of the old Court of Appeals in Cases of Capture. The decision is an important one. Speaking for the Court, Justice Paterson rejected the position urged by New Hampshire: "The truth is, that the States, individually, were not known nor recognized as sovereign, by foreign nations, nor are they now; the States collectively, under Congress, as the connecting point, or head, were acknowledged by foreign powers as sovereign." Somewhat vaguely, he continued: "Before Articles of

Confederation were ratified, or even formed, a league of some kind subsisted among the States; and whether that league originated in compact, or a sort of tacit consent, resulting from the situation, the exigencies of the times, and the nature of the warfare, or from a combination, is utterly immaterial."(7)

It is difficult to follow Paterson in his reasoning. The States were, in fact, "recognized as sovereign" by the highest possible authority—the authority of Great Britain, in the treaty ending the war. They were recognized, individually, not as one nation, but rather as entities. They had declared themselves, in 1776, to be "Free and Independent States." Mr. Justice Iredell, dissenting, emphasized some of these points: Each of the States, or provinces, he said, was a separate body politic, "and the several provinces were not otherwise connected with each other than as being subject to the same common sovereign."(8)

Citizens of the different States were as foreigners to one another. They had formed themselves into different States, and as States had conveyed "by each body politic separately, and not by all the people in the several provinces, or States, jointly."(9) Thus, in Iredell's view, what New Hampshire had done in 1777 was peculiarly the business of New Hampshire, and no longer subject to review.

But the majority of the Court prevailed. New Hampshire again protested strongly, and her second remonstrance, of January 16, 1795, merits quotation for twentieth century readers. Do these views sound familiar? The New Hampshire legislators, again remonstrating against "a violation of State independence and an unwarrantable encroachment in the courts of the United States," declared that the attempts "repeatedly made to render the laws of this State . . . null and void [are] a flagrant insult to the principle of the Revolution. . . ." Then the resolution asked:

Can the rage for annihilating all the power of the States, and reducing this extensive and flourishing country to one domination make the administrators blind to the danger of violating all the principles of our former government, to the hazard of convulsions, in endeavoring to eradicate every trace of State power, except in the resentment of the people. . . .

Forced by events, the Legislature of New Hampshire have made the foregoing statements; and while they cheerfully acknowledge the power of Congress in cases arising under the Constitution, they equally resolve not to submit the laws made before the existence of the present government by this (then independent State) to the adjudication of any power on earth, while the freedom of the Federal Government shall afford any constitutional means of redress. Impressed with the singular merits of the present case, and deprecating the many and complicated evils which must be the necessary consequence of establishing the power claimed by the courts of the United States, and its tendency to produce disaffection to our government, the Legislature of New Hampshire rest assured that a speedy and just decision will be had, and that the rights of State Governments and the interests of their citizens will be secured against the exercise of a power of a court, or any body of men under Congress, of carrying into effect an unconstitutional decree of a court instituted by a former Congress, and which, in its effects, would unsettle property and tear up the laws of the several States.

Thus spoke New Hampshire, but Congress and the Court were deaf. Back in Connecticut, however, Olmstead took heart. Hoping to emulate Doane's success, he dug out of his sea chest the records of his suit in 1792, and in 1802 filed a new proceeding in the United States District Court at Philadelphia, this time against Elizabeth Sergeant and Esther Waters, daughters and executrices of the late State Treasurer, David Rittenhouse. In January, 1803, Judge Peters ruled in Olmstead's favor, but prudently declined to issue process until the matter could be reviewed once more by the Supreme Court of the United States.

This time it was the Pennsylvania Legislature's turn to take action. In the summer of 1803, it pronounced this Federal opinion "null and void," but prudently arranged for Mrs. Sergeant and Mrs. Waters to pay into the State Treasury the contested sum. Five more years elapsed before Olmstead, by now an old man, set in motion the final chain of events: Through the United States Attorney General, he applied for a mandamus against Judge Peters, compelling issuance of process for a judgment he had won almost thirty years earlier; to this, the judge replied that Pennsylvania had passed an act to protect the Rittenhouse executrices against the process of any Federal court in the Olmstead case; that he was unwilling to embroil the United States with Pennsylvania; and that he wished the Supreme Court itself to take the responsibility.

Chief Justice John Marshall took it: "If the legislatures of the several States," he said "may at will annul the judgments of the courts of the United States, and destroy the right acquired under these judgments, the Constitution becomes a solemn mockery, and the nation is deprived of the means of enforcing its laws by the instrumentality of its own tribunals."(10) The act passed by Pennyslvania, he noted, did not assert "the universal right of the State to interpose in every case whatever." What Pennsylvania had done was to question the Federal court's jurisdiction on two grounds: First, that the old Congress, under the Articles of Confederation, had no authority to reverse the original finding of fact by a jury in Judge Ross' Admiralty Court in 1778, with the result that the case had been finally settled many years before; and secondly, that Olmstead, as a citizen of Connecticut, could not, under the new Eleventh Amendment, bring suit against Pennsylvania. Marshall brushed off the first objection by saying that the Penhallow case had settled that issue; of the second, he insisted that Pennsylvania was not actually a party to the suit—the defendants were Mrs. Sergeant and Mrs. Waters: "It is deemed perfectly clear that no title whatever to the certificates in question was vested in the State of Pennsylvania."

Marshall's opinion aroused an astonishingly bitter reaction in Pennsylvania. It is a little difficult, looking back, to understand why this should have been true. The amount in controversy was not large; the right of a State jury to hear prize cases had been abandoned in 1780, two years after it had been created; by 1809, of course, all questions of Revolutionary prizes were moot; the main point in Marshall's opinion—that Federal courts under the new Constitution could dispose of cases heard by the Prize Court many years earlier—established no dangerous precedent for the future. Nevertheless, Pennsylvania reacted strongly.

On February 27, 1809, Governor Simon Snyder advised the Legislature that he intended to call out the State militia to protect Mrs. Sergeant and Mrs. Waters against the service of process. His firmness was warmly approved, and when late in March the writ finally was issued, and Marshal John Smith went to the Rittenhouse mansion at Seventh and Arch streets to serve the papers, a delegation of the Pennsylvania militia awaited him. They had been called out on orders of Governor Snyder addressed to General Michael Bright, commander of the First Brigade, First Division. "It is my express orders," Governor Snyder had said, "not to injure any person attempting to serve such process as aforesaid, unless imperious necessity compels you to do it in execution of the orders it has become my duty to issue." Nevertheless, General Bright was to see to it that the ladies were protected.

Let Marshal Smith tell the story: On March 25, he went to Mrs. Sergeant's house, but "Upon my approach a sentinel who was placed at the door presented his bayonet at my breast." When he attempted to get past Sergeant Cole and his detachment, "I was driven from the pavement . . . and was repelled by the whole guard with charged bayonets."(11) Marshal Smith then called for a chair, and when this was provided, hoisted himself upon it to read a proclamation to the assembled crowd. He lectured them on the subject of Federal authority, promised to summon a posse of two thousand men if need be, and then retired.

For three weeks, General Bright's detachment held "Fort Rittenhouse," but at last Marshal Smith eluded the guard. "I got into the house," he was to testify, "went into the back parlour, where I saw two young ladies and young gentlemen, who were exceedingly alarmed." But doing his duty as he saw it, the marshal served his papers and departed.

Scarcely had this obligation been fulfilled before United States District Attorney Alexander J. Dallas swore out a warrant against General Bright and his troops, charging them with obstructing justice. On April 28, they came on for trial in Philadelphia before Supreme Court Justice Bushrod Washington and District Judge Richard Peters. Meanwhile, on April 3, the Pennsylvania Legislature had adopted certain resolutions that will be noted hereafter, and had appropriated $18,000 to Governor Snyder's discretion as a fund for settling the case.

It was a curiously Wonderland trial that unfolded in Philadelphia that spring. Reading the record, one is reminded of Alice's hedgehog, that kept unrolling itself and wandering away. General Bright, for one thing, did not bother to show up to hear the indictment read. When Dallas asked the court to be patient, waiting on him, Judge Peters put in a wary remark: "The defendants are bound in a recognizance to appear and not depart the court without license; but I do not want to hurry on the trial. I am content for my own part to wait still longer on this business, though God knows it has been so long before me I am tired of it." Eventually General Bright showed up—a bailiff had been sent to the docks to find him, where the general was engaged as inspector of flour for the port of Philadelphia—and all hands pleaded not guilty. A jury then was sworn, and counsel for the government and the defense launched into long and absorbing reviews of the powers of Federal and State authorities.

It was the government's position that Pennsylvania's interposition should be ignored altogether: If Judge Peters' original order were void, the action of the Pennsylvania Legislature was needless; if his order were valid, Pennsylvania's action could not make it less so. It was the position of the defense that Pennsylvania had acted throughout in defense of her sovereign rights, and that General Bright was wholly within the State's authority in interceding against an arbitrary and unconstitutional action by the marshal. On this division, the case went to trial.

Mr. Justice Washington had a difficult jury to contend with. Never a specially shrewd or knowledgeable man, he delivered a charge in which he argued obtusely with himself. He noted that the Eleventh Amendment prohibited suits "in law and equity" by citizens of one State against another State. Could he, as a member of the Supreme Court, interpret this prohibition also to apply to cases in admiralty? "I think not. In our various struggles to get at the spirit and intention of the framers of the Constitution, I fear that this invaluable charter of our rights would, in a very little time, be entirely construed away, and become at length so disfigured that its founders would recollect very few of its original features." It was a comment of singular prophecy. But Mr. Justice Washington wondered also about the right of Pennsylvania to pass upon judgments of a Federal court and declare them null and void: "Could such a power be granted to them, without sapping the foundations of the government, and extinguishing the last sparks of American liberty?" Mr. Justice Washington thought not, but his confusion was evident to the jury. He had asked them, sarcastically, if "they have the vanity to think themselves wiser than all those who have passed opinions upon this important question of the law?" and finally he had suggested to the jury that "If there is any misapprehension, or difficulty about the law, the court are ready now, or will be at any time hereafter, to give any further information, or elucidation, you may require." To this offer, the record shows this response:

One of the jurors: We seem to want no information on this head, for there are three or four jurors who think they understand the law as well as the judges themselves.

The jury went out between five and six o'clock on the evening of Saturday, April 30. After supper, the clerk summoned them back to the court to inquire if they had reached a verdict. "One of the jurors said they had not, and he saw no prospect that they ever would, and therefore hoped they might be discharged." Instead, Washington ordered them back to the jury room. At ten-thirty they came back in, but mainly to report that "one of the jurors has had a strong convulsion fit, and another was very much indisposed." Washington ordered them locked up over the weekend. On Sunday afternoon, it was to develop later, one of the jurors, Mathias Corless, slipped out the back door of the court house at Sixth and Chestnut streets, and merrily made his way across to the Shakespeare Hotel, a tavern, intent on a cooling drink.

On Monday morning, the jury reluctantly brought in a verdict finding General Bright and his soldiers guilty, but with so many mitigating circumstances that no decree could be readily reduced to writing. It was the jury's view that the defendants had not opposed "Any law of the United States acknowledged to be so by the military authority of Pennsylvania." After considerable argument, a decree was agreed upon, and Justice Washington sentenced General Bright to three months in jail and a fine of $200, and each of his eight soldiers to one month in jail and a fine of $50. That was on May 2, 1809. Four days later, President Madison, commenting upon the court's finding that the defendants had acted under "a mistaken sense of duty," pardoned all of them. So ended the trial of General Bright.

But if the trial proved a short-lived fiasco, some of the things said by the Pennsylvania Assembly in its April resolution merit a more permanent place. This is Pennsylvania speaking, let it be noted—*Pennsylvania,* no part of the South, in a time when Pennsylvania felt keenly about her own State rights:

And whereas the causes and reasons which have produced this conflict between the general and State government should be made known, not only that the State may be justified to her sister States, who are equally interested in the preservation of the State rights; but to evince to the Government of the United States that the Legislature, in resisting encroachments on their rights, are not acting in a spirit of hostility to the legitimate powers of the United States courts; but are actuated by a disposition to compromise, and to guard against future collisions of power, by an amendment to the Constitution; and that, whilst they are contending for the rights of the State, that it will be attributed to a desire for preserving the Federal government itself, the best features of which must depend upon keeping up a just balance between the general and State governments, as guaranteed by the Constitution,

Be it therefore known, that the present unhappy dispute has arisen out of the following circumstances. . . . (12)

And Pennsylvania thereupon proceeded to spell out her case. In one aspect, it was a good and sound case. "It is clear," said the resolution, "that David Rittenhouse could not have received a farthing of the money as David Rittenhouse, but as Treasurer of the State only, and by order of the State." Hence it was, in actual fact, the State itself that was being sued, in violation of the Eleventh Amendment. "If this can be done, the amendment . . . is a dead letter. The State can act under its laws only by its agents. Its moneys remain in the hands of its Treasurers. If the officers can be converted by the decree of a judge, into mere stakeholders, there can, perhaps, be no possible case in which the Constitution may not be invaded."(13)

Then Pennsylvania had this to say, and let it be read in the context of the mid-twentieth century:

Although the Legislature reverence the Constitution of the United States and its lawful authorities, yet there is a respect due to the solemn and public acts, and to the honor and dignity of our own State, and the unvarying assertion of her right, for a period of thirty years, which right ought not to be relinquished. . . .

An assertion of right for a period of thirty years. May a question be interpolated? What do the good people of Pennsylvania say today of a State right asserted unvaryingly for a period of nearly *ninety* years? Is this not entitled to respect? Pennsylvania once thought so.

And the resolution of April 3, 1809, went on to say other things worth repeating today. The Legislature of Pennsylvania acknowledged the supremacy of the general government, and cheerfully submitted to its authority "*so far as that authority is delegated by the Constitution of the United States.*" But beyond that point?

Whilst they yield to this authority, when exercised within Constitutional limits, they trust they will not be considered as acting hostile to the General Government, when, *as guardians of the State rights,* they can not permit an infringement of those rights by an unconstitutional exercise of power in the United States' courts. [Emphasis in the original.]

Again let it be noted: Here was the old and rightly respected State of Pennsylvania, declaring in the most solemn fashion, that the "United States' courts" themselves violate the Constitution. Is it so unthinkable that Pennsylvania could have been right then, and that Southern and Southwestern States are equally right in making identical assertions in our own time?

The April resolution went on to recognize that "it is impossible" for a boundary to be marked precisely between "the powers granted to the general government, and rights reserved to the States." Difficulties were bound to arise "from a collision of powers." And because the Constitution had made no provision for determining such disputes, the Pennsylvania Legislature proposed that a new tribunal be created by constitutional amendment. Otherwise, "the harmony of the States, if they resist encroachments on their rights, will frequently be interrupted." And if the States, to prevent the evil, "should on all occasions yield to stretches of power, the reserved rights of the States will depend on the arbitrary power of the courts." Therefore, it was

Resolved, that should the independence of the States, as secured by the Constitution, be destroyed, the liberties of the people in so extensive a country cannot long survive. To suffer the United States' courts to decide on STATE RIGHTS will, from a bias *in favor of power,* necessarily destroy the FEDERAL PART of our Government: And whenever the government of the United States becomes consolidated, we may learn from the history of nations what will be the event.(14) [Emphasis in the original.]

Pause for a moment. Let us note the language. Pennsylvania, in April of 1809, was speaking: Should the States keep yielding to usurpations of power by the Federal courts, *the rights of the States would be swept away.* Is that not precisely what has happened in our own time? By failing to resist judicial encroachments, the States have indeed seen their rights one by one swept away, as the United States have become more consolidated and the liberties of the people more inexorably infringed.

That is about all that remains to be said of the Olmstead case. On April 17, 1809, some ten days before General Bright went on trial, counsel for Mrs. Sergeant had applied for a writ of habeas corpus to free her from the marshal's custody. Chief Justice Tilghman, of the Pennsylvania court, concluded that he had power to free her from Federal custody, if the evidence justified him in doing so: His right to issue a writ "flows from the nature of our Federal Constitution, which leaves to the several States absolute supremacy in all cases in which it is not yielded to the United States."(15) "The United States have no power, legislative or judicial, except what is derived from the Constitution," Chief Justice Tilghman said.

When these powers are clearly exceeded, the independence of the States, and the peace of the Union, demand that the State courts should, in cases brought properly before them, give redress. There is no law which forbids it; their oath of office exacts it, and, if they do not, what course is to be taken? We must be reduced to the miserable extremity of opposing force to force, and arraying citizen against citizen; for it is vain to expect that the States will submit to manifest and flagrant usurpations of power by the United States, if (which God forbid) they should attempt them.

Nevertheless, Judge Tilghman regretfully held that Federal authority had been exercised properly, and refused to release Mrs. Sergeant. At long last, on April 26, Governor Snyder released the contested sum to Olmstead.

The following January of 1810, it must be confessed to Virginia's shame, the General Assembly at Richmond adopted resolutions that were far removed from her resolutions of 1798 and 1799. This time, replying to Pennsylvania's resolution of 1809, the Virginia Assembly declared that the Supreme Court of the United States had been provided "to decide disputes between the State and Federal judiciary," and Virginia praised the Supreme Court judges as men "selected from those in the United States who are most celebrated for virtue and legal learning."(16) The duties they have to perform, said Virginia then, "lead them necessarily to the most enlarged and accurate acquaintance with the jurisdiction of the Federal and several State courts together, and with the admirable symmetry of our government." Further, "the tenure of their offices enables them to pronounce the sound and correct opinions they may have formed, without fear, favor, or partiality." In time, it may be interpolated, Virginia's view on this score was to change radically.

To this resolution from Virginia, Pennsylvania put in the last word on February 3, 1810. A committee report was brought forward in the State Senate declaring flatly that

the committee are of opinion, that the Constitution of the United States has been violated by the decision of the judge, and the constitutional rights of the State invaded. The question then occurs, *in what manner is a State to defend her rights against such invasion?* It has already been observed, that the Constitution of the United States guarantees to each State a republican form of government; that the powers not delegated to the United States are reserved to the States respectively. Without entering into a detail of the rights reserved or not delegated, suffice it to say that "the right of acquiring, possessing and protecting property" is one. If this be not one of the powers not delegated, then indeed a State is in a worse and more degraded situation than the most obscure individual, whose property cannot be taken from him when fairly acquired, without his consent, even for publick use, without compensation. . . .

It may be asked, *who is to decide the question?* If it be alleged that the State has not the right, it may justly be replied, the power invading it, has not. It is a case unprovided for in the Constitution, *and there is no common umpire*. . . . [Emphasis supplied.]

There remains "no common umpire." By every rule of sound common sense and rightful Constitutional construction, it is the States themselves, parties to the compact, who should decide, in the last resort, if their compact has been violated. To leave such arbitraments to an agency of the Federal government, even as Jefferson and Madison made clear, is to substitute the discretion of the agent for the will of the principals; and it is to make the decision of a court, rather than the Constitution as agreed upon by the States, the supreme law of the land.

Notes

Go to top.

2

The Case of the Lands of Lord Fairfax

IN CHRONICLING some of the more spirited conflicts between State and Federal authority, necessarily one must place first emphasis upon the resistance by State legislatures and State governors. To this day lawmakers and chief executives speak in less inhibited fashion than judges, in protesting usurpation of power by the Supreme Court of the United States.

Yet it is important to note that the States frequently have interposed their sovereign powers through their own judiciary. As early as 1791, it was noted earlier, North Carolina's Supreme Court bluntly refused to comply with a Federal court order attempting to transfer a case from State to Federal jurisdiction.(17)

But it was in Pennsylvania, in 1798, that the position of the State judiciary was expounded at length for the first time. The expounder was one of the most remarkable jurists of the early years of our country, the redoubtable Judge Thomas McKean.

He was born in 1734; he rose to manhood in the turbulent decades of revolution against Great Britain; he was a signer of the Declaration of Independence. For several years, he held the remarkable distinction of occupying public office simultaneously in two States—as Assemblyman and later Congressman from Delaware, and as Chief Justice of Pennsylvania. Toward the middle of the 1780's, however, he settled permanently in Philadelphia, and took an active part in the Pennsylvania Convention of 1787, by urging adoption of the new Constitution. Never at a loss for a well-turned phrase, he there compared the arguments of those who opposed the Constitution to "the feeble noise occasioned by the working of small beer."(18) An active and partisan Federalist, he nevertheless reserved strong apprehensions against excessive power in the Federal government. These apprehensions burst forth in 1798, when he wrote the unanimous opinion of his court denying a petition filed by one William Cobbet in a certain libel proceeding.(19)

This was a criminal case, in which the defendant Cobbet had been placed under bond as a common libeller. When he continued his libelous publications, an action was instituted against him. Cobbet pleaded that he was an alien, a subject of Great Britain, and demanded that his case be removed for trial into the United States Circuit Court. Counsel for the

Commonwealth argued that to grant such a motion "would prostrate the authority of the individual States." The mischief that had been apprehended prior to the Eleventh Amendment, in allowing States to be sued in the Supreme Court, would be recreated by allowing them to be forced into the Circuit courts.

Chief Justice McKean and his associates unanimously rejected Cobbet's petition; and what McKean had to say[20] merits quotation at some length.

"Our system of government," said Chief Justice McKean, "seems to me to differ, in form and spirit, from all other governments that have heretofore existed in the world." Following the reasoning of Madison in the *Federalist*[21] and in the Virginia Convention of 1788,[22] McKean found the Union "as to some particulars national, in others Federal, and in all the residue territorial, or in districts called States." Continuing, he said:

The division of power between the national, Federal, and State governments (all derived from the same source, the authority of the people) must be collected from the Constitution of the United States. Before it was adopted, the several States had absolute and unlimited sovereignty within their respective boundaries; all the powers, legislative, executive and judicial, excepting those granted to Congress under the old Constitution. They now enjoy them all, excepting such as are granted to the government of the United States by the present instrument and the adopted amendments, which are for particular purposes only.

The government of the United States forms a part of the government of each State; its jurisdiction extends to the providing for the common defense against exterior injuries and violence, the regulation of commerce, and other matters specially enumerated in the Constitution; all other powers remain in the individual States, comprehending the interior and other concerns. These combined, form one complete government.

Should there be any defect in this form of government, or any collision occur, it cannot be remedied by the sole act of the Congress or the State; the people must be resorted to, for enlargement or modification. If a State should differ with the United States about the construction of them, there is no common umpire but the people, who should adjust the affair by making amendments in the constitutional way, or suffer from the defect. . . .

There is no provision in the Constitution, that in such a case the judges of the Supreme Court of the United States shall control and be conclusive; neither can the Congress by a law confer that power. There appears to be a defect in this matter. . . .

As events proved, of course, the remedy—if it was a remedy—was found in John Marshall's bold assertions of power. It is here contended that the defect described by McKean more than one hundred fifty years ago remains a major defect to this day.

The Cobbet case is important in part because it was cited at length in the next major contest that arose between State and Federal judiciaries—the prolonged litigation in Virginia over the lands of Lord Fairfax. The case began in 1796, and did not end until 1816. Things moved at a far more leisurely pace in those days. The suit was enormously complicated. It will suffice for our purposes to note that a contest arose involving the validity of a grant made by the General Assembly of Virginia in 1789 to one David Hunter. The land conveyed was a part of the vast holding that earlier (in 1736) had been granted by the English crown to Thomas Lord Fairfax. It was contended by the heirs of Lord Fairfax that Virginia's grant to Hunter was prohibited by the terms of the treaty of 1783 which ended the Revolutionary war. It was contended by Hunter, as plaintiff, that the State grant was wholly valid. On the question, so drawn, the trial court at Winchester ruled in favor of the Fairfax heirs, but on appeal, the Virginia Supreme Court of Appeals reversed the trial court and found for Hunter. (23) It was a split decision. Judge Fleming felt the treaty of 1783 had some effect, but on balance he felt title should go to Hunter. Judge Roane felt the treaty had nothing to do with the case, and he too felt title should go to Hunter.

But the heirs appealed, and in 1813 the Supreme Court of the United States reversed the Virginia Supreme Court and ordered the judgment of the Winchester court affirmed.(24) Now, that was not the first time the Supreme Court of the United States had reversed a State court, and it is not clear why this case, above all cases, should have "excited all that attention from the bench and bar which its great importance truly merited."(25) The fact is that the Supreme Court's action did stir great resentment; and matters were not helped by a tactlessly worded mandate which "hereby commanded" that further proceedings be had agreeable to the judgment and instructions of the Supreme Court.

Six days were consumed in argument before the Virginia Supreme Court on the disposition of this mandate. What the Virginia court had to say is set forth fully in the old reports. It still has meaning today. Judge Cabell led off: "My investigations," he said, "have terminated in the conviction that the Constitution of the United States does not warrant the power which the act of Congress"—that was the Judiciary Act of 1789—"purports to confer on the Federal judiciary." He went on to lay down, precisely and cogently, the essential separation of powers for which Virginians are contending to this very day. He said:

To the Federal government are confided certain powers, specially enumerated, and principally affecting our foreign relations and the general interest of the nation. These powers are limited, not only by their special enumeration, but by the positive declaration that all powers not enumerated or not prohibited to the States, are reserved to the States, or to the people.

The Tenth Amendment, it will be seen, still had some meaning then.

Cabell continued:

This demarcation of power is not vain and ineffectual. The free exercise by the States of the powers reserved to them is as much sanctioned and guarded by the Constitution of the United States as is the free exercise, by the Federal government, of the powers delegated to that government. If either be impaired, the system is deranged. The two governments, therefore, possessing each its portion of the divided sovereignty, although embracing the same territory, and operating on the same persons, and frequently on the same subjects, are nevertheless separate from, and independent of, each other . . . The Constitution of the United States contemplates the independence of both governments, and regards the residuary sovereignty of the States as not less inviolable than the delegated sovereignty of the United States.

Then Cabell went on to echo what McKean had said in the Cobbet case, what Jefferson and Calhoun were to say later:

It must have been foreseen that controversies would sometimes arise as to the boundaries of the two jurisdictions. *Yet the Constitution has provided no umpire., has erected no tribunal by which they shall be settled.* [Emphasis supplied.]

Why was no such tribunal provided to settle disputes between the States and the Federal government the States mutually had created? Cabell thought that probably the omission proceeded from the belief "that such a tribunal would produce evils greater than those of the occasional collisions which it would be designed to remedy." But in any event, he observed, "to give to the general government, or any of its departments, a direct and controlling operation upon the State departments, as such, would be to change at once the whole character of our system." The result, he said, would be this: "The independence of the State authorities would be extinguished, and a superiority, unknown to the Constitution, would be created, which would sooner or later terminate in an entire consolidation of the States into one complete national sovereignty." It was a prophetic remark.

Judge Cabell turned to the nature of the State and Federal judiciaries. Suppose the Virginia Supreme Court should comply with this "command" from the Supreme Court of the United States? The Virginia judges, in doing so, "must act either as Federal or as State judges." But they could not be made Federal judges without their consent, or without commissions. So they were not Federal judges. Thus they remained State judges. But how could they, as State judges, be required "to enter up a judgment, not our own, but dictated and prescribed to us by another court"? Obviously, they must act either ministerially or judicially—but no one contended that the Supreme Court of the United States had any authority to convert State judges into mere ministerial agents. Could the Virginia court, then, act judicially? Cabell thought not.

Before one court can dictate to another the judgment it shall pronounce, it must bear to that other the relation of an appellate court. The term appellate, however, necessarily includes the idea of superiority. But one court cannot be correctly said to be *superior* to another, unless both of them belong to the same sovereignty. It would be a misapplication of terms to say that a court of Virginia is *superior* to a court of Maryland, or vice versa. The courts of the United States, therefore, belonging to one sovereignty, cannot be appellate courts in relation to the State courts, which belong to a different sovereignty—and of course, their commands or instructions impose no obligation. [Emphasis in the original.]

Cabell argued that to admit this appellate jurisdiction would be to place the State courts "at the feet of the Federal courts, and make them the unwilling instruments of their usurpation of State rights." He would have no part of it.

Justice Brooke then took up the argument. He harked back to the Virginia Resolution of 1798, in commenting that "the right to resist infractions of the Federal Constitution, proceeding from the general government, or any department thereof, has been solemnly asserted in Virginia." The twenty-fifth section of the Judiciary Act, he declared flatly, was unconstitutional; the Virginia court should refuse obedience to the mandate.

Next, Judge Spencer Roane leaped into the fray. He had been sitting back too long, fidgeting, waiting upon his colleagues. He denounced the idea that State courts could be made arms of the Federal judiciary simply because "in the course of their ordinary jurisdiction, [they] incidentally acted upon the Constitution, laws or treaties of the United States." He found this "a circumstance which would equally make the Supreme Court of Calcutta a part of the judicial system of the United States, when enforcing the laws of this country and that." Striking at John Marshall, he declared that the Supreme Court had "gained ground by piece-meal," that its assertions of power were "at war with the idea of limited and specified powers in the general government." Then he quoted at some length from the Cobbet case, and wound up in this fashion:

Upon the whole, I am of the opinion that the Constitution confers no power upon the Supreme Court of the United States to meddle with the judgments of this court in the case before us . . . and that this court is both at liberty and is bound, to follow its own convictions on the subject, anything in the decisions, or supposed decisions, of any other court, to the contrary notwithstanding.

It remained only for Judge Fleming to concur with his brothers. Together, they joined in a unanimous opinion "that the appellate power of the Supreme Court of the United States does not extend to this court, under a sound construction of the Constitution of the United States . . .and that obedience to its mandate be declined by this court."

Happily or unhappily—men will disagree on the point—the case then went back to Story and Marshall, and in 1816 Mr. Justice Story made the Supreme Court's opinion stick.(26) It had been a wonderful fight, as they say, while it lasted. There are many Americans, not thought of as devout men, who pray earnestly that one day the fight may be resumed.

Notes

Go to top.

3

The Embargo Crisis

THE INTERPOSITION of Pennsylvania in the Olmstead case, and Virginia's spirited resistance in the Fairfax suit, coincided with massive resistance by other States to Federal authority on a matter of far greater importance. In a brief chronicle of the Embargo Crisis, and the measures of the New England States against the embargo laws, may be found some notable precedents for the resistance of Southern States to unconstitutional decrees in our own time. It will be seen that Massachusetts, Connecticut, and Rhode Island once equally cherished their State powers as they conceived them; they, too, interposed to arrest the progress of what seemed to them a deliberate, palpable, and dangerous evil. It will be recalled that the war between France and England, which erupted with such fury following the Reign of Terror in the spring and summer of 1793, subsided for a time in the closing years of the century. But in 1803, when sale of the Louisiana Territory enriched Napoleon's treasury, the conflict broke out anew. Before the end of 1804, Napoleon had crowned himself emperor at Notre Dame; in May of 1805, at Milan, he placed upon his head the iron crown of the old Lombard kings. Great Britain, Russia and Austria, breathing new life into their Triple Alliance of 1795, arrayed themselves against him, but the conquering Napoleon swept onward: Nelson's victory at Trafalgar in October of 1805 was more than offset by Austria's defeat at Ulm that same month, and by Napoleon's triumph at Austerlitz in December. By mid-summer of 1806, German opposition to Napoleon had all but collapsed; in the fall, the victorious French dealt the Prussians a cruel blow at Jena.

Napoleon accompanied these conquests by land with harsh measures at sea, and it is with these that the young United States were most deeply concerned. By his "decrees" at Paris and Berlin, and late in 1807 at Milan, Napoleon undertook to impose a strong blockade against Britain. To these impositions, Britain responded with equally stringent decrees of her own.

The effect of the British pronouncements, backed by the Royal Navy in its greatest hour, was virtually to deny the seas to neutral nations.

The United States, under Jefferson, at first responded feebly to the insults of the belligerent powers. In view of the sharp division of political sentiment, perhaps no more could have been expected: The Federalists, loving Britain and hating France, were in many quarters almost equally arrayed against the Republicans, loving France and hating Britain. To the Federalists, Napoleon embodied worldwide French imperialism in a way that Stalin, nearly one hundred fifty years later, was to embody the menace of Soviet conquest. Yet to the Republicans, the hypothetical threat of French domination was subordinate to the reality of British humiliations. These sentiments of high politics on the part of the Federalists, as is so often the case, reflected less lofty considerations of commerce: Trade with Britain was the lifeblood of New England. That blood was being drained away.

In the summer of 1807, the balance of national sentiment tipped against Britain in the outrageous affair of the *Chesapeake,* an American vessel halted by the British *Leopard* and contemptuously boarded by British sailors. For the first time, Republican measures against Britain began to gain widespread support; and on December 18, 1807, a month after new British decrees were imposed against neutral trade, Jefferson asked Congress for an embargo against all shipping. Four days later, the Embargo Act was law.

For the space of a month or so, even parts of New England went along. The Massachusetts General Court, which soon was to level against Jefferson the spirit of States' rights he himself had advanced in the Kentucky Resolutions just ten years earlier, at first praised the embargo as "a wise and highly expedient measure,. . . calculated to secure to us the blessings of peace."(27)In Southern States, though the embargo would hurt them gravely also, hostility to the British gave support to Jefferson's plan.

But the first Embargo Act of December, 1807, was followed by supplementary laws in January and March of 1808, and finally by the severe law of April 25, which authorized the President to detain all coasting vessels upon suspicion of intent to evade the embargo. With this last enactment, New England revived her bitter resentment. Two years earlier, when Congress had adopted a non-importation act to prohibit the admission of British products, the people of New England had rendered it ineffective by widespread smuggling. Now this smuggling trade was defiantly expanded, especially in Vermont and New Hampshire. On Lake Champlain and in Passamaquoddy Bay, all along the St. Lawrence, and from Newport, Portland, Nantucket, and Martha's Vineyard, smugglers actively plied their trade.(28) To these measures of the resentful people, the State governments added official harass-ments of their own. During the summer of 1808, Rhode Island actively interposed through her judiciary, when State courts at Newport effectively prevented detention of vessels under the April enactment. In August, New York's Governor Tompkins coldly refused to assist a Federal collector at Oswego who sought help in enforcing the embargo regulations.

Throughout the autumn, members of Congress from New England States continued strenuously to assert the unconstitutionality of the Embargo Acts. Across the seas, the hated Napoleon, his tide of empire not yet turned, swept triumphantly into Madrid and turned his eyes toward Rome. And as American vessels swung idly at anchor in New England harbors, a spirit of secession began to kindle among a rebellious people.(29)

In the light of that brief and oversimplified chronology, it is useful now to turn to the resolutions of the various State legislatures in the early months of 1809. The Southern States of today, interposing their sovereign powers in another cause, may perhaps be forgiven a gentle reminder to old friends north of the Potomac: This, gentlemen, is what you said then.

Delaware came first, on January 30, 1809. The Embargo Acts (and especially the new "Force Act" just signed by Jefferson on January 9) were "an invasion of the liberty of the people and [of] the constitutional sovereignty of the State governments." And while Delaware would submit to "unwise and arbitrary laws, rather than resort to violence," Delaware would seek every constitutional remedy that could be found for the evils under which her people suffered.(30)

Then Massachusetts. The Lieutenant Governor, Levi Lincoln, an ardent follower of Jefferson, having succeeded to the chief magistracy on the Governor's death, sent to the Legislature a message deprecating Federalist agitation against the laws of the land and asking an end to opposition. To this address, both Senate and House responded with ringing statements. These merit attention in our own not less turbulent time.

The government of the Union, said the Massachusetts Senate then, "is a confederation of equal and independent States with limited powers." The Senate agreed, of course, with a comment by Governor Lincoln that while measures "are pending and ripening" in Congress, the States have every right to question the justness or policy of any proposal." But do State rights end there? Governor Lincoln thought so. The Senate did not. Its resolution observed:

. . . we learn with concern from your Honour, that there are stages when questions involving unalienable rights—"can be no longer open to controversy and opposition"—"stages when an end must be put to debate and a decision then resulting be respected by its prompt and faithful execution, or government loses its existence and the people are ruined." . . . We owe it to ourselves and to the people distinctly to deny this doctrine, at once novel and pernicious.(31)

A distinction must be drawn, said the Senate, between the respect that is owed to valid laws, and the respect that cannot be required of the people for laws "unwarranted by the commission given to their rulers." In this case, the people manifestly regarded the Embargo Acts as a usurpation of their most cherished liberties. What, then, was the duty of the General Court? "The people have not sent us here to surrender their rights, but to maintain and defend them."

The Massachusetts House also responded warmly to Governor Lincoln's assertion that a time had come to end objection and opposition to a distasteful law:

We cannot agree with your Honour that in a free country there is any stage at which the constitutionality of an act may no longer be open to discussion and debate; at least it is only upon the high road to despotism that such stages can be found.

At such a point the Government, undertaking to extend its powers beyond the limits of the Constitution, degenerates into tyranny.(32)

It may be inquired, perhaps, by this citizen of Virginia who offers these notes for public review, if there be any essential difference between an unconstitutional decree by a court, and an unconstitutional enactment by its separate but equal branch of the Federal government? The paragraph that follows from the resolution of the Massachusetts House, it may be urged, applies no less to the judgment of a court than to an act of the Congress.

Were it true, that the measures of government once passed into an act, the constitutionality of that act is stamped with the seal of infallibility, and is no longer a subject for the deliberation or remonstrance of the citizen, to what monstrous lengths might not an arbitrary and tyrannical administration carry its power. . . . Were such doctrine sound, what species of oppression might not be inflicted on the prostrate liberties of our country? If such a doctrine were true, our Constitution would be nothing but a name—nay, worse, a fatal instrument to sanctify oppression, and legalize the tyranny which inflicts it. (33)

On February 15, 1809, both houses of the Massachusetts General Court concurred in a resolution declaring their solemn conviction that the Embargo Acts are "in many particulars, unjust, oppressive, and unconstitutional." To be sure, mere expression of opinion could not in itself be "decisive of the question." But through the interposition of "peaceful and legal remedies," Massachusetts proposed to protect her citizens against violations of their rights. "While this State maintains its sovereignty and independence, all the citizens can find protection against outrage and injustice in the strong arm of the State government."(34)

Massachusetts then solemnly declared that in the view of its Legislature, the embargo was "*not legally binding on the citizens of this State.*" (Emphasis supplied.) Yet until the embargo were repealed, it was urged not that the law be obeyed, but only that "all parties aggrieved by the operation of this act . . . abstain from forcible resistance."

We may look also to Connecticut. Do her press, and her professors, and her legislators now frown upon the South? This was what Connecticut said then:

The General Assembly are decided in the opinion, and do Resolve, that the acts aforesaid are . . . grievous to the good people of this State, dangerous to their common liberties, incompatible with the Constitution of the United States, and encroaching upon the immunities of this State.(35)

But Connecticut did not stop with mere expression of opinion. Her resolution directed all persons holding executive office in the State not to afford "any official aid or co-operation in the execution of the act aforesaid." And more ominously still, Connecticut's Legislature directed that the Governor be requested, "as commander in chief of the military force of this State," to cause the resolution to be published in general orders. Let us note also this paragraph:

Resolved, that to preserve the Union, and support the Constitution of the United States, it becomes the duty of the Legislatures of the States, in such a crisis of affairs, vigilantly to watch over, and vigorously to maintain, the powers not delegated to the United States, but reserved to the States respectively, or to the people; and that a due regard to this duty, will not permit this Assembly to assist, or concur in giving effect to the aforesaid unconstitutional act, passed, to enforce the embargo.(36)

(Are the legislatures of the Southern States, today, it may be asked, fairly to be condemned by their New England brethren for viewing their responsibilities exactly as Connecticut and Massachusetts viewed their own responsibilities a century and a half ago? Is it to be urged that both were wrong, Connecticut then, Virginia now? Or is it not equally possible that New England legislatures were right then, in protecting the most intimate concerns of their people, and Southern legislatures are equally right today?)

Finally, brief note may be made of a concluding resolution on the embargo, adopted by the General Assembly of Rhode Island on March 4, 1809, the very day that the hated laws expired at the direction of Congress. The embargo, said Rhode Island flatly, had been an "unconstitutional" proscription on the people. In resisting it, the people of Rhode Island *as one of the parties to the Federal compact,* had a right to express their opposition; and the General Assembly, for its part, had a duty as the organ of their sentiments and the depositary of their authority,

to interpose for the purpose of protecting them from the ruinous inflictions of usurped and unconstitutional power.(37)

The duty of the States to interpose, thus expressed by Rhode Island at the time of the Embargo Crisis, remains in the view of this citizen of Virginia a high and undiminished duty of the States in our own generation.

Notes

Go to top.

4

Matters of the Militia

LET US remain in New England for a while. It is a strong land, strong peopled, strong principled; and for all the blood they have shed against each other, the South and New England hold much in common. The row houses of Beacon Street are brothers to those of King Street, and the many-steepled valleys of Vermont have their clean and quiet counterparts in the Great Smokies and the Shenandoah Valley. The Southerner, traveling in New England, often finds a spiritual kinship in the courtesy and reserve of the people he meets; and no less certainly does the advocate of States' rights, searching the history of Massachusetts, Connecticut, Rhode Island, and Vermont, find in their high-spirited past repeated expressions of New England's devotion to the responsible role assigned to the States.

The detested embargo was abandoned, we have noted, in March of 1809, only to give way to a non-intercourse act almost equally resented. In April of 1810, John Randolph of Roanoke described this proscription in characteristic language: "It has been reprobated and reviled by every man, of every political description, in this House and out of it, from one end of the country to another." Why, then was it kept on the books? "Is it a sort of scarecrow, set up to frighten the great belligerents of Europe? Or is it a toy, a rattle, a bare plaything, to amuse the great children of our political world?"(38)

Certainly New England was not amused. Her commerce still suffered, her ships still were idled. Worse yet, blundering British diplomacy (by which Madison first was encouraged to believe that Britain would suspend her restrictions on trade, only to be abruptly disabused of the thought) added to national feeling against the government of George III. Bitterly, the Federalists saw Republicans make large gains in Congress and in State legislatures; and to the insult of affairs abroad was added fresh injury at home, in the furious controversy of 1811 over the admission of Louisiana. To an angered New England, this was fresh evidence of the declining influence of the East. Secession was talked openly on the village greens, and in Congress a melancholy Josiah Quincy commented sadly that it soon would be the duty of some of the States "to prepare definitely for a separation."(39)

It was in this spirit of total discontent that the Federalists voted solidly against Madison's request in June 1812 for a declaration of war against Great Britain. The resolution carried by the feeble vote of 19-13 in the Senate and 79-49 in the House. To the Federalists, it was Madison's war—and Clay's and young Calhoun's; it was "a party and not a national war," entered into by a "divided people." In Massachusetts, the Legislature rebelliously adopted resolutions urging her male citizens not to volunteer except for defense operations; the Governor proclaimed a public fast to atone for the wickedness of the administration's action.(40)

Nevertheless, as Southern States are so often reminded in another context these days, the declaration of war was the supreme law of the land. There was no question of the constitutional power of Congress to declare war. But we may well inquire: Where was the "spirit of willing compliance," to which Southern States are abjured so strenuously just now, in the New England of 1812?

War was declared on June 18. On the 22nd, General Dearborn, by authority of the President, called upon both Massachusetts and Connecticut to supply detachments of their militia for coastal defense. Governor Caleb Strong of Massachusetts flatly refused to comply. Under the Constitution, he said, Congress could provide for calling forth the militia on three grounds only: To execute the laws of the Union, to suppress insurrection, or to repel invasion. For his own part, he could not perceive that any of these exigencies was present. The Supreme Judicial Court of Massachusetts agreed with him: Judges Parson, Sewall, and Parker, asked for an advisory opinion, agreed that the right to decide when the militia would be ordered to duty was a right "not delegated to the United States by the Constitution, nor prohibited by it to the States; it is reserved to the States respectively, and from the nature of the power, it must be exercised by those with whom the States have respectively entrusted the chief command of the militia."(41)

Governor Griswold of Connecticut took precisely the same view. On June 29, he convened his executive council, which advised him to reject General Dearborn's requisition. In August, the General Assembly of Connecticut warmly concurred in the Governor's course of resistance. If the State militia could be called out upon the sole decision of Federal authority, said the Assembly's resolution of August 25, it would have the effect of converting the militia into standing troops of the United States. The Assembly was "not able to discover that the Constitution of the United States justifies this claim."

Let us note carefully what the Assembly next declared—this is Connecticut speaking:

The people of this State were among the first to adopt that Constitution. . . . They have a deep interest in its preservation, and are still disposed to yield a willing and prompt obedience to all the legitimate requirements of the Constitution of the United States.

But it must not be forgotten, that the State of Connecticut is a FREE SOVEREIGN andINDEPENDENT State; that the United States are a *confederacy* of States; that we are a confederated and not a consolidated Republic. The Governor of this State is under a high and solemn obligation, "to maintain the lawful rights and privileges thereof, as a sovereign, free and independent State," as he is "to support the Constitution of the United States," and the obligation to support the latter imposes an additional obligation to support the former. The building cannot stand, if the pillars upon which it rests, are impaired or destroyed.(42) [Emphasis in the original.]

And because Connecticut, as a State, did not agree that Madison had authority to requisition her militia "to assist in carrying on an offensive war," Connecticut refused to participate until New England should in fact be threatened "by an actual invasion of any portion of our territory."

So, too, with Rhode Island. On October 6, Governor William Jones, on the advice of his Council and with the approval of the General Assembly, advised Federal authorities that he alone, as Governor of the State, would judge "whether those exigencies provided for by the Constitution exist or not."

So, also, with Vermont. On October 23, 1813, Governor Chittenden declared in a message to the Assembly that he always had regarded the militia as a force "peculiarly adapted and exclusively assigned for the service and protection of the respective States." It never could have been contemplated by the framers of the Constitution, "who, it appears, in the most cautious manner guarded the sovereignty of the States, or by the States who adopted it, that the whole body of the militia were, by any kind of magic, at once to be transformed into a regular army for the purpose of foreign conquest."

In the case of Vermont, there is a sequel to the story that may be briefly noted. By a proclamation of November 10, Governor Chittenden commanded the recall of a part of the Vermont militia that was then serving under Federal command "for the defense of a neighboring State." Vermont's troops refused to obey this command and arrested the Governor's agent. A resolution then was offered in Congress instructing the prosecution of the Governor for treason. A counter resolution was offered in Massachusetts, "pledging the support of the State to the Governor and people of Vermont in their efforts to maintain their constitutional rights."(43) Quite a rash of other resolutions then broke out. New Jersey, in February of 1814, regarded "with contempt and abhorrence, the ravings of an infuriated faction, either as issuing from a legislative body, a maniac Governor, or discontented and ambitious demagogues." In March, Pennsylvania also denounced Governor Chittenden, and viewed "with utmost concern and disapprobation every attempt to screen from just punishment any individual or individuals, however exalted by station, who may violate the Con-stitution or laws of the United States."

What may we learn from this today? This citizen of Virginia, taking note of these events, does not profess to say who was right and who was wrong on the matter of the militia. Certainly it would appear that the question of contested power, having been raised by responsible States in mid-summer of 1812, could have been settled promptly had it been submitted to the arbitrament of all the States. The one point that may be emphasized, for the purposes of this essay, is that for two solid years—from the summer of 1812 until New England actually was invaded in the summer of 1814—Massachusetts, Connecticut, Rhode Island, and Vermont interposed their sovereign powers against *what they regarded* as an encroachment by Federal authority upon their rights. They stood granite-like upon what was to them a question of high constitutional principle.

Notes

Go to top.

5

Events of 1814

NEW ENGLAND'S contribution in this period to the story of State and Federal relations is by no means ended. Even as the bitter controversy continued over the control of State militia, Congress in December, 1813, added a fresh grievance to the Federalists' overflowing cup: A new embargo law was adopted, more stringent than all the embargoes of the preceding five years. Even shore fisheries and coastal trade were proscribed. In Massachusetts, a flood of memorials and remonstrances poured in from town meetings. These petitions were assembled and referred to a committee of the State Legislature headed by William Lloyd; and on February 18, 1814, the General Court of Massachusetts overwhelmingly approved what still is remembered as "Lloyd's Report." It merits respectful attention.

The report first reviewed the protests of the town meetings against the December embargo:

This act is denounced by all the memorialists in the warmest and most energetic language as a gross and palpable violation of the principles of the Constitution; and they express decidedly their opinion, that it cannot be submitted to without a pusillanimous surrender of . . . rights and liberties. . . .

The Massachusetts legislators were wholly prepared to accept this view of the law, and to interpose their powers against it. The people, they said, had given Congress no right to enact the law. And now let us read closely—this is Massachusetts speaking:

A power to regulate commerce is abused, when employed to destroy it; *and a manifest and voluntary abuse of power sanctions the right of resistance, as much as a direct and palpable usurpation.* The sovereignty reserved to the States, was reserved to protect the citizens from acts of violence by the United States, as well as for purposes of domestic regulation. We spurn the idea that the free, sovereign and independent State of Massachusetts is reduced to a mere municipal corporation, without power to protect its people, and to defend them from oppression, from whatever quarter it comes. Whenever the national compact is violated, and the citizens of this State are oppressed by cruel and unauthorized laws, this Legislature is bound to interpose its power, and wrest from the oppressor his victim. [Emphasis supplied.]

This is the spirit of our Union, and thus has it been explained by the very man [Madison], who now sets at defiance all the principles of his early political life.(44)

What course could the Legislature pursue? Three avenues had been suggested. One was a memorial to Congress, but that would be useless: "It has been again, and again resorted to, and with no other effect than to increase the evils complained of." Secondly, laws might be adopted to punish violations of the security of the people of Massachusetts in their property; but sufficient State laws already existed: "No act of this Legislature can afford any additional security." Thirdly, following the proposal of Madison himself in the Virginia Resolution, a convention of States could be urged, "for the purpose of devising proper measures to procurethe united efforts of the commercial States, to obtain such amendments or explanations of the Constitution, as will secure them from future evils."

It was this course that ultimately was to be sought, but Massachusetts, in February, thought the time not yet right to take it. Some negotiations had begun toward ending the war, and if these were successful the burdens would be removed. For a second reason, it was thought better to let the people themselves pass on the question of summoning a convention among the offended States, by making it a campaign issue in the next election to the General Court. Meanwhile, the people were urged patiently to wait "for the effectual interposition of the State Government for their relief." The embargo, in the State's official view, was "unconstitutional and void."

It is difficult, considering the many forces and counter-forces leveled against each other in that tempestuous year, to appraise the weight that should be accorded the resolute posture taken by the Massachusetts Legislature. But the fact is that the embargo act of December, 1813, was not effectively enforced and soon was repealed, *largely because of the interposition of the*

New England States. The effect of their resistance was to nullify the law.

Similarly, it is impossible to say whether, in the late fall of 1814, the oratory of Daniel Webster or the militant opposition of Massachusetts and Connecticut was the more responsible for defeat of a conscription bill proposed by Madison's desperate administration. At its October session, the Connecticut Legislature condemned the conscription plan as "not only intolerably burdensome and oppressive, but utterly subversive of the rights and liberties of the people of this State." Should the bill actually be passed, "it will become the imperious duty of the Legislature of this State to exert themselves to ward off a blow so fatal to the liberties of a free people." Hence the Governor was instructed to summon an immediate session of the Assembly if the bill became law.

As events worked out, the conscription bill was defeated. Webster, tossing his massive head in a roaring denunciation of the conduct of the war, condemned the bill as "this horrible lottery"—not only unconstitutional, but worse than unconstitutional: "'tis murder."(45) But Congress did pass, however, a "Bill in regard to the Enlistment of Minors"; and Connecticut, in January, 1815, promptly undertook to nullify its provisions by adopting her own "Act to Secure the Rights of Parents, Masters and Guardians." The act required judges to release on habeas corpus all minors enlisted without the consent of their parents or guardians, and provided for fines and imprisonment against any person concerned in such enlistment who should remove any such minor out of the State.(46) Massachusetts, the following month, enacted a similar law.

Notes

Go to top.

6

The Hartford Convention

WE MAY now profitably turn back to the strongly-worded resolution that Massachusetts had adopted in February of 1814. Should all else fail, the Legislators had said, and negotiations with Britain prove fruitless, a convention of the aggrieved New England States should be summoned.

All else did fail. The peace commission, in the spring, had nothing of a favorable nature to report. Meanwhile, the British, who earlier had capitalized upon Federalist sentiment in New England by leaving her ports relatively free of blockade, now began turning on pressure. During the summer, the blockade was extended, and coastal raids became a matter of increasing concern. In August came the capture of Washington, and near collapse of the national government. New England Federalists were not greatly concerned.(47) But when British troops began to occupy parts of

Maine and Massachusetts, New England States, which earlier had been so indifferent to needs of the United States Army, now cried out for Federal forces. When these were not promptly provided, the Legislatures turned to their own militia. Early in September, Governor Strong of Massachusetts called out 5,000 militiamen, and summoned a special session of the General Court for October 5. A committee of the Legislature brought in a report accusing the national administration of deliberately neglecting the defense of Massachusetts. The day of salvation had passed, said the committee, unless Massachusetts discarded an administration "which made war for party purposes."(48)

It was evident, said the committee, that the present Constitution did not give the Eastern States their proper rights; the usual means of amending the Constitution were inadequate to the emergency. It was recommended, therefore, that a convention be called to undertake the task.

The resolution thereupon adopted, in addition to providing for the raising of a State army of ten thousand men, called for the appointment of twelve delegates to confer with delegates from other New England States. They were to discuss measures of common defense, and also, "should they deem it expedient," were "to lay the foundation for a radical reform in the national compact, by inviting to a further convention, a deputation from all the States in the Union."

Rhode Island accepted warmly on November 5. "The Legislature and the whole people of this State already but too well know how frequently and fruitlessly they have petitioned the Federal government for some portion of those means of defense for which we have paid so dearly, and to which, by the Constitution, we are so fully entitled." But these petitions had gone unheeded, or been answered only by "unmeaning professions and promises never performed, but generally by telling us to protect ourselves." Rhode Island and her sister States were not compelled to continue to accept such mistreatment "by a government we have ourselves created."

Connecticut also accepted the invitation of Massachusetts, and though neither Vermont nor New Hampshire officially accepted, both were represented when the convention began at Hartford on December 15.

Now, the Hartford Convention of 1814 has often been ridiculed. It has been described as a "purely party assemblage, lacking the united support of New England."(49) Its proposals for constitutional amendment later were to be "unqualifiedly rejected" by New Jersey, denounced severely by New York, condemned in a long report from Pennsylvania, and rejected without comment by Vermont, Virginia, North Carolina, Ohio, Tennessee, and Louisiana.

Yet this assemblage ought not to be so cavalierly disdained. The twenty-six delegates who met in the counsel chamber of the State House at Hartford included some outstanding men—the Chief Justice and an associate justice of the Supreme Court of Connecticut, the Chief Justice of Rhode Island, former United States Senator George Cabot of Massachusetts, and Harrison Grey Otis, an outstanding Federalist who had represented Massachusetts in Congress. Among others present were Nathan Dane, author of the Ordinance of 1798; Stephen Longfellow, father of the poet; Timothy Bigelow, Speaker of the Massachusetts House of Representatives; Chauncey Goodrich, Lieutenant Governor of Connecticut; Senator James Hillhouse of New Haven, Treasurer of Yale College, and several leading members of the State legislatures.

The convention met in closed session from December 15 until January 4, when its report was formally adopted. It is true, as William Edward Buckley said of it, that much of the report "took the tone of a party platform."(50) It opened with an account of the virtues of Federalist administrations and the general incompetence and corruption of the Republican administrations. Among the amendments proposed to the Constitution was a patently political proposal, aimed at ending the Virginia dynasty, by which no President could be eligible for reelection, nor could Presidents be elected from the same State for successive terms. Another proposed amendment, recalling Jefferson's Secretary of the Treasury, Albert Gallatin, would have barred naturalized citizens from serving in Congress or holding any civil office under the national government. Other proposed changes in the Constitution would have based representation in Congress (and votes in the electoral college) solely upon the number of free inhabitants of the States; required a two-thirds vote of both Houses of Congress to admit new States or to declare war; limited any embargoes laid by Congress to sixty days; and required that any act shutting off commercial relations with a foreign nation must pass Congress by a two-thirds vote. The last group of proposals, it will be seen, were concerned not with partisan politics as such, but with the concerns that had dominated New England since the first embargo six years earlier.

These resolutions became public on January 6. But unknown to the delegates at Hartford, while they met, a peace treaty ending the war had been signed at Ghent on December 24; even then the treaty was on its way to Washington for ratification. Then, on January 8, Jackson defeated the British at New Orleans. As soon as these events became known, the whole purpose of the Hartford Convention vanished, and jubilant Republicans leaped upon the resolutions with vengeful cries of "treason!" and "disunion!" and "folly!"

But was the Hartford Convention so futile? Was it, in retrospect, as great a blunder as some historians have termed it?

There is some reason to believe that this drastic interposition by the New England States achieved at least some of the objects which were sought, and that the convention itself was not nearly so repudiated by the people at the time as it has been denounced by historians of a much later era.

Harrison Gray Otis, who was to spend much of the remainder of his life defending the Hartford Convention,(51) made some of these points in *A Short Account of the Hartford Convention,* which he published at Boston in 1823. Here he notes, for example, that the Massachusetts House of Representatives, which had approved the call of the convention in October of 1814 by a vote of 260 to 90, the following year adopted a new report, defending and approving the Hartford resolutions, by an equally impressive vote of 159 to 48. Also, the year after the "blundering" Hartford Convention, Massachusetts voters returned Caleb Strong to the Governorship by the same "relative majority as he had received the year before." Evidently the delegates were not repudiated by their own people.

More important, however, is this: The Hartford Report concluded with a resolution urging adoption of a law by which State troops would be used in State defense. This was exactly the substance of a law, Otis notes, "incredible and unlooked for as it certainly was, which was enacted by the national government on the 27th day of January, 1815." The law authorized and required the President to receive into the service of the United States any troops which might have been raised and organized under the authority of a State, whose term of service was not less than twelve months, subject to the rules and articles of war, with the provision that such troops could be employed "in the State raising the same, or in an adjoining State, and not elsewhere, except with the assent of the Executive of the State so raising the same."

"Now, we declare," said Otis, "and we appeal most solemnly to every honest man who lived in those disastrous days, if the whole bone and muscle, and marrow of the controversy was not touching the exact and precise point which this law absolutely and entirely settled."

Another major grievance of the New England States, repeatedly emphasized by their members in Congress, was the refusal of the United States to pay members of the State militia who had served in defending any part of the United States. The Hartford Convention also had asked for redress on this score, and a bill carrying out the proposal had passed the United States Senate and was on its way to the House when news of peace arrived. "What is this," asked Otis, "but acknowledging in plain and direct terms the justice and propriety of all the proceedings of New England during the war?" Up until the very moment that news of the peace arrived, he insists, "the government was not only disposed but prepared to comply with every proposition contained in the commission."(52)

It is not the purpose of the author of these notes either to applaud or to condemn the conduct of the New England States in this period of 1808-15; the purpose is simply to recount what happened. The States interposed, and to a very large extent, they succeeded in obtaining the ends which they, as States, deemed so vitally important to *their own interests:* They undertook to nullify the whole series of acts relating to non-intercourse, non-importation, and embargo. Taking a strict construction of the constitutional provision relating to calling forth the militia, they succeeded in challenging national authority throughout the whole of the war. Their interposition was influential in defeating a conscription bill they regarded as unconstitutional; and when a corollary bill actually was approved, relating to the enlistment of minors, they effectively nullified it with State laws of their own. Until the day that news was received in Washington of Jackson's victory and the Treaty of Ghent, they were well on their way to achieving two of the most important objects sought by the Hartford Convention. Throughout this period, the interposing States repeatedly asserted, in the strongest and most unequivocal terms, their view of the Union as a confederacy in which the sovereignty and the broad reserved rights of the States must be respected. They did not hesitate to term actions of the Federal government "unconstitutional and void," and they laid down, as a deliberate, and considered public policy, a program of steadfast resistance to what they deemed encroachments upon their powers.

Notes

Go to top.

7

The Bank of the United States

SOME of the greatest embarrassments of the Madison administration during the War of 1812 stemmed from the inability of the government efficiently to finance its operations. The charter of the first Bank of the United States expired in 1811, and a hostile Congress, divided by factionalism and genuinely concerned at the constitutional issues of a national bank, stubbornly refused to renew it. By 1813, the Treasury was desperate. Efforts to float war loans met with the resentful disdain of State banks. Legitimate revenues of the government could not be transferred for lack of a national common medium of exchange. By 1814, the Treasury itself could no longer pay interest on the national debt. In Boston, Philadelphia, and New York, the Federal government found itself unable to redeem treasury notes. The War Department could not pay a bill for $3,500. The State Department could not even pay for its stationery.(53)

In this chaotic state of affairs, many Republicans deserted their principles of strict construction: Even Calhoun came to support the second Bank of the United States, and took a decisive part in the leadership that led finally to the act of April 10, 1816, recreating the bank under a twenty-year charter.

Scarcely had the bank been revived, however, before it ran into grave difficulties through mismanagement, speculation, and fraud.(54) Stock-jobbers and gamblers manipulated its securities shamefully. In Baltimore, some especially fraudulent transactions ironically centered around Cashier

James W. McCulloch, whose name soon was to be identified with the bank's preservation.(55)

In a desperate effort to retrieve itself from difficulties, the Bank of the United States began calling upon State banks for repayment of loans. But the State banks themselves were far overextended, and often unable to pay. In the resulting constriction of credit, hundreds of merchants, farmers, and storekeepers found themselves in bondage to "the monster." At one point, the bank owned "a large part of Cincinnati" through such foreclosures,(56) but communities in North Carolina, Kentucky, and Indiana were scarcely less afflicted. As trade began to dry up and merchants dunned their impoverished creditors, a wave of hostility toward the Bank of the United States swept the country.

The animosity of the people was soon reflected in acts of their State governments. Indiana in 1816 and Illinois in 1818 inserted provisions in their Constitutions prohibiting the Bank of the United States from establishing branches within their jurisdictions. North Carolina imposed a tax of $5,000 on the Fayetteville branch. Georgia ordered a tax of 31¼¢ on every $100 of the bank's stock. Maryland in 1817 undertook to impose a tax of $15,000 a year on the bank's Baltimore branch. Tennessee levied a tax of $50,000 per year, and Kentucky exceeded this with a tax of $60,000 per year.(57)

Believing that these State taxes would bring destruction of the bank, Federal authorities hastily drummed up a contest in Maryland, in the certain conviction that John Marshall would bring home a decision in their favor. He did not disappoint them. In February of 1819, Marshall handed down one of his half-dozen most important decisions, in the renowned case of *McCulloch vs. Maryland*.(58) This decision is so well known, and so widely quoted, that no good purpose would be served by reviewing it at any length. Here Marshall gave the broadest possible construction to that clause of the Constitution which authorizes the Congress to pass whatever laws may be "necessary or proper" to carry out functions of the Federal government. On this point, Marshall held that "necessary" should be understood to mean no more than "convenient," or "useful," or "conducive to." "Let the end be legitimate," he said, "let it be within the scope of the Constitution, and all means, which are appropriate, which are plainly adapted to that end, which are not prohibited, but consist with the letter and spirit of the Constitution, are constitutional."(59)

On the second point, he explored at great length Maryland's contention—an entirely sound and proper contention, in the view of the author of these notes —that the Constitution did not emanate from the broad mass of the people, but "as the act of sovereign and independent States." But Marshall, of course, found it "difficult to sustain" this self-evident proposition that the powers of the General government had been delegated by the States. It was true, he had to admit, that the Constitution had been ratified by the people in their respective States, but what of this? "Where else should they have assembled?" No political dreamer was ever wild enough, Marshall asserted, "to think of breaking down the lines which separate the States, and of compounding the American people into one common mass. Of consequence, when they act, they act as States." But Marshall, dogmatically refusing to distinguish between a "State" and a "State government," thoroughly confused the essential point here at issue. He threw a sop in the direction of strict construction: "The principle that [the Federal government] can exercise only the powers granted to it, would seem too apparent to have required to be enforced by all those arguments which its enlightened friends . . . found it necessary to urge." But prophetically, he remarked that "the question respecting the extent of the powers actually granted, is perpetually, arising, and will probably continue to arise, as long as our system shall exist." Then, agreeing that the States have an undoubted power to tax within their jurisdictions, he denied that the bank was within their reach; it was a creature of the Federal government, of all the people, beyond the power of any State or group of States. "That the power to tax involves the power to destroy," he observed, in the most famous line from this decision, is a proposition not to be denied.

"The court has bestowed on this subject its most deliberate consideration," said Marshall, "The result is a conviction that the States have no power, by taxation or otherwise, to retard, impede, burden, or in any manner control, the operations of the constitutional laws enacted by Congress to carry into execution the powers vested in the general government. This is, we think, the unavoidable consequence of that supremacy which the Constitution had declared."

And who would declare and define that supremacy of the Federal government? Why, John Marshall, to be sure, Chief Justice of the Federal government's Supreme Court. The States that had created the Constitution, and bound themselves by their mutual compact, were to have no effective voice in saying what the compact meant. Presumably all the people, through the Congress, had approved the bank; therefore none of the people, through their States, could disapprove it. When the people acted nationally, as Marshall thought, to aggrandize the powers of the Federal government, the people were right; when the identical people acted as States, to restrict the Federal agency, they were wrong.

His opinion, to be sure, did not go unchallenged. One of the most lucid, and indeed overwhelming criticisms of Marshall's doctrines, came in Virginia from Spencer Roane, chief judge of the State's Supreme Court. It was an accident of fortune, and a most unlucky one, that saw Roane writing letters to the Richmond *Enquirer* while Marshall wrote law on the Court. Their positions could easily have been reversed. Historians are agreed that had Ellsworth not retired from the Court in time for Adams to name Marshall Chief Justice, the incoming Jefferson would have appointed Roane to the place Marshall was to occupy.(60) In that event, we might have enjoyed a government as our government constitutionally was intended to be, by a federation of sovereign States jointly controlling their mutual agent, the Federal government. Roane ranks among the greatest "might have beens" of our history. He was a man of towering integrity, great eloquence, and profound convictions on the nature of the Union. He was a States' Righter in a way that his high-tempered father-in-law, Patrick Henry, could never have been, for Roane's views were grounded in a depth of penetrating thought that the more colorful Henry rarely brought to his public statements.

The Supreme Court's decision in the McCulloch case, Roane was to write, served to expunge the words "necessary and proper" from the Constitution. And "great as is the confidence of the nation in all its tribunals, they are not at liberty to change the meaning of our language" or effectively "to change the Constitution."(61) More than this, in Roane's view, the court "had no power to adjudicate away the reserved rights of a sovereign member of the confederacy, and vest them in the general government."

With great insight, Roane observed that it is ever the tendency of man to submit, little by little, to infractions of the fundamental law; the American people had not rebelled against George III until a *general* declaration had come along, asserting for the British Parliament a right to legislate for the American colonies "in all cases whatsoever." In the McCulloch case, Roane perceived the same sort of general declaration: "If the limits imposed on the general government, by the Constitution, are stricken off, they have *literally,* the power to legislate for us 'in all cases whatsoever': and then we may bid a last adieu to the State governments."

Roane went on to examine, with great care, the basic nature of the Union. The Federal government, it was intended, should have no powers beyond those specifically delegated by the States; all other powers were reserved then, in 1788, and must always remain reserved to the States or to the people, until delegated by Constitutional amendment. Was it not apparent, he asked, that Congress was to have, under the Constitution, only the powers "herein granted"? And was it not a reasonable construction, that the power of Congress to adopt laws "necessary and proper" for carrying out its enumerated powers, related only to those laws fairly incident to such powers? The phrase, said Roane, "created no extension of the powers previously granted." Neither could the Supreme Court, by fiat, extend or stretch the language; if Federal powers were to be extended, or State powers further limited, let it be done "by amendment to the Constitution." Let it be an "act of the people, and not that of subordinate agents."

By its opinion in the McCulloch case, said Roane, the Court had laid down principles that "tend directly to consolidation of the States, and to strip them of some of the most important attributes of their sovereignty." Yet the truth was, that the respective States never had consented to a consolidated government. As sovereign States, true, they jointly had delegated some of their powers, but they did not become less sovereign thereafter. They remained separate, respective States. He asked incredulously how Marshall could hold otherwise: "The States . . . gave birth to the Constitution; they support its existence, and they alone are capable of reforming or changing its form and substance, and yet we are informed by a solemn adjudication that its powers are not derived from that source, and consequently, that they are not parties to it!"

To be sure, Roane conceded, Marshall's nationalist doctrine was not new. It had been advanced by Chase and Washington and Paterson, among others, at the time of the Alien and Sedition Acts. But the doctrine had then been "exposed and refuted, and I did not expect that it would be brought forward at this day under the proposed sanction of the highest judicial authority."

One more paragraph from Roane's exposition, and reluctantly this citizen of Virginia will resume his own narrative notes. But let this be attended carefully:

The doctrine [which denies that the States are parties to the Federal compact], if admitted to be true, would be of fatal consequence to the rights and freedom of the people of the States. If the States are not parties to the compact, the legislatures of the several States, who annually bring together the feelings, the wishes, and the opinions of the people within their respective limits, would not have a right to canvass the public measures of the Congress, or of the President, nor to remonstrate against the encroachments of power, nor to resist the advances of usurpation, tyranny and oppression. They would no longer be hailed as the sentinels of the public liberty, nor as the protectors of their own rights. *Every government, which has ever yet been established, feels a disposition to increase its own powers.* Without the restraints which are imposed by an enlightened public opinion, this tendency will inevitably conduct the freest government to the exercise of tyrannized power. If the right of resistance be denied, or taken away, despotism inevitably follows.

It has, however, been supposed by some that the Constitution has provided a remedy for every evil: That the right of the State governments to protest against, or to resist encroachments on their authority is taken away, and transferred to the Federal judiciary, whose power extends to all cases arising under the Constitution; that the Supreme Court is the umpire to decide between the States on the one side, and the United States on the other, in all questions touching the constitutionality of laws, or acts of the Executive. There are many cases which can never be brought before that tribunal, and I do humbly conceive that the States never could have committed an act of such egregious folly as to agree that their umpire should be altogether appointed and paid by the other party. The Supreme Court may be a perfectly impartial tribunal to decide between two States, but cannot be considered in that point of view when the contest lies between the United States and one of its members.(62) [Emphasis supplied.]

Thus, in Roane's view, the States not only had a right to tax the Bank of the United States; they also had a right to resist the Supreme Court's pronouncement *until the States themselves had settled the question of contested power by their own arbitrament.* It is evident that his views were widely shared. Despite the McCulloch opinion, many of the States continued to resist the bank. Georgia in 1819, and again in 1821, adopted particularly harassing enactments, designed to bar the bank from suing in Federal Courts. (63)

It was in Ohio, however, that events came to a climax. No State had suffered more grievously than Ohio from the disastrous inflation brought about by the bank's first years of blundering mismanagement.(64) This hatred of the bank was manifested by an act of the Ohio Legislature in 1819—enacted in the teeth of the McCulloch decision—levying a tax of $50,000 per year on each of the bank's two branches in the State. This tax was to become due on September 15, 1820, but the bank, having protested vainly against the levy, refused to pay and instead obtained an injunction from a Federal judge against its collection.

Before the injunction could be served, however, State Auditor Osborn ordered one of his deputies, John L. Harper, to collect the tax by persuasion if he could, but by violence if he must. Entering the bank's branch office at Chillicothe, on the morning of September 17, Harper made one last request for voluntary payment. When this was denied, he leaped over the counter, strode into the bank vaults, and helped himself to $100,000 in paper and specie.(65) He then turned this over to a deputy, one H. M. Currie; and Mr. Currie, stuffing this considerable hoard into a small trunk, with which the party thoughtfully had come equipped, loaded the trunk into his wagon and set off down the road to Columbus.

The bank furiously brought suit against Osborn and Harper for recovery of the money, relying, of course, upon Marshall's opinion in the McCulloch case. But Ohio was in no mood to regard the Supreme Court's pronouncements as the supreme law of the land. In December of 1820, Ohio's House of Representatives brought in a blistering report, substantially concurred in by the Senate on January 3, 1821, condemning the bank's suit as a suit against the State itself. "To acquiesce in such an encroachment upon the privileges and authority of the States, without an effort to defend them, would be an act of treachery to the State itself, and to all the States that compose the American Union."

Particular attention may be directed to the statement that next follows. Gentlemen, this is Ohio speaking:

The committee are aware of the doctrine, that the Federal courts are exclusively vested with jurisdiction to declare, in the last resort, the true interpretation of the Constitution of the United States. To this doctrine, in the latitude contended for, they never can give their assent.(66)

An express provision of the Constitution, said Ohio, places the States, in suits brought against them by individuals, beyond the jurisdiction of the Federal courts. Citing the Kentucky and Virginia Resolutions, and quoting at length from Madison's Report of 1799, the Ohio Legislature declared that the elections of 1800— the "Jefferson Revolution"—gave the sanction of the people themselves to the view that even the Supreme Court must bow to the supreme people of the States.

Thus has the question, whether the Federal Courts are the sole expositors of the Constitution of the United Slates in the last resort, or whether the States, "as in all other cases of compact among parties having no common judge," have an equal right to interpret that Constitution for themselves, where their sovereign rights are involved, been decided against the pretension of the Federal judges by the people themselves, the true source of all legitimate powers.

John Marshall's Court was wrong, said Ohio bluntly, in the McCulloch case; and because the Court's opinion had encroached so unwarrantably upon the reserved powers of the States, there was no obligation upon Ohio to acquiesce therein. After all, the resolution continued, it was one thing for the Court to define a right, and another for the right to be exercised. Had not William Marbury, the appointee of Adams, been told that he had a right to his commission as justice of the peace? Yet was it not true that Marbury had never received it? Similarly, the Court had ruled that purchasers of the Yazoo lands were entitled to their property. "But the decision availed them nothing, unless as a make-weight in effecting compromise."

These two cases are evidence that in great questions of political rights and political powers, a decision of the Supreme Court of the United States is not conclusive of the rights decided by it. . . . Surely the State of Ohio ought not to be condemned because she did not abandon her solemn legislative acts as a dead letter upon the promulgation of an opinion of that tribunal.

If the Bank of the United States would agree to get out of Ohio, close its branches, and settle its business, Ohio proposed in its resolution to return the tax money. But whether or not such a compromise should be effected,

It behooves the General Assembly . . . to take measures for vindicating the character of the State, and also for awakening the attention of the separate States to the consequences that may result from the doctrines of the Federal courts upon the questions that have arisen. And besides, as it is possible that the proposition of compromise may not be accepted, it is the duty of the General Assembly to take ulterior measures for asserting and maintaining the rights of the State by all constitutional means within their power.

And what were some of these "ulterior measures" by which Ohio would interpose her sovereign powers against the Supreme Court's decree?

For this purpose the committee recommend that provisions be made by law, forbidding the keepers of our jails from receiving into their custody any person committed at the suit of the Bank of the United States, or for any injury done to them; prohibiting our judicial officers from taking acknowledgments of conveyance where the Bank is a party, or when made for their use, and our recorders from receiving or recording such conveyances; forbidding our courts, justices of the peace, judges and grand juries from taking any cognizance of any wrong alleged to have been committed upon any species of property owned by the Bank, or upon any of its corporate rights or privileges, and prohibiting our notaries public from protesting any notes or bills held by the Bank or their agents or made payable to them.

Ohio concluded her resolution by expressly approving the "Doctrine of '98" (by a vote of 59-7), denouncing the Federal courts for violation of the Constitution, pledging her best efforts to maintain "by all legal and constitutional means" the right to tax the bank, and resolving—by a vote of 64-1:

That this General Assembly do protest against the doctrine that the political rights of the separate States that compose the American Union, and their powers as sovereign States, may be settled and determined in the Supreme Court of the United States, so as to conclude and bind them, in cases contrived between individuals, and where they are no one of them parties direct.

The Ohio Assembly went on to carry out many of these legislative recommendations, beginning with an act in January, 1821, withdrawing from the Bank of the United States "the protection and aid of the laws of the State in certain cases." Meanwhile, the bank continued to prosecute its suit against the State auditor and State treasurer, and in September of 1821 obtained a decree in the Circuit Court ordering the State officials to restore the money. The State treasurer, one Sullivan, refused to obey this command. An attachment for contempt was issued against him, and he wasthrown into prison. The bank then obtained the appointment of commissioners who went into Sullivan's cell, forcibly took from him the key to the State vaults, and thereupon helped themselves to the original $98,000—evidently still in the same trunk where Currie had placed it the year before.(67)

This action on the bank's part served only to fan the public's indignation, with the result that for three more years Ohio continued to harass the bank's operations in every way that could be devised. The State officials took a further appeal to the Supreme Court, and in February, 1824, John Marshall wrote an end to the stormy litigation in an opinion reviewing and confirming the court's position in the McCulloch case, and declaring Ohio's tax law unconstitutional.

The opinion is an interesting exposition of Marshall's strongly nationalist views, and is the more interesting for the evidence it offers of the Chief Justice's progressively stronger attitude in this regard. Fifteen years earlier, in another case that curiously paralleled the Osborn case, officials of Georgia had forcibly entered the Savannah branch of the first Bank of the United States and seized $2,000 in payment of a State tax; but when the bank appealed, Marshall cautiously held that the bank had no power to sue in the Federal courts. Though it would appear that the first Bank of the United States was equally an instrument of national policy with the Second Bank of the United States, in 1809 Marshall took a narrower view. Or perhaps he felt that his opinion against Pennsylvania in the case of Judge Peters, announced at the same term, would be about all the resentful States would stand; in any event, he ducked the bank case in Georgia in 1809, but he managed it with characteristically Marshallian aplomb: The Supreme Court has an equal duty, he said piously, "to exercise jurisdiction where it is conferred, and not to usurp it where it is not conferred."(68)

But in 1824, Marshall did not hesitate to declare that Federal courts had jurisdiction over the Bank of the United States' various proceedings against State officers or State banks. If he were thus reversing the Georgia case of 1809, as Justice Johnson, dissenting, believed, Marshall was not concerned. Whether the decision of 1809 "be right or wrong," he said briskly, a new case entirely was presented from Ohio. He brushed aside the State's defense that the bank's suit was in essence a suit against the State of Ohio itself: The State was not a party on the record. Further, if the agents of a State government were permitted to arrest the execution of Federal laws, or to prevent Federal instrumentalities from carrying on their functions, then each member of the Union would be capable, at its will,

of attacking the nation, of arresting its progress at every step, of acting vigorously and effectually in the execution of its designs; while the nation stands naked, stripped of its defensive armor, and incapable of shielding its agent or executing its laws. . . .(69)

Yet it may be asked, in reviewing these olympian pronouncements of Marshall's Court, *is not precisely the same objection valid as to Federal assaults upon State prerogatives?* When Federal judges are free to attack the States, arrest the progress of their institutions, strip them naked of their reserved powers—what, then, are the States to do to shield their agents or execute their laws? Marshall's response, presumably, to judge from his comments in the McCulloch case, would have been that the Federal government "is supreme within its sphere of action," and a branch of the Federal government, the Supreme Court, will determine the boundaries of that sphere, blowing it up like a balloon as the Court pleases.

To be sure, no such authority to umpire State and Federal disputes ever had been given to the Supreme Court. As Calhoun and John Taylor of Caroline often noted, the power had indeed been expressly denied to the Court by the Convention of 1787, and for the obvious reason that Roane (and Madison, and Jefferson) so frequently laid down: "The Supreme Court is but a department of the general government. A department is not competent to do that to which the whole government is inadequate. . . . They cannot do it unless we tread underfoot the principle which forbids a party to decide his own cause."(70)

But Marshall, having decided the Federal government's own cause in 1819 and again in 1824, in the end could not prevail. The constitutional issues raised so vigorously by Ohio continued to hold widespread support. Resistance by the States to the bank was never abandoned.

In Kentucky in 1825, Governor Desha warmly adopted Ohio's position: "When the general government encroaches upon the rights of the State," he asked, "is it a safe principle to admit that a portion of the encroaching power shall have the right to determine finally whether an encroachment has been made or not? In fact, most of the encroachments made by the general government flow through the Supreme Court itself, the very tribunal which claims to be the final arbiter of all such disputes. What chance for justice have the States when the usurpers of their rights are made their judges? Just as much as individuals when judged by their oppressors. It is therefore believed to be the right, as it may hereafter become the duty of the State governments, to protect themselves from encroachments, and their citizens from oppression, by refusing obedience to the unconstitutional mandates of the Federal judges."(71)

Nor was Kentucky alone. Despite the Court's opinion in the McCulloch and Osborn cases, Tennessee did not repeal her tax law until 1827, and then by the narrowest of margins. Connecticut in 1829 devised a new scheme to harass the bank, and South Carolina in 1830 imposed a tax upon the dividends of stockholders resident in that State. With the election of Jackson, who hated all banks, this hostility on the part of the States gained new strength. New York and New Hampshire adopted strong resolutions urging that the bank not be rechartered, and Jackson's veto of a premature recharter bill (July 10, 1832) won wide approval.

In the face of this unrelenting warfare, the bank could not survive. Withdrawal of the public deposits began in August of 1833, under Jackson's order; and when Pennsylvania's Governor Wolf, who had been one of the bank's staunchest supporters, denounced the institution in his message to the Legislature in March of 1834, public opinion was fatally influenced against the bank.(72) The Pennsylvania Senate adopted fresh resolutions urging that the bank ought not to be rechartered. The following month, the United States House of Representatives adopted the same view, and the bank's days came to an end.

Notes

Go to top.

8

Internal Improvements

IT HAS been suggested earlier in these notes that interposition by the States against Federal encroachments may take a wide variety of forms, ranging from the mildest remonstrance at one extreme to resolute nullification at the other. In the militant postures taken by Pennsylvania in the Olmstead case, by New England during the War of 1812, and by Ohio in its resistance to the Bank of the United States, one may find examples of relatively strong efforts by the States to invoke their sovereign powers against what they regarded as unwarranted and unconstitutional actions of Federal authority.

Yet these notes would be less complete than they are if reference were not made to some of the more modest protests offered from time to time by the States. Among these, the objections voiced in the 1820's against the growth of "internal improvements" offer a fair example.

Let Governor Wilson of South Carolina be recognized. He is speaking to the General Assembly in December, 1824:

There is one subject of deep and vital importance to the stability of general and State governments, to which I beg leave to invite your attention. Every friend of our present Constitution, in its original purity, cannot but have witnessed the alarming extent to which the Federal judiciary and Congress have gone toward establishing a great and consolidated government, subversive of the rights of the States and contravening the letter and spirit of the Constitution of the Union.

The act of the last session of Congress appropriating money to make surveys [act of April 30, 1824] is but an entering wedge which will be followed, no doubt, by the expenditure of millions.

Unless the people apply the proper corrective, the day, I fear, is not far distant when South Carolina shall be grievously assessed to pay for the cutting of a canal across Cape Cod. . . .(73)

What Governor Wilson might have said of a Central Arizona Project or an Upper Colorado Project can be imagined. His point, and assuredly it remains a valid point to this day, is that the Constitution at no point directly sanctions the vast "internal improvements" made under congressional authority. The power is at best an implied power, said to be necessary and proper to national defense, or to the establishment of post roads, or to the regulation of commerce among the States. So loose a construction, in Wilson's view, was "an open violation of that which has heretofore universally been admitted the true rule for expounding all grants."

The Senate of South Carolina agreed with Governor Wilson's view of the internal improvements program, but the House of Representatives did not. Indeed, the South Carolina House adopted a resolution reciting stiffly that "the people have conferred no power upon their State Legislature to impugn the acts of the Federal government or the decisions of the Supreme Court of the United States." By the following year, however, this view had changed: Both houses of the South Carolina Assembly agreed that "among those rights retained in this [Federal] Constitution to the people, is, the unalienable right of remonstrating against any encroachments upon that Constitution by the Congress of the United States, or any other officer belonging or acting under the general government."(74) To restrain this birthright of protest "would be to establish that odious doctrine of non-resistance and perfect obedience." In South Carolina's view, "Congress does not possess the power, under the Constitution, to adopt a general system of internal improvements as a national measure."

Just a week after South Carolina adopted this resolution, it is interesting to note, Thomas Jefferson, in a letter to Madison, suggested the desirability of Virginia's passing new resolutions, in the spirit of 1798, denouncing the internal improvement laws as not warranted by the Constitution.(75) He enclosed with this letter a draft of a proposed "Virginia Protest," to which every friend of States' rights profitably may repair. Here Jefferson set forth in the clearest and most explicit language that "the right to construct roads, open canals, and effect other internal improvements within the territories and jurisdictions exclusively belonging to the several States" had never been delegated to the Congress, "but remains to each State among its domestic and unalienated powers, exercisable within itself and by its domestic authorities alone."(76) But Jefferson was entirely agreeable to seeing this power specifically vested in the Federal government by appropriate constitutional amendment. He had commented in a letter to Edward Livingston the year before that he felt "there is not a State in the Union which would not give the power willingly."(77) Surely, he felt, that would be better than to witness the continued distortion of the Constitution by the doctrine of "implied powers," and the continued practice among Congressmen of the custom "which, with us, is called logging,' the term of the farmers for their exchanges of aid in rolling together the logs of their newly-cleared grounds."(78)

Madison, however, advised against Virginia's adoption of the protest drafted by Jefferson,(79) and Jefferson dropped the idea. But on January 14, Maryland's General Assembly adopted a resolution, replying to South Carolina's action of the preceding month, in which Maryland asserted that Congress did indeed "possess the power . . . to adopt a general system of internal improvement."(80) Virginia's General Assembly then went ahead, in March, with a resolution very much along the lines Jefferson had suggested.

Here Virginia specifically revived and confirmed her Resolution of 1798, and held that the right of the States to interpose, then asserted, applies "with full force" against the act directing a survey of routes for roads and canals. By an overwhelming vote (127-26 in the House, 12-8 in the Senate), Virginia declared that the appropriation of money for such purposes would be "a violation of the Constitution." This "most solemn protest" was renewed in March of 1827 in further resolutions, temperately phrased, against Federal efforts to make internal improvements within the State.

Manifestly, nothing came of this interposition by South Carolina and Virginia. The issue of internal improvements, in their view, was not of sufficient magnitude to warrant further, more drastic action. Besides, a far more significant problem, still no bigger than a man's hand, could be seen in the distance: The same resolutions that protested the policy of internal improvements also protested the tariff act of 1824.

Notes

Go to top.

9

Kentucky vs. the Court

BEFORE a review is attempted, however, of the dramatic events that stemmed from the tariff laws of this period, attention may be usefully directed to the determined, violent—and largely successful—interposition of Kentucky and Georgia against Federal decrees that seemed to them gross encroachments upon their reserved powers. Let us consider the case of Kentucky first.

In the period immediately following the Revolutionary War, Virginia, in common with other States, made widespread grants of land to the soldiers, officers, sailors, and marines who had fought in the war. In other cases, speculators and land companies acquired enormous tracts of property, parts of which they then sold or leased—or abandoned. Many of these grants conveyed land by exceedingly vague metes and bounds; conflicts of title were the rule, not the exception.

Thus, when the time came in 1789 for Kentucky to be split off from Virginia, some provision necessarily had to be made covering the rights and interests of persons who held land in the Kentucky territory under grant from Virginia. By an act of the Virginia General Assembly on December 18, 1789, it was provided that as a condition of Kentucky's formation, all such interests must remain as valid in the new State of Kentucky as they were in the parent State of Virginia. Kentucky accepted this condition and embodied the provision in her Constitution. In June, 1792, Kentucky entered the

Union.

Immediately, Kentucky authorities encountered what Justice Johnson later was to describe as "the very peculiar nature of the land titles created by Virginia, and then floating over the State of Kentucky."(81) Virginia had left matters "in a state of confusion [which] rendered it impossible for Kentucky to guaranty any specific tract to an individual."(82) In an effort to achieve some stability, Kentucky in February, 1797, adopted an act concerning occupying claimants of land, and followed this with a supplementary act in January, 1812. Briefly, both acts provided that when any claimant to land, occupying property under a title he had some reason to regard as valid, should be ousted by a new claimant having a better title, the incoming owner should reimburse the former occupant for improvements made upon the land; further, the original occupant was to be excused from payment of rents to the owner who displaced him.

Obviously, these acts of 1797 and 1812, while they achieved some stability, achieved it largely in favor of Kentucky's local interests and adversely to the interests of Virginia claimants. Inevitably, a series of acrimonious suits arose; and at last, one of these actions, brought by John Green and others against Richard Biddle, reached the Supreme Court of the United States. It was, like *Fletcher vs. Peck* (to be noted in the next section), a generally spurious piece of litigation: Biddle did not even appear by counsel.

On March 5, 1821, Justice Story handed down a unanimous opinion by the Court. It was held that the rights and interests of the rightful owners of the land had been secured by the agreement between Kentucky and Virginia in 1789; thus a contract had been entered into by Kentucky; under the Constitution, no State may impair the obligations of a contract; the two acts of 1797 and 1812, in the Court's view, materially impaired these interests; their effect was to compel a rightful owner to pay "for improvements which he has not authorized, which he did not want, or which he may deem useless."(83) Under Virginia law—under common law—this could not be sanctioned. Kentucky's two occupying claimant laws, said the Court, were unconstitutional and void.

The decision created consternation in Kentucky. Henry Clay immediately came before the Court, as amicus curiae, to ask—and win—a rehearing. The Constitution, Clay insisted, prohibited the States from entering into compacts *without the consent of Congress;* in his view, Congress never had consented to the compact between Kentucky and Virginia in 1789—"It was no compact: It was mere negotiation." It was not enough that Congress might have acquiesced tacitly over a period of nearly thirty years; some affirmative act of congressional consent was required.

The following October, Kentucky's General Assembly adopted a long and generally temperate statement of protest against the Court's decision. (84) Here it was pointed out that the two laws in question had been approved by Kentucky's State courts over a long period of years. Virginia had acquiesced in Kentucky's handling of the matter. The decree of the Supreme Court, in this "fictitious" case, was "incompatible with the powers of the State, and highly injurious to the best interests of the people." Kentucky appointed commissioners to discuss the problem with Virginia, and confidently awaited a reversal by the Court when the case was reargued.

This hope proved vain. On February 27, 1823, in an opinion by Justice Washington, the Court again declared the acts of 1797 and 1812 invalid as an impairment of Kentucky's compact of 1789 with Virginia. In the Court's view, Congress had given all the consent required by the Constitution in the act admitting Kentucky into the Union.

From this opinion, Justice Johnson warmly dissented. Adverting to the chaotic condition of Virginia's grants in the post-Revolutionary period, he observed that "land they were not, and yet all the attributes of real estate were extended to them."(85) As often as not, these grants were no more than surveyor's entries. In the nature of things, Kentucky had to take some action to quiet titles: It never was intended "that Kentucky should be forever chained down to a state of hopeless imbecility."

Again, Kentucky reacted strongly to the Court's decree, this time in far sharper temper than before. In November of 1823, Governor John Adair denounced the opinion in hard-ringing words: It was not the "incalculable litigation and distress" that would be produced by the Court's two decisions, nor yet the pecuniary loss to many innocent persons, that concerned him most.

The principles they would establish, and the effects they would produce, sink much deeper and would produce infinitely more permanent evils. They strike at the sovereignty of the State, and the right of the people to govern themselves.(86)

In December, the Assembly approved a long statement of Kentucky's views. If the Court's doctrines were correct, that "one unalterable system of laws was destined to regulate, in perpetuity, the concerns of the republics of America," then why had not the States, on formation of the Union, been "melted down and their existence abolished"? Was sovereignty meaningless? Were the States no more than "dwarf vassals"?(87) The Assembly again protested firmly; and because the Court's opinion the preceding February had been handed down by a 3-1 count, with three justices absent, it was urged that Congress provide by statute that no question growing out of the Constitution of the United States, involving the validity of State laws, could be decided without the concurrence of two-thirds of the full Court.

Again in January, 1824, the Kentucky Legislature assailed the Court for an opinion "which disrobes Kentucky of her sovereign power, and places her in a posture of degradation which she never would have consented, and never can consent, to occupy."(88) Gentlemen, this is Kentucky speaking:

The construction of the Court which thus disfranchises the State of Kentucky, can neither exact the homage of the people upon whom it acts, for the intellect employed in making it, nor conciliate their patience under its humiliating and afflicting effects. If the same privative effects were attempted to be produced upon the individual and political rights of the people of Kentucky, by a foreign armed force, and they were not to repel it at every hazard, they would be denounced as a degenerate race, unworthy of their patriotic sires, who assisted in achieving the American Independence; as a people unworthy of enjoying the freedom they possessed. In that case, the United States, too, would be bound, at whatever hazard, to vindicate the right of the people of Kentucky to legislate over the territory of their State; to guarantee to them a republican form of government, which includes the right insisted on. And can it make any difference with the people of Kentucky, whether they are deprived of the right of regulating by law the territory which they inhabit, and the soil which they cultivate, by the Duke de Angoulême at the head of a French army, or by the erroneous construction of three of the judges of the Supreme Court of the United States? To them the privation of political and individual rights would be the same.

Again the Assembly denounced the manner of the Court's decision. The mandate had been delivered by three, a minority of the Court: "There was a fourth judge on the bench; he dissented." Had the third agreed with the fourth, Kentucky had not been disfranchised. Thus, in this particular case, "the political destiny of a State was decided by a solitary judge." Kentucky strongly demanded that Congress adopt the two-thirds rule.

But though such a bill was reported favorably by the Senate in 1824, and debated approvingly over a period of months, in the end Congress took no action on Kentucky's plea. In January of 1825, the Kentucky Legislature continued to protest, more angrily now than ever, against judicial control: "If the judges possessed the purity and wisdom of archangels, it would be unwise to concede to them the power contended for, unless they were also immortal; for however wisely and beneficently they might exercise it, their successors might exert it wickedly and oppressively."(89) Was not the Constitution, in effect, the Bible of the people? Was it not their right to read it and construe the book of faith for themselves?

Would they be bound to adopt the exposition of it by their preacher, which was at war with the fundamental principles of their association and their creed? And which ought they to change—their creed or their pastor?(90)

Kentucky's interposition reached its peak the following winter, when Governor Joseph Desha, in November, 1825, came before the Assembly. Reference already has been made to his denunciation of the Supreme Court, especially in regard to its decisions in the McCulloch and Osborn cases. He also pilloried the Court for its opinion in *Green vs. Biddle,* which was "spreading its baneful influences" across the State.

That same month, Kentucky's Supreme Court added its potent strength to the State's resistance. On November 15, having before it a case in which a claimant advanced the identical contention that Kentucky's laws of 1797 and 1812 were void, the State court flatly refused to abide by the Supreme Court's decree. Kentucky judges would respect any "settled" mandate of constitutional law, they said, but *Green vs. Biddle* had been decided by only three members of the Court; thus "it cannot be considered as having *settled* any constitutional principle." The Kentucky judges hinted plainly that even if the full Court had been unanimous, they still would not have regarded the decision as having settled a point of law so plain to them. (91)

In December, the Kentucky House of Representatives supported the State judges with a bellicose resolution addressed to the Governor: Would he please inform them of

the mode deemed most advisable in the opinion of the Executive to refuse obedience to the decisions and mandates of the Supreme Court of the United States, considered erroneous and unconstitutional, and whether, in the opinion of the Executive, it may be advisable to call forth the physical power of the State to resist the execution of the decisions of the Court, or in what manner the mandates of the Court should be met by disobedience.(92)

To this Governor Desha replied, on December 14, with a suggestion that the Assemblymen "restrain their ardor and try yet a little while the pacific measures of an application to Congress."(93)

That pretty well ended matters. Kentucky's State courts and State officials continued adamantly to defy the Supreme Court's decision in *Green vs. Biddle;* titles were recorded and land conveyed according to Kentucky's claimant laws; and six years later the Supreme Court, in effect, surrendered. This time Justice Johnson spoke for the majority of the court. He coolly observed that the 1823 decision in *Green vs. Biddle* had been misunderstood; and over Baldwin's dissent, the Court upheld a seven-year limitation act, adopted by Kentucky on title contests, which surely was as much an "impairment" of the compact of 1789 as anything that had gone before.

Kentucky had interposed her sovereign powers; and Kentucky had remained in the Union; and Kentucky had won.

Notes

Go to top.

Georgia vs. the Court

CONSIDER Georgia. And consider the Supreme Court. The one has ever been at war with the other. No State in the Union has more clearly perceived the dangers of judicial encroachment than Georgia, and no State—into our own time—has been more resolute in resisting them.

Attention already has been directed to Georgia's remarkably successful interposition in the Chisholm case: There Georgia flatly refused to abide by a decree of the Court, took the issue to the country in the form of a constitutional amendment, and won hands down. The Eleventh Amendment today attests her success. But even as the Eleventh Amendment was pending before the Union for ratification, a new case arose that was to pit Georgia squarely against the Court.

This was the case of the Yazoo lands. It is so well known that only the briefest reference is necessary here. Subsequent to 1787, by reason of an agreement between Georgia and South Carolina, Georgia became possessed of vast lands south and west of the Savannah River extending to the Mississippi. These were the Yazoo lands, named for a river that formed a key boundary point. One effort to dispose of this enormous area ended abortively in 1789. But in January, 1795, a bill to dispose of the land was approved by the Georgia Legislature and reluctantly signed by the Governor—reluctantly, because the Legislature, almost down to the last man, had been shamefully bribed by a pack of scoundrels headed by U.S. Senator James Gunn. Under this fraudulent act, some 35,000,000 acres of land passed into the hands of speculators for $500,000. Some accounts place the total at 50,000,000 acres. But no account denies the total corruption of the Georgia Legislature. Scarcely had the bill been passed before the people, suddenly shocked into awareness, turned on their venal Legislators and threw them out of office. On February 13, 1796, the new Legislature passed an elaborate act rescinding the sale of 1795. Under this act, every reference to the Yazoo infamy was to be expunged from the records of the State, and any State official who thereafter took note of it was to be fined $1,000, and rendered forever incapable of holding public office. A fire was built in front of the Capitol, and as members of the newly chosen House and Senate filed around, a messenger of the House consigned the act of 1795 to the flames (kindled, symbolically, from the rays of the sun, as from "the burning rays of the lidless eyes of justice"), the while crying out, "God save the State! And long preserve her rights!! And may every attempt to injure them perish as these corrupt acts now do!!!"

But it was not so easy a matter, as Georgia was to discover, to expunge an act obtained by "atrocious peculation, corruption, and collusion." For the Legislature of 1796 to void an act of the bribed Legislature of 1795, and render it "null and void," was to encounter the objection of John Marshall's Court that the act of 1795 constituted a contract between Georgia and the land purchasers, which contract could not constitutionally be impaired later on.(94) This was the gist of the Court's famous ruling in *Fletcher vs. Peck,* by which it decided an obviously contrived piece of litigation brought by a pair of Massachusetts citizens who well knew of the potential cloud on the Yazoo title. John Peck technically sold 15,000 acres of Yazoo land to Robert Fletcher for $3,000, covenanting that his title of 1795 was valid. Justice Johnson penetrated the spurious nature of this suit in an acid comment that the proceeding "appears to me to bear strong evidence, upon the face of it, of being a mere feigned case." But John Marshall, who had no objection to looking beyond the record when it suited him, this time stuck tenaciously to the record itself: "If the title be plainly deduced from a legislative act, which the legislature might constitutionally pass, if the act be clothed with all the requisite forms of a law, a court, sitting as a court of law, cannot sustain a suit brought by one individual against another, founded on the allegation that the act is a nullity, in consequence of the impure motives which influenced certain members of the legislature which passed the law."(95)

This was in 1810, fifteen years after the original Yazoo act, eight years after Georgia had ceded all claim to the lands to the United States. But it was the first time the Supreme Court had held an act of a State unconstitutional, and the Court's decision aroused a bitter reaction. This hostility is in a sense paradoxical; the Court's opinion actually has served as a magnificent buttress for the rights of the States. Had the Court ruled otherwise, the door would have been opened for assault upon any act of a State legislature upon contentions of corruption or bribery. Nevertheless, Georgia wrathfully denounced the Court, and her representatives in Congress succeeded, over a period of several years, in frustrating the claims of the Yazoo purchasers.

Resentment on this issue scarcely had died down, however, before new controversies claimed Georgia's concern. These involved two Indian tribes, the Creeks, and more importantly the Cherokees, which persisted in holding lands within the territorial limits of Georgia. Getting rid of the Creeks proved sufficiently difficult. When negotiations, petitions, memorials, and finally the Treaty of Indian Springs, in 1825, failed to dislodge them, Georgia's fiery Governor Troup ordered a land survey launched by which the troublesome tribe would at last be ousted. Secretary of War Barbour, in May of 1825, advised Troup that this survey "could not be permitted." To this Troup replied with a message denouncing "officious and impertinent intermeddlings" with domestic concerns.(96) "Stand by your arms," he advised the Assembly; and the Assembly, for its part, "approved the exhortation with its whole heart." There followed a series of letters between Troup and Barbour, chiefly notable for the extreme stand of State sovereignty the Georgia Governor maintained throughout. In his eyes, the Federal government was a foreign power with whom he engaged in "diplomatic intercourse." In his letters to the War Department, Troup consistently requested the officer addressed to convey Georgia's views to "your government."

In 1826, the United States Senate undertook to ratify a new treaty with the Creeks, more favorable to the Indians than the one before. At this added injury, Georgia threw herself into the conflict with new zeal. Troup furiously ordered his surveyors back to work; and when Barbour, early in 1827, threatened to use "all the means" at the President's command to stop it, Troup dispatched orders to the generals commanding the Sixth and Seventh Divisions of the State Militia to hold their troops in readiness "to repel any hostile invasion of the territory of this State."(97) Then he wrote Barbour, with deadly effect, that from the first decisive act of hostility on Barbour's part, "you will be considered as a public enemy."

He took one more step also. Anticipating that an effort would be made by the Adams administration to obtain a ruling from the Supreme Court, upholding the President's actions, Troup fired a message to the Georgia Assembly. "I am not wanting in confidence in the Supreme Court of the United States," he said, "in all cases falling within their acknowledged jurisdiction."

As men I would not hesitate to refer our cause to their arbitration or umpirage. On an amicable issue made up between the United States and ourselves, we might have had no difficulty in referring it to them as judges, protesting at the same time against the jurisdiction, and saving our rights of sovereignty. . . . But according to my limited conception, the Supreme Court is not made by the Constitution of the United States, the arbiter in controversies involving rights of sovereignty between the States and the United States . . . because that court, being of exclusive appointment by the government of the United States, will make the United States the judge in their own cause. . . .(98)

Shortly thereafter, the Federal government backed down; the surveyors continued peacefully at their assignment, and in time the Creeks went west.

Getting rid of the 10,000 Cherokees remaining in Georgia proved still more difficult. At that time, the Cherokees were well entrenched in what they chose to call their own "nation," in the land now defined by Carroll, DeKalb, Gwinnett, Hall, and Haber-sham counties. There was some substance for their claim: The Cherokees had their own constitution, their own language, their own laws, their own courts, their own well-advanced civilization; they exchanged what amounted to ambassadors with Washington; they entered into treaties with the United States. But Georgia was not impressed by these amenities: The Cherokees occupied land that was plainly Georgia's land, and the Federal government, in Georgia's view, was doing nothing effective to remove them.

As one consequence of this resentment, Georgia in December, 1828, adopted an act extending her own criminal jurisdiction into the Cherokee territory. (A rumored discovery of gold in the Cherokee lands probably had something to do with this.) And soon thereafter, a nondescript Indian named George "Corn" Tassels was arrested under Georgia law, convicted of murder, and sentenced to be hanged. His counsel appealed to the United States Supreme Court, and the Court thereupon commanded Georgia to appear and make answer. The peremptory tone of Marshall's order was a mistake: It aroused all the smoldering hostility of aproud and impatient people. Governor Gilmer, who had succeeded to the office, said flatly that Marshall's order "will be disregarded; and any attempt to enforce such order will be resisted with whatever force the laws have placed at my command. If the judicial power thus attempted to be exercised by the courts of the United States is submitted to, or sustained, it must eventuate in the utter annihilation of the State governments, or in other consequences not less fatal to the peace and prosperity of our present highly favored country." The Georgia Assembly vigorously supported him. In a resolution adopted in 1830, it declared that the right to punish crimes against the peace and good order of the State "is an original and a necessary part of sovereignty, which the State of Georgia has never parted with." The Assembly viewed Marshall's interference as "a flagrant violation" of Georgia's rights, and directed the Governor and all other State officers "to disregard any and every mandate and process that has been or shall be served upon him or them purporting to proceed from the Chief Justice, or any associate justice, . . . for the purpose of arresting the execution of any of the criminal laws of this State." More ominously still, the Assembly directed Governor Gilmer "to resist and repel any and every invasion, from whatever quarter, upon the administration of the criminal laws of this State" with all the force and means placed at his command.

Tassels was forthwith hanged, on Christmas Eve of 1830.(99) There seemed to be nothing more to be said.

Two days prior to Tassels' demise, the Georgia Legislature adopted further laws designed to extend State jurisdiction over the Cherokee territory. The most important of these provisions undertook to prohibit any white person from residing in the Cherokee lands after March 1, 1831, without specific permission from the Governor. Meanwhile, the Cherokees had attempted to invoke the aid of John Marshall's Supreme Court, and had won his sympathy but not his jurisdiction.(100) Marshall had termed the Cherokees not a nation, but rather a dependent domestic territory; the Chief Justice was not willing (considering President Jackson's views and the demonstrated hostility of Georgia) to attempt to "control the legislature of Georgia, and to restrain the exertion of its physical force."(101)

This opinion came down on March 18, 1831. Meanwhile, a band of Presbyterian missionaries, headed by Elizur Butler and Samuel A. Worcester, had deliberately settled in Cherokee land without consent of Governor Gilmer. The missionaries were arrested, brought on for trial in Gwinnett County, convicted, and sentenced September 15, 1831, to four-year terms in prison for violation of the December enactment. They appealed to the Supreme Court, and in January, 1832, Marshall ordered the convictions reversed.(102) But Governor Lumpkin, a gentleman imbued with the spirit, and succeeding to the office, of Troup and Gilmer, bluntly refused to release them. It was at this time—the comment is most probably apocryphal—that Jackson was said to have remarked, "John Marshall has made his decision—now let him enforce it."(103) It was not until two full years later that the missionaries, having sought pardon, were released. In their first application, they made the tactical error of saying that there had been no change in their views "in regard to the principles on which we have acted." To this, Governor Lumpkin replied that if they regarded these principles so highly, "they might stand on them in the penitentiary." The desperate missionaries then wrote from the Milledgeville prison, apologizing, and at long last were released.

Georgia's defiance of the court led both Massachusetts and Connecticut, in the spring of 1831, to adopt resolutions commending the Supreme Court and criticizing Georgia's resistance. These good New England States had forgotten that fifteen or twenty years earlier, they too had resisted Federal authority in what seemed to them a palpable encroachment upon their rights. But they must have been impressed, even as they adopted their resolutions, by the self-evident fact that in the Tassels case and in the Worcester case, Georgia had interposed; and Georgia had remained in the Union; and Georgia had won.

Notes

Go to top.

11

Calhoun and Nullification

THE GREAT nullification controversy of 1832 goes to the heart and soul of the constitutional doctrines advanced in this essay, and, as a consequence, must be treated at some length. In the interests of an orderly presentation, it is proposed first merely to chronicle what happened in this period, and to touch briefly upon the great personalities who figured in that drama; secondly, it is proposed to argue the essential soundness and constitutionality of nullification, when it is invoked as a last resort against dangerous and deliberate usurpations of authority by the Federal government.

The second act adopted by the First Congress of the United States, in 1789, was a tariff law which imposed duties on "goods, wares and merchandise imported." Significantly, the act recited that its purpose was not alone to raise revenues for the support of government and the discharge of public debts, but also "for the encouragement and protection of manufactures."(104)From that day until comparatively recent times, (105) students of the Constitution have vigorously debated the authority of Congress to utilize its taxing power beyond the aim of raising revenue. This first tariff law was so mild in its provisions, however, that few serious apprehensions were aroused; it was not until the tariff of 1816, imposing duties averaging about 20 per cent upon the covered imports, that a few cries of alarm began to be heard.(106) Again, these protests were not loud—Calhoun himself supported the tariff of 1816 (in an impulsive speech he was to regret all his life), and later was agreeable to accepting it as the basis for a permanent law.(107) But with the sharply increased tariff of 1824, which very nearly doubled the average rates of 1816, all the latent fears of free traders were aroused. The higher tariffs imposed a severe hardship upon Southern States especially: Cotton shirts, woolen blankets, and other staple items of an agrarian society, became suddenly more expensive, and this at a time when the South had virtually no industries of its own that might benefit from a protectionist policy.

At first, the protests of the Southern States were firm but temperate. South Carolina resolved, in December of 1825, that "a right to impose and collect taxes, does not authorize Congress to lay a tax for any other purposes than such as are necessarily embraced in the specific grants of power, and those necessarily implied therein."(108) The following March, Virginia spoke through her Assembly: "The imposition of taxes and duties, by the Congress of the United States, for the purpose of protecting and encouraging domestic manufactures, is an unconstitutional exercise of power, and is highly oppressive and partial in its operation."(109)

Advocates of high protective tariffs were firmly in the saddle, however, and though the woolen interests lost an important bill by Calhoun's tie-breaking vote in February of 1827, the enthusiasm generated by the protectionists' "Harrisburg Convention" the following summer set in motion an irresistible force. In considerable alarm, South Carolina's Assembly spoke up with new resolutions in December of that year: Tariff laws designed not to raise revenue or to regulate commerce but for "the promotion of domestic manufactures," are "violations of the Constitution in its spirit, and ought to be repealed."(110) A week later, Georgia raised a truculent and sarcastic voice: "While manufacturing companies and self-created delegates, pretending to represent whole States, assemble for the purpose of directing the Congress what measures they must adopt, surely the Legislature of a State, without much violence to any known rule of modesty, may respectfully offer a counter remonstrance to such a growing temper of dictation." And then, putting subtlety aside: "An increase of Tariff duties will and ought to be RESISTED by all legal and constitutional means, so as to avert the crying injustice of such an unconstitutional measure."(111)

North Carolina, in January of 1828, interposed her objections: "The People of North Carolina . . . have seldom expressed a legislative opinion upon the measures of the general government." But now, "a crisis has arisen in the political affairs of our country, which demands a prompt and decisive expression of public opinion." Whenever policies of the Federal government strike "at the very foundation of the Union, it is the right of every member of the Confederacy to call their attention to the fundamental principles upon which the government was formed." Should the offensive policies be persisted in, then "the question may fairly be discussed . . . whether the benefits of the Union are not more than counterbalanced by the evils." In North Carolina's considered view, Congress might have the naked power under the Constitution to impose a tariff for protective purposes, but such tariffs were a "direct violation of the spirit of that instrument." Manufactures, in their essence, were not objects of general welfare but of local interest; and to protect the woolen interests of New England, at the price of an enormous tax upon the agriculture of the South, would be "fatal to the happiness, the morals, and the rights of a large portion of our common country."(112)

Alabama also spoke up: "Let it be distinctly understood that Alabama, in common with the Southern and Southwestern States, regards the power assumed by the General Government to control her internal concerns, by protecting duties beyond the fair demands of the revenue, as a palpable usurpation of a power not given by the Constitution." And Alabama pledged "the most determined and unyielding resistance" to this effort "to pamper the gentlemen wool-growers and wool-carders of the Northeast . . . at a time when agriculture is languishing and prostrate, yielding a bare support to those who pursue it."(113)

To these warning cries from the South, Massachusetts, Ohio, Pennsylvania, Rhode Island, Indiana, and New York responded with resolutions of their own, defending the policy of protective tariffs and indeed urging higher levies.(114) The Northeastern forces prevailed. On May 19, 1828, Congress adopted what came to be known thereafter as the "Tariff of Abominations." Measured by any yardstick, it was a bad bill. The tariff on woolens climbed again, but the act was so rigged that on the cheaper grades of woolen cloth, a tax of nearly 200 per cent was imposed. To the Southern farmer, the act imposed disastrous burdens on hemp, cotton bagging, iron, clothing for slaves. Just as the embargo and non-intercourse laws, twenty years earlier, had heavily damaged the economy of New England, so the Tariff of Abominations, coinciding with other adverse factors, now caused intense hardship among the agrarian States.

Again the aggrieved South erupted with protesting resolutions, but at this point a new and powerful force began to be felt: It was the intellect and leadership of John Caldwell Calhoun. He had become Vice-President in March of 1825, after seven years in Monroe's Cabinet as Secretary of War. Now, in the administration of John Quincy Adams, he sat brooding, solitary, upon the rostrum of the Senate. Beneath him, his old mentor, mad Jack Randolph, eloquently denounced the protective tariff as an infringement upon the sovereignty of States. Day after day, debate raged upon the nature of the Union, and day by day Calhoun's concern grew deeper for some means by which the rights of a minority of the States—or even a single State—might be protected from the tyranny of a majority.

In the spring of 1827, Calhoun came home. He had been in Washington for almost sixteen years, living first in a boarding house, later in the gracious brick mansion in Georgetown Heights that would be known as Dumbarton Oaks. He was badly in need of a rest, of a period of quiet away from the tensions of Washington. Hence he came home to the quiet land of Up-Country Carolina, to the Seneca River, to the peaceful fields of Pendleton District. He came back to his white-pillared home at the crest of a hill, and there he did something few men in public life find time to do today: He sat and thought, undisturbed, gazing across the fields, now rising to consult a book or document, now composing a letter to Littleton Waller Tazewell in Norfolk, but mostly he engaged in that hardest of all exercises: Pure thought. What was the nature of the Union? Where was sovereignty, he asked himself, and what was sovereignty, and how was it exercised? How could a "great local interest" be preserved?(115)

Out of those long days of thought and reading and correspondence, that summer of 1827, there began to emerge a pattern. If the federal character of the Union were to be maintained, then the dignity of the respective States must be maintained. At some point, he came to realize, there must be a power inherent in the nature of each member State by which it could protect its constitutionally reserved rights *without withdrawing from the Union.*

The following summer, with the Tariff of Abominations now written into law, Calhoun came home again. He found all South Carolina in ferment. The leaders of the State were not talking of petitions or compromise; they were talking openly of secession. Among them was the colorful George McDuffie, a tall, slender man, possessed of passionate convictions in the field of States' rights and gifted with an eloquent voice to defend them. Another was Charleston's "Jimmy Hamilton," who four years later, as Governor, was to face the enraged Andrew Jackson with a spirit as resolute as Old Hickory's. A third was twenty-one-year-old James H. Hammond, in time to edit the nullification paper, the *Southern Times*. And present at Fort Hill in spirit, as Margaret Coit wrote, "if not in his fat, aging flesh," was that fascinating old Republican, Thomas Cooper, who had come to South Carolina after his conviction at the hands of Justice Chase for sedition nearly thirty years before.(116)

Calhoun swiftly came to realize that if the hot-blooded agitation of the secessionists were not channeled into a calmer course, a resort to arms was imminent. Hence, as Vice-President, he employed the device Jefferson had employed in espousing the Kentucky Resolution in 1798, and for the same reason: Vice-Presidents, are, or were, to be seen and not heard. In secrecy, Calhoun drafted the South Carolina *Exposition and Protest*. Though it was not formally adopted by the South Carolina Assembly,(117) it was published under legislative authority. Its impact upon South Carolina, though somewhat delayed by the length of the document and the difficulties of Calhoun's prose style, ultimately was to have the greatest significance.

In the *Exposition*(118) Calhoun devoted himself first to the problems of an agricultural South, whose people had become "serfs" to the industrial North. The South would not complain, he said, of a moderate tariff which afforded incidental protection: "We would rejoice to see our manufacturers flourish on any constitutional principle consistent with justice." But the tariff of 1828 was neither constitutional nor just. It was a device through which a majority in Congress had utilized their powers as "an instrument of aggrandizement." In this process, they had gravely encroached upon the rights of the States, but—and here the doctrine of nullification in its most drastic form was asserted for the first time—the States had one remedy remaining to them: They could invoke their inherent right "to interpose to protect their reserved powers," and by interposing, *suspend the operation of a law they regarded as unconstitutional pending a decision by all the States in convention assembled.*

Whatever may be said of South Carolina, and of the many Southern farmers and small businessmen who approved her *Exposition,* a lack of forebearance cannot be attributed to them. Calhoun's striking doctrine of State powers went forth in December of 1828. Nearly four years elapsed before South Carolina, her patience at last exhausted, pursued the remedy Calhoun had outlined.

Meanwhile, a dozen States had engaged in a battle of resolutions over the tariff and the theory of interposition. Georgia had called upon the States to unite in "a policy of self preservation" in a "continued and strenuous exertion to defeat that general pernicious and unconstitutional policy, contemplated and pursued by the advocates of the tariff." Mississippi, in February of 1829, had agreed that the tariff should be resisted "by all constitutional means." The same month, Virginia had revived her Doctrine of '98: "The Constitution [is] a Federal compact between sovereign States, in construing which no common arbiter is known," thus "each State has the right to construe the compact for itself." On the opposite side, Pennsylvania, Ohio, Delaware, New Jersey, Connecticut, Vermont, Louisiana (where sugar interests predominated), and most notably, Kentucky, had replied in language almost equally strong.(119) Kentucky's resolution of January 27,1830, may especially be noted; it summarized the objections most generally voiced against the Calhoun doctrine:

The General Assembly of Kentucky cannot admit the right of a minority, either of the States or of the people, to set up their opinion not only in opposition, but to overrule that of the majority. . . . The consequences of such a principle, if practically enforced, would be alarming in the extreme. . . . If one State had a right to obstruct and defeat the execution of a law of Congress because it deems it unconstitutional, then every State has a similar right. . . .

The Kentucky resolution conceded that, of course, there may be acts of government of such extreme oppression as to justify an appeal to arms—but this was not asserted by South Carolina in protesting the tariff law. On the contrary, it was South Carolina's position that without going to war or seceding, South Carolina could suspend the operation of the tariff within her jurisdiction. In Kentucky's view, this could not be sanctioned. Nor was this position in 1830 inconsistent with Kentucky's more famed Resolutions of 1798 and 1799: In protesting the unconstitutionality of the Alien and Sedition Acts, "it neither interposed nor threatened the adoption of any measures to defeat or obstruct their operation within the jurisdiction of Kentucky." The Assembly in 1798 had expressed, in very strong language, its disapprobation of the laws and its firm conviction that they were unconstitutional and void.

There it stopped, and that is the limit which no State should pass, until it has formed the deliberate resolution of lighting up the torch of civil war. Every State, as well as every individual, has the incontestable right freely to form and to publish to the world its opinion of any and every act of the Federal government. It may appeal to the reason of the people, enlighten their judgements, alarm their fears, and conciliate their support, to change Federal rules or Federal measures. But neither a State nor an individual can rightfully resist, by force, the execution of a law passed by Congress.(120)

These objections on the part of Kentucky will be considered hereafter. It is best, at this point, simply to hew to the chronology of events. Thus it may be noted that during the years immediately following the *Exposition* of December, 1828, the spirit of nullification grew rapidly in South Carolina. McDuffie and Hamilton and Hayne were aided by Robert J. Turnbull's belligerent essays, gathered together in *The Crisis, or Essays on the Usurpations of the Federal Government,* which gained wide circulation following their publication as the letters of "Brutus" in the Charleston *Mercury.* Many other prominent Carolinians joined the nullification movement. They were opposed, from the beginning, by a strong Unionist group, but the continued deprivations blamed upon the tariff brought recruits in increasing numbers to Calhoun's camp.

James Madison, meanwhile, was busily engaged in denying the very theories he had espoused so warmly thirty years before. In a stream of public letters, he insisted that Virginia's Resolution of 1798 gave no sanction to South Carolina's doctrine.(121) As a pointed reply, South Carolina's Legislature, in December, 1830, adopted a resolution quoting verbatim from the first four paragraphs of the Virginia Resolution and the first paragraph of the Kentucky Resolution, in order to make its point that whenever a State has lost all reasonable hope of redress from Federal departments, "it will be its right and duty to interpose, in its sovereign capacity, for the purpose of arresting the progress of the evil occasioned by the said unconstitutional acts."(122)

In the summer of 1831, President Jackson, whether unwittingly or deliberately, added fuel to the fire. He had been invited to attend a dinner in Charleston on July 4. To this invitation heresponded with a letter severely criticizing nullification as leading to "disorganization" of the Union. At its first opportunity, the embittered South Carolina Assembly responded with a strong resolution declaring that if by "disorganization" Jackson meant "disunion," no constitutional or legal authority imposed any duty on the President to prevent it. "This is a confederacy of sovereign States, and each may withdraw from the confederacy when it chooses; such proceedings would neither be treason nor insurrection nor violation of any portion of the Constitution. It is a right which is inherent in a sovereign State, and has not been delegated by the States of this Union." Should South Carolina, exercising her deliberate judgment, acting in her sovereign capacity, declare an act of Congress unconstitutional, "that judgment is paramount—and if the Executive, or all the combined departments of the general government endeavor to enforce such enactment, it is by the law of tyrants, the exercise of brute force."(123)

Less than three weeks after the publication of Jackson's reply to the dinner invitation, Calhoun brought forth, on July 21, 1831, his justly renowned "Fort Hill Address." If the student of State and Federal relations, interested in Calhoun's beliefs, is able to read one of Calhoun's papers only, he would do well to read this clear and cogent statement. It may be found in Volume Six of Calhoun's *Works,* though it is widely available elsewhere.

The following summer, Congress undertook to amend the hated Tariff of Abominations, but its act of July 14, 1832, accomplished no significant changes. To the rebellious Carolinians, their last chance of congressional redress had passed. On the Charleston Battery and up and down Meeting and King streets, the blue cockades of the nullifiers flourished. Calhoun, by this time thoroughly identified, publicly and privately, with the nullificationist cause, added fresh ammunition in a long and clearly reasoned letter to Governor Hamilton.(124)

By the fall of 1832, no influence other than Calhoun's despised "metaphysics" could have prevented a violent secession by South Carolina. Hamilton, a brigadier general in the militia, was busily engaged in problems of gunpowder and logistics; groups of "volunteers" were ready to make war for the defense of South Carolina's rights. President Jackson, never one to pass up a fight, ordered General Winfield Scott to Charleston and directed that a special guard be maintained at Fort Sumter.

In this tense situation, the best thing that could have happened was what did happen. Pursuant to a call of the Legislature, a convention of the people of South Carolina met at Columbia on November 19, 1832. The ordinance they adopted on November 24 is the final and most drastic expression of the right of a State to interpose against Federal encroachment. It was not the "State government," let it be emphasized, that here acted; it was rather *a convention of the people, speaking with the voice of ultimate sovereignty,* that declared the tariff acts of 1828 and 1832 "are unauthorized by the Constitution of the United States, and violate the true meaning and intent thereof, and are null, void, and no law, nor binding upon this State, its officers, or citizens." Again, this was not a "resolution"; it was styled an "ordinance." Here the people, sovereign, made law for their State: All judicial proceedings in affirmance of the tariff acts "shall be hereafter . . . utterly null and void." After February 1, 1833, all enforcement of the tariff acts was to be suspended in South Carolina. Should any cases in law or equity be decided in South Carolina State courts, involving the authority of the convention's ordinance or the validity of the tariff acts, no appeal was to be allowed to the Supreme Court of the United States, nor was any copy of a court record to be permitted for that purpose. Should Federal officials retaliate by employing naval forces against South Carolina, or attempting to close her ports, such action would be viewed "as inconsistent with the longer continuance of South Carolina in the Union." South Carolina then would hold herself absolved from all ties of the Union, and her people would "forthwith proceed to organize a separate government, and to do all other acts and things which sovereign and independent States may of right do."(125)

On November 27, the South Carolina Assembly reconvened and speedily passed a series of acts to implement the ordinance. And on December 10, Jackson issued his blistering proclamation (largely composed by Edward Livingston) denouncing nullification, denying the sovereignty of States, and pledging force to compel obedience in South Carolina to the laws of Congress.

This proclamation left the South Carolinians unimpressed. On December 20, the Assembly adopted further resolutions, describing Jackson's opinions as "erroneous and dangerous." And in a pointed aside, the Assembly noted that Jackson's statement "is the more extraordinary, in that he had silently, and as it is supposed, with entire approbation, witnessed our sister State of Georgia avow, act upon, and carry into effect, even to the taking of life, principles identical with those now denounced by him in South Carolina." Insisting upon the right of peaceable secession, in the last resort, the resolution denied Jackson's power to employ force to keep South Carolina in the Union, and declared that the Legislature "regards with indignation the menaces which are directed against it, and the concentration of a standing army on our borders." It was resolved that South Carolina "will repel by force, and relying upon the blessings of God, will maintain its liberty at all hazards."

Now, it should be made clear, in the interests of a fair presentation of these events, that other States—even other States in the South—strongly disapproved the course taken by South Carolina. Massachusetts, Ohio, and Delaware promptly rejected South Carolina's invitation for a convention to consider Constitutional amendment; Delaware, joined by Maryland and New Jersey, declared that questions of contested power should be settled in the Supreme Court, as a tribunal expressly provided for the settlement of controversies between the United States and the respective States. New York and Pennsylvania, among others, declared expressly against the right of secession. Even belligerent Georgia termed nullification "neither a peaceful, nor a constitutional remedy." Alabama, though agreeable to a convention, termed it "unsound in theory and dangerous in practice . . . leading in its consequences to anarchy and civil discord." North Carolina, again denouncing the protective tariff, thought nullification "revolutionary in its character," and "subversive of the Constitution." Mississippi regarded the doctrine as "heresy, fatal to the existence of the Union."

If these replies disheartened South Carolina, it was not evident in the determined preparations she made to enforce her ordinance. Calhoun, distraught, saw his hopes for a peaceful settlement glimmering. Word spread that Jackson, his temper high, had promised to have 100,000 troops in South Carolina in three months' time. Indeed, Jackson had grimly threatened, in several conversations, to hang Calhoun "as high as Haman." It was in this taut situation that Calhoun resigned as Vice-President in order to accept appointment to the Senate, succeeding Hayne; and on December 22, 1832, he set out for Washington and a head-on clash with Jackson.

The rest of this story is quickly told. Once Calhoun took his seat in the Senate, quiet negotiations toward a settlement became possible. Under the aegis of Clay, a compromise tariff bill was worked out. It passed the House on February 26, the Senate on March 1; simultaneously, Jackson's "Bloody Bill," a Force Act, also was approved.(126) Meanwhile, word was relayed to Charleston for the nullifiers to wait upon Congressional action. When the compromise yielded substantially what South Carolina had demanded, (127) the November ordinance, so far as it related to the tariff acts, was repealed. And within a few years, as it will be noted hereafter, the very States that had denounced South Carolina so strenuously for direct and plain-spoken nullification of Federal acts were busily engaged themselves in effective nullification of the laws and the Constitution in the matter of fugitive slaves.

Notes

Go to top.

12

The Case for Nullification

AT THIS point, it is proposed to pause in this review of State and Federal conflicts, in order to argue the basis, the soundness, and the wisdom of the constitutional doctrines of John Calhoun. In undertaking this task, the author of these notes asks of his readers no more than the open mind which he himself brought to the subject at first encounter some months ago. To one reared in the custom of docile obedience to Federal authority, to the tradition of a strong "national" government, Calhoun's cold and logical reasoning comes with the shock of an icy plunge.

Because the best exposition of this argument is Calhoun's own exposition, let us go first to his Fort Hill Address of 1831. "The great and leading principle," he began, "is that the general government emanated from the people of the several States, forming distinct political communities, and acting in their separate and sovereign capacity, and not from all the people forming one aggregate political community."

The evidence in support of that proposition already has been marshaled, and seems undeniable: The colonies, under British rule, were separate colonies; with the Revolution, they declared themselves individually "free and independent States." As separate and distinct States they entered into the Articles of Confederation. As separate and distinct States they bound themselves under the new Constitution in 1787 and 1788. At no time did "we the people," meaning the people *en masse,* take any action affecting the creation of the Union; at every juncture, the people acted solely as *people-of-States.* Had the States abandoned this proud characteristic of individual sovereignty, it is reasonable to believe that their act of divestiture would have been set forth, at some point, in unmistakable terms. No such evidence can be adduced. On the contrary, the plain language of the Constitution shows repeatedly that the States formed a "Union." Under this compact, their sovereignty was not surrendered, and only certain of their sovereign powers were granted or delegated. The States were the principals in this agreement; they created a common Federal government whose powers were to be derived solely from the Constitution—and the power of amending the Constitution they reserved solely to themselves.

If this be granted, that the Federal government emanated from the States, and the premise scarcely can be challenged, Calhoun's second premise flows directly from the first: In any compact among equal parties, each party to the compact has an equal right to judge for itself if the compact be violated. Is this not the rule of international law? Is it not, on a more mundane basis, the everyday rule of ordinary commerce? A, B, and C enter into a partnership by which X is made their agent and trustee as to certain affairs. If X oversteps his authority, and treads upon the rights reserved by one of the contracting parties, who is to allege a violation of the compact if it be not the aggrieved party himself? And if A believes that he has been wrongfully treated—if he believes the infraction is truly of a grave and serious nature—what is his remedy? He submits the dispute to B and C; surely it is not for X to decide, for the trustee, however powerful, *is no party to the compact.*

As in the world of commerce, so among the States: Doubtful assertions of authority by the Federal government, inconsequential invasions of the rights of contracting States, unimportant differences of opinion—these may be dismissed with mild objections, or may be tacitly accepted. Love of the Union lies deeply engrained in the people; their affections are long suffering. But what is to be done, in the last resort, when remonstrance fails and protests go unheeded *in matters of the most vital nature?* "In the case of a deliberate, palpable and dangerous exercise of power not delegated," said the Virginia Resolution, and said Calhoun, the States in the last resort have a right "to interpose for arresting the progress of the evil, and for maintaining within their respective limits, the authorities, rights, and liberties appertaining to them." This right of interposition, said Calhoun,

I conceive to be the fundamental principle of our system, resting on facts historically as certain as our revolution itself, and deductions as simple and demonstrative as that of any political or moral truth whatever; and I firmly believe that on its recognition depend the stability and safety of our political institutions.

What are the consequences, Calhoun inquired, of the opposite doctrine, which holds that the States have no such right to protect their reserved powers? Inevitably, it must be conceded that this is to vest in the Federal government—whether in the President, the Congress, or the Supreme Court, it matters not—the right of determining, exclusively and finally, the powers delegated to it. In Jefferson's phrase, this is to make the *discretion of Federal office holders,* and not the Constitution the measure of the powers of Federal agencies. It means that the States, having created the Constitution and bound themselves by it, are in practical effect unable to pass finally on the meaning of their compact. The people, meaning the people-as-States (which is the only meaning to be given to the term "people" as employed in the Constitution), no longer control; *they are controlled.* And by this theory, the whole meaning and foundation of our government must be destroyed.

Let it be inquired, Calhoun asked, what is the object of a Constitution? Plainly, he replied, *the object of a Constitution is to restrain the government, as that of laws is to restrain individuals.* (128) And the necessity for a restraint upon the abuses and excesses to which all governments are inclined, arises largely from the fact that the governed people have dissimilar interests and concerns. Were all the people alike, and all interests of a community identical, no such restraints would be required; a simple majority division would justly decide every question submitted to it. But this identity of interest does not exist among the several States who jointly form the American Union. From the very inception of the Republic, the different States zealously have cherished differing institutions: To one, foreign trade may be vital; to another, domestic manufactures; to a third, agriculture; to a fourth, water power and irrigation; to a fifth, the operation of public schools and parks. It is only to a limited extent that these most vital concerns may be subordinated to the "national good." At some point, Calhoun argued, compromise must end and oppression begin. And it is "to guard against the unequal action of the laws, when applied to dissimilar and opposing interests, in fact, what mainly renders a constitution indispensable."

This recognition of the diversification and contrariety of interests among the States of the American Union lies at the essence of our Constitution. That was the whole purpose of delegating to the central government, as it was thought, only those powers supposed to be necessary "to regulate the interests common to all States," while reserving to the States *respectively* (the adverb is of the keenest significance) the control of those interests of a local character. By this means, the interests of the whole were to be subject to the will of the whole, while the peculiar interests of a particular State were to be left to its own people exclusively. "This distribution of power, settled solemnly by a constitutional compact, to which all the States are parties, constitutes the peculiar character and excellence of our political system."

The question next must be asked, how is this perfect distribution of powers to be maintained? There is but one mode, replied Calhoun, by which such political organization can be preserved— "the mode adopted in England, and by all governments, ancient and modern, blessed with constitutions deserving to be called free"—

to give to each co-estate the right to judge of its powers, with a negative or veto on the acts of the others, in order to protect against encroachments the interests it particularly represents: a principle which all of our Constitutions recognize in the distribution of power among their respective departments, as essential to maintain the independence of each, but which, to all who will duly reflect on the subject, must appear far more essential, for the same object, in that great and fundamental distribution of powers between the General and State governments. So essential is the principle, that to withhold the right from either, where the sovereign power is divided, is, in fact, *to annul the division* itself, and *to consolidate* in the one left in the exclusive possession of the right *all* powers of government; for it is not possible to distinguish, practically, between a government having all power, and one having the right to take what powers it pleases. [Emphasis is in the original.]

Calhoun's argument still holds good. It may be fairly assumed that it is not the will of the American people, or of the States as such, that the Federal government simply should "take what powers it pleases." We are not yet so conditioned to despotic rule. On the contrary, our political system still holds, however perilously, to a division of powers between State and Federal authority. And should the State and Federal governments come into serious conflict—into a clash that imperils the most essential institutions of a State —what is to be done? Are the alternatives two only: Submission, or arms? Is the choice truly confined to an acceptance of tyranny on the one hand, or a resort to the sword on the other? Every consideration of reason, common sense, and constitutional theory demonstrate that in a civilized and enlightened society, disputes are not to be so resolved.

We must examine, then, the various remedies that may be suggested. Our supposition is that Congress has enacted a bill, or the President has issued an executive order, or the Supreme Court has entered a decree clearly not authorized by the Constitution, the effect of which, if consented to, would be to endanger or destroy a plainly reserved power of a State. The question first must be asked, is not every such unconstitutional act absolutely void, and void *ab initio?* Obviously it is, and on the highest authority of our law. Are the States, then, bound to submit to laws or decrees which are unconstitutional and void? No such obligation can be inferred. On the contrary, it would appear that those States which refuse to submit to them are right, and that other States, undertaking to compel submission and to coerce obedience to usurped power, are guilty of oppression of the worst sort.

But it is asked, who is to ascertain that the purported law or decree is in fact a palpable and dangerous violation of the Constitution? The answer most commonly given is that the Supreme Court, under the Constitution, is appointed the common umpire in conflicts between State and Federal authority. *But this is plainly and demonstrably not so.* The Court derives its powers, just as its co-equal branches of the Federal government derive theirs, from the Constitution and from the Constitution alone. Let Article III be read from first to last, and not the first phrase will be found by which the jurisdiction of the Court may be implied over political contests between the States and the Federal government, each claiming a contested power. As we have noted earlier, precisely this power was suggested for the Court during the Convention of 1787, and was emphatically rejected.

Three reasons may be advanced to support the assertion that the Court is not, in fact, the common umpire in such contests.

First, the powers of the Court are judicial, not political, and under the Constitution extend primarily to *cases in law and equity.* The Court's jurisdiction over "controversies to which the United States shall be a party" never was regarded by the framers of the Constitution as authority in the Court to decide questions of political contest. It was not until 1890, more than a century after the ratification of the Constitution, that the Supreme Court claimed jurisdiction in any suit brought by the United States against a State—in this case, a suit against North Carolina to recover upon bonds issued by that State.(129) As recently as 1935, the Court refused to accept jurisdiction in a proceeding sought by the Federal government against West Virginia to determine the navigability of the New and Kanawha rivers, on the ground that its jurisdiction *did not extend to the adjudication of differences of opinion between officials of the two governments.*(130)

Not until the Tidelands Oil cases of 1947 and 1950, in a drastic overreaching of its powers, did the Court undertake to snatch the very authority that properly had been denied it.(131) The Tidelands question did not involve any petty question of bonds or any minor controversy over a boundary(132) or any inconsequential issue of title to particular tracts. (133) It involved a grave contest of power between the coastal States and the Federal government on an issue that, in the view of many leaders of those States, seriously affected their most vital interests.

Secondly, it is regrettably clear, even as Madison foresaw in his report of

1799, "that dangerous powers, not delegated, may not only be usurped and executed by the other departments, *but that the judicial department may also exercise or sanction dangerous powers,* beyond the grant of the Constitution." It is not to be supposed, in this democratic republic, that our Congressmen are mortal, but our judges divine. To regard the Court as the sole expositor of the Constitution and to vest in it the unchecked power not merely to interpret but *substantively to amend* the Constitution, is to relinquish unto a majority of the judges the sovereign power reserved to not fewer than three-fourths of the States. On this theory, the Court, by advancing specious reasons or no reasons at all, could in one bold move blot out the veritable existence of half-a-dozen States that displeased the judges; and the States would be powerless to resist effectively.

Thirdly, it is not to be forgotten that the Supreme Court, by the very nature of the instrument creating it, is *a portion of the Federal government itself.* It is the judicial branch of the trinity whose other branches are the Presidency and the Congress. Just as the President is the executive representative of this general government, and the Congress its legislative representative, *so is the Court its judicial representative.* The Justices are confirmed by a majority of the Senators, which is to say, by a majority of the States; they can be removed, if at all, only by a majority of the States. And in Calhoun's phrase: "To confide the power to the judiciary to determine finally and conclusively what powers are delegated and what reserved, would be, in reality, to confide it to the majority, whose agents they are, and by whom they can be controlled in various ways; and, of course, to subject . . . the reserved powers of the States, with all the local and peculiar interests they were intended to protect, *to the will of the very majority against which the protection was intended.*"

Littleton Waller Tazewell, a great Virginia jurist, made the same point in a series of essays in which he demolished Jackson's proclamation of December, 1832: "Can the human mind conceive a more audacious proposition," he asked, "than that which suggests that in a controversy between the parties to a covenant [under which] an agent is created, where the matter in dispute . . . regards the authority exerted by the agent, the decision of this controversy must be referred to the agent himself?"(134) What would have been the result, in the matter of the Sedition Act, if it may be supposed, first, that the act carried no expiration date, and secondly, that the Federalists had retained control of the House and refused to consent to its repeal? The Federalist judges—Chase, Paterson, Washington—already had held this wickedly unconstitutional law to be valid. An appeal by the States, on behalf of their gagged and persecuted people, surely would have been vain had it been addressed to the Court: The judges would have been asked to decide if the judges themselves had done right.

Before completing this phase of the discussion, a hostile witness may be called—the widely regarded Edward Livingston of Louisiana, Secretary of

State under Jackson, a member of the Senate during the Webster-Hayne debates, principal author of Jackson's proclamation. "I think," he said, "that by the institution of this government, the States have unequivocally surrendered every constitutional right of impeding or resisting the execution of any decree or judgment of the Supreme Court, in any case of law or equity, between persons, or on matters, of whom, or on which, that court has jurisdiction, even if such decree or judgment should, in the opinion of the States, be unconstitutional." But then Livingston, who strongly opposed Calhoun's theory of nullification, went on to concede that

in cases in which a law of the United States may infringe the constitutional right of a State, but which in its operation cannot be brought before the Supreme Court, under the terms of the jurisdiction expressly given to it over particular persons or matters, *that court is not created the umpire between a State that may deem itself aggrieved and the General Government.* [Emphasis supplied.](135)

What is to be deduced from Livingston's fuzzy thinking? First, that in *cases,* the Court is the supreme and final umpire, though the effect of its judgment upon the parties may be to deprive the State of what the State regards as its constitutionally reserved power; but secondly, if no*case* can be devised, the *Court* is not the umpire at all. But whence comes this limitation of the court's jurisdiction to *cases?* Why, as we have seen, from Article III of the Constitution. It is, then, the Constitution that controls the Court; it is, as it ever must be, the *Constitution* that is the supreme law of the land. But if the Constitution is over the Court, who or what finally is over the Constitution? *It can only be the States,* who under Article V alone have the power to amend or rewrite it. How, then, may it be urged that the States "unequivocally surrendered" the control of their most fundamental rights, in the last resort, to a Court they themselves created? So trusting a confidence in fallible man is unknown in human affairs; it cannot be imputed to the great men who as delegates of States drafted the Constitution.

Let us return, now, to a further inquiry into the alternative courses said to be available to a State, or several States, whose most vital institutions have been imperiled by an act or a decree regarded as unconstitutional. What we are seeking, it must be emphasized, is a peaceable remedy within the Union, and within the framework of the Constitution.

Livingston, in this same speech, suggested that an aggrieved State may resist in this way: (1) By remonstrating to Congress against the act; (2) by an address to the people, in their elective functions, to change or instruct their Representatives; (3) by a similar address to the other States, in which they will have a right to declare that they consider the act as unconstitutional, and therefore void; and (4) by proposing amendments to the Constitution, in the manner pointed out by that instrument.

But it must be evident that petition and remonstrance to Federal authority are vain, for such petitions are addressed *to the source of the oppression itself;* nor is a suppliant posture to be expected of a free people before their government. Neither can it be expected that an "address to the people" would achieve the desired end, or that mere resolutions, dispatched to the Legislatures of other States, could arrest the evil complained of. The proposing of constitutional amendments is fine, and to be presumed in every case of major contest, but is the proposing of amendments sufficient?

None of Livingston's remedies will answer, in the grievous and dangerous case supposed, and for this reason: None of them serves *to arrest the progress of the evil.* They are paper locks for barn doors when horses have been stolen. Before the most eloquent remonstrance could move an oppressor to provide relief, before the most justified amendment to the Constitution could be proposed by the Congress (assuming that two-thirds of the members of each house could be persuaded promptly to act upon it), before a new President could be chosen to appoint new judges to be confirmed by new Senators—the mischief would be done, the challenged liberty irretrievably lost, the cherished institution overthrown beyond restoration.

In the phrase, *"to arrest the progress of the evil"* lies the whole end and purpose of State interposition. The evil, as Abel Parker Upshur observed long ago, "is the exercise of an usurped power." The aim is to suspend this usurpation alone, within the limits of the objecting State, and thus to force a decision by the arbitrament of the ultimate umpire—the sovereign people themselves, acting in their respective States. In the grave and extraordinary crises for which outright nullification may be invoked, said Calhoun, "the States themselves may be appealed to, three-fourths of which, in fact, form a power, whose decrees are the Constitution itself, and whose voice can silence all discontent." And he added:

The utmost extent, then, of the power is, that a State acting in its sovereign capacity, as one of the parties to the constitutional compact, may compel the government, created by that compact, to submit a question touching its infraction to the parties who created it.

The alternative is to give to the Federal government "the sole and final right of interpreting the Constitution, thereby reversing the whole system, making that instrument the creature of its will,. . . and annihilating, in fact, the authority which imposed it, and from which the government itself derives its existence."

Now, Calhoun emphasized throughout his writings, as did Jefferson, that it is not to be supposed that this drastic remedy would be lightly invoked. Jefferson, late in his life, undertook to correct the impression that the States are subordinate to the Federal government. "This is not the case," he said—

They are coordinate departments of one simple and integral whole. But you may ask, If the two departments should claim each the same subject of power, where is the umpire to decide between them? In cases of little urgency or importance, the prudence of both parties will keep them aloof from the questionable ground; but if it can neither be avoided nor compromised, a convention of the States must be called to ascribe the doubtful power to that department which they may think best.(136)

So, too, with Calhoun: "The spirit of forbearance, as well as the nature of the right [of nullification] itself, forbids a recourse to it, except in cases of dangerous infractions of the Constitution; and then only in the last resort, when all reasonable hope of relief from the ordinary action of the government has failed; when, if the right to interpose did not exist, the alternative would be submission and oppression on one side, or resistance by force on the other." So, also, it will be recalled that Madison emphasized, in the Report of 1799, that an infraction of the Constitution must be "deliberate, palpable and dangerous." Interposition, he said, is not to be invoked "either in a hasty manner or on doubtful and inferior occasions." It can be called for by the States only on those occasions that "deeply and essentially affect the vital principles of their political system."

It is perfectly true that, under Calhoun's reasoning, a determination of the gravity of the infraction, and of the mode and measure of redress, remains with each respective State. Like every other right known to man, the "right to interpose" is susceptible to abuse. It was Jackson's criticism, in the December proclamation, that if a State may declare *one* law to be void, it could pick and choose those laws it would obey, and those it would defy. And meanwhile, every other State would be making the same capricious choice, and all government would collapse in disorder.

Yet while this is possible, it is by no means probable, and the reverse must be considered also: If power-hungry Federal judges may impose one unconstitutional mandate, they may impose a thousand, each more oppressive than the one before, until all liberties are extinguished. No one imagines that this will happen, though it is a plain fact that Federal inroads upon State responsibilities are progressing at an alarming pace.

Neither should it be imagined that Calhoun's right to interpose, if it were accepted fully into our political system, would be arbitrarily and frivolously invoked. Upshur, in his beautifully composed letters of 1833, provided the clearest answer on this point:

Although governments are primarily founded in distrust, yet there is, of necessity, some degree of confidence in all of them. The wisest statesman can do no more than repose that confidence in the safest hands, while at the same time, he surrounds it with all practicable safeguards against abuse. If the States may abuse their reserved rights in the manner contemplated by the President, the Federal government, on the other hand, may abuse its delegated rights. There is danger from both sides, and as we are compelled to confide in the one or the other, we have only to inquire, which is most worthy of our confidence.

It is much more probable that the Federal government will abuse its power than that the States will abuse theirs. And if we suppose a case of actual abuse on either hand, it will not be difficult to decide which is the greater evil.

If a State should abuse its right of interposition by arresting the operation of a constitutional law, the worst that could come of it would be to suspend the operation of the law, for a time, as to that State, while it would have all its effects within the other States. This would certainly be unjust, but in most cases, would be attended with very little practical evil.

Besides, according to the doctrine for which I am contending, this evil would be temporary only; it must cease in some way or other, as soon as the other States act upon the subject. I acknowledge, however, that it is at best an evil, but it is an evil inseparable from our system, and one which cannot be avoided except by submitting to a greater evil.(137)

May it be earnestly submitted, to those friends of constitutional government who are concerned at the aggrandizement of the Federal government, that careful consideration be given to Calhoun's reasoned doctrines? They rest upon the structure of the Union itself as a Union of co-equal States, in which each State rightfully should be responsible for the management of its most intimate domestic concerns; yet his doctrines do not deny to the Federal government one iota of the power and authority delegated to it by the Constitution.

Were the powerful weapon of State interposition carried by the States as a well-sheathed sword, its very existence would exert upon Federal departments a restraining influence of incalculable value. The judge, contemplating some bold engraftment on the fundamental law, could be expected to ask himself: *Will this be acceptable to three-fourths of the States should an infraction be charged?* The Congress, proposing to seize from a few States the control of their own natural resources, might pause in its ambitious course if there were reason to believe that an appeal would be taken, as from a ruling of the chair, to the source of ultimate sovereignty. Yet the States themselves, for their part, it may be imagined, seldom would risk an immediate and decisive rebuke by their brethren for interposing on light or unwarranted grounds. Year after year, it would be supposed, the States would accept the interpretations placed upon their Constitution by the Court, and would acquiesce without objection in the acts of Congress; indeed, for the past half-century, they have done so with few exceptions.

The object must be to preserve in the hands of the people, which is to say *in the people of the States,* some effective power that may be utilized, in great and extraordinary instances, by which an asserted usurpation of power may be checked, suspended, and submitted for decision to the principals in the constitutional compact. John Calhoun, building upon the foundation of Madison and Jefferson, offered a means by which that object may be attained. His adversaries have offered nothing.

Notes

Go to top.

13

The Personal Liberty Laws

WE MAY now resume, may it please the court, a discussion of those instances of particular State interposition, by which it may be discerned that every portion of this Union, at some point in its history, has recognized the imperative necessity of a State veto upon acts of the Federal government.

In commencing this section, it ought not to be necessary to make one disavowal:(138) The author of these notes utterly disclaims any affection or admiration for the detestable institution of human slavery that cursed the South for a century and a half. It was an abominable custom, indefensible in any light; no one could condemn it more severely than this citizen of Virginia. As many objective students of Southern history have fairly noted, the citizens of an older Virginia condemned it also. Governor Randolph, addressing the Virginia Convention of 1788, grimly described Virginia and North Carolina as "both oppressed with debts and slaves."(139) George Mason, in addressing the Virginia convention, referred to the "nefarious" and "detestable" and "disgraceful" slave trade,(140) but Mason foresaw, as many others did not, the "Northern and Eastern States meddling with our whole property of that kind."(141)

For a correct understanding of Mason's apprehension, it is necessary to shift some mental gears violently, in order to comprehend an economy, in our own country, revolving entirely around slave labor. We must recall that there was a time, nauseously distasteful as the thought may be, when many of the finest and most cultured leaders of our Republic owned slaves and rather helplessly defended slavery. They trafficked in human beings, bought and sold them like cattle. There is no condoning it now.

But for the purposes of this essay, it must also be comprehended *that the Constitution of the United States specifically sanctioned slavery.* Nailed into our fundamental law were three provisions that in 1787 were essential to the adoption of any Constitution whatever: It was provided in Article I that representation in the House would be based upon "the whole Number of free Persons . . . and . . . three fifths of all other Persons." It was further provided that "the Migration or Importation of such Persons as any of the States now existing shall think proper to admit, shall not be prohibited by the Congress prior to the Year 1808." And it was provided, finally, in Article IV, that

> A Person charged in any State with Treason, Felony, or other Crime, who shall flee from Justice, and be found in another State, shall on Demand of the executive Authority of the State from which he fled, be delivered up, to be removed to the State having Jurisdiction of the Crime.
>
> No Person held to Service or Labour in one State, under the Laws thereof, escaping into another, shall, in Consequence of any Law or Regulation therein, be discharged from such Service or Labour, but shall be delivered up on Claim of the Party to whom such Service or Labour may be due.

Those provisions related expressly to the slave trade and to slavery. They were a part of the many compromises that had to be made in order to assure ratification of the compact—but more than that: Once ratified, *they became a part of the fundamental constitutional law of the Union,* as respectable at law, as binding upon the States and the people, as any provision relating to the coinage of money or the election of Senators. It is in that light that these clear and unmistakable provisions are viewed here: Stripped of moral values, and considered only as binding law.

With that understanding, it may be noted that among the earlier acts of Congress was the Fugitive Slave Act of February 12, 1793, by which the foregoing constitutional provisions were implemented with legislation clearly "necessary and proper" to carry them out.(142) From the very beginning—even from the Northwest Ordinance in the prior Congress of 1787, abolition of the slave trade was widely urged. Prior to 1810, half-a-dozen States—among them North Carolina, Maryland, and Tennessee—proposed constitutional amendments toward that end. An act providing for an end to this traffic, with the expiration of the constitutional limitation in 1808, received overwhelming support. Yet even among those who condemned slavery most severely, the ugly practice was recognized unhappily as an inescapable part of the economy of the affected States.

Various schemes were devised to ameliorate the condition. Most prominent among these was the colonization plan, which early had the support of Jefferson and late the support of Lincoln. As far back as 1802, the General Assembly of Virginia could be found urging that land be acquired, in Africa or South America, for colonization of free Negroes.(143) In 1816 and 1817, States as far apart as Georgia and Vermont endorsed the proposal. Indeed, the idea came and went over a period of nearly forty years, as Pennsylvania, Delaware, Illinois, Indiana, Connecticut, and Massachusetts one by one approved it.

Yet the colonization plan, if it were desirable in theory, proved unacceptable in practice. Nothing came of it, and in time the sponsors fell out. Meanwhile, other events came along that served to drive a terrible wedge between the States. The bitter fight of 1819-20 over the admission of Missouri saw at least nine States (Vermont, New Hampshire, Massachusetts, New York, New Jersey, Pennsylvania, Delaware, Ohio and Indiana), strongly interceding against any terms of admission by which slavery might be extended. (144) Their opposition, as New Jersey and Vermont freely conceded, was not on moral grounds alone: Every 1,000 voteless slaves in Missouri would be counted as 600 free citizens in providing representation in the House of Representatives. The question was political as well as moral. But it was a constitutional question also, as Virginia, among others, repeatedly pointed out: Every new State, entering the Union, necessarily had to be admitted with exactly the same equal rights and privileges that obtained to every other State. It could not be otherwise.

The wrath of the North, and the resentment of the South, were further aroused in this period by the almost incredible outpourings of the abolitionist press. William Lloyd Garrison's *Liberator* began publication in Boston January 1, 1831, but it was merely the best known of a hundred publications that began to flood the country. "I do not wish to think, or speak, or write with moderation," said Garrison,(145) and he set the tone for the others. To the Southern States, these violently inflammatory newspapers and pamphlets were a serious and dangerous aggravation.(146) The white residents, in many areas overwhelmingly outnumbered by their subject slaves, justifiably feared insubordination or insurrection; they dreaded the "torch of the incendiary, and the dagger of the midnight assassin."(147) And they were heartily outraged by "officious and impertinent intermeddling with our domestic concerns."(148) After all, as South Carolina grimly pointed out, "The evils of slavery have been visited upon us by the cupidity of those who are now the champions of universal emancipation."(149)

In a spirit of desperate self-preservation, many of the Southern States embarked upon a program of retaliation. Following a potentially disastrous Negro uprising in Charleston in May of 1822, South Carolina adopted a "Negro Seaman's Act," the effect of which was to deny free Negroes, arriving as crew members aboard sailing vessels, permission to land at South Carolina ports. Virginia earlier had adopted a somewhat similar law, (150) and in time other seaboard States were to follow. New England shipowners angrily protested the law, and in the fall of 1833 arranged a test case of its provisions. Mr. Justice Johnson promptly declared the South Carolina statute unconstitutional. He was not interested in South Carolina's anxieties and fears: "The plea of necessity is urged," he said, "and of the existence of that necessity, we are told, the State alone is to judge. Where is this to land us? Is it not asserting the right in each State to throw off the Federal Constitution at its will and pleasure? If it can be done as to any particular article, it may be done as to all, and, like the old Confederation, the Union becomes a mere rope of sand."(151) Yet South Carolina, in the face of this decision, continued to enforce her law.(152) Indeed, two years after Johnson's opinion, South Carolina added some fresh teeth to it. (153) Alabama and Florida, and later Louisiana and Georgia, in 1842, paralleled the statute. And the offended New Englanders, in a gesture not wholly appreciated, dispatched missions southward to arrange fresh test cases. Mr. Samuel Hoar, when he explained his purpose in South Carolina, was abruptly expelled from the State by legislative resolution.(154) A mission to Louisiana met the same inhospitable treatment.

But meanwhile, Northern States were far more industrious in seeking to nullify both Constitution and courts. Very early in the period, they began to adopt what were known as "Personal Liberty Laws"—State statutes designed shrewdly and deliberately to nullify the Federal Fugitive Slave Act. That this was their intention, few Northerners denied; that the enactments presented an outright defiance of law was generally conceded. Even the great Webster, no friend of slavery or the South, once commented of Southern outcries against the personal liberty laws, "The South, in my judgment, is right, and the North is wrong."(155) The laws took a dozen ingenious forms. The Southern slave-owner, who came North seeking his escaped servant or farmhand, was susceptible of arrest himself on a trumped up charge of "kidnapping." Should the slave-owner actually capture his fugitive, it was necessary for him to prove ownership by the most elaborate evidence— presented before a jury of hostile abolitionists. State officials were prohibited under pain of heavy punishment from cooperating in any way in enforcement of the Federal act. It was made a serious misdemeanor for any person to assist in the recapture of a fugitive slave. In Vermont, all fugitives were declared automatically free men; any person who attempted to detain such a fugitive thereafter made himself liable, on conviction, to a prison term of five to twenty years or a fine of up to $10,000.(156)

All told, fourteen respected and honored Northern States engaged in this prolonged, and generally successful interposition of their sovereign powers. Let the roll be called: Connecticut, Iowa, Maine, Massachusetts, Michigan, Pennsylvania, New York, Ohio, New Hampshire, Rhode Island, Vermont, Illinois, Indiana, Wisconsin. Theirs was a planned and deliberate program of nullification, pursued with relentless vigor, in defiance of the Constitution, over a period of nearly forty years. Each of them enacted laws willfully intended to veto the Act of Congress of 1793, and to render nugatory any effort to enforce it. As rapidly as their acts were held unconstitutional, (157) they enacted new evasions, or simply ignored the court decrees.

This steadfast resistance to the Constitution, as might be surmised, led to some angry conflicts between the States. Virginia for example, tangled bitterly with New York, when New York's Governor Seward refused to surrender three men charged with stealing slaves. Repeated requests for their extradition, phrased in the most respectful terms, went unanswered, and finally Virginia's Governor Gilmer lost his temper. Seward's refusal, he declared, was "monstrous."(158) It was "a palpable and dangerous violation of the Constitution and laws of the United States . . . [which] cannot be acquiesced in."(159)

New York, unimpressed, added injury to insult by enacting in 1840 a new and more ingenious Personal Liberty Law than any the State had adopted in the past.(160) To this Virginia retaliated, in 1841, with "An act to prevent citizens of New York from carrying slaves out of the Commonwealth."(161) And Gilmer, still aroused, also refused to surrender a forger to New York until Seward chose to return the slave-stealers. Notably, Virginia's General Assembly regarded this action on Gilmer's part as dishonorable, censured him for it, and accepted his resignation from office. Virginia's act of 1841, which required an inspection of every New York vessel (at the shipowner's expense), to make certain no slaves were being carried away, was repealed by Virginia's Assembly in 1845.(162)

An even more dramatic conflict arose between Georgia and Maine, involving a twenty-two-year-old slave by the name of Atticus who turned up, in May of 1837, aboard the schooner Susan, bound for Maine. According to the ship's master, Daniel Philbrook of Camden, and the mate, Edward Kelleran of Cushing, the slave was a stowaway. According to the aggrieved owners, James and Henry Sagurs of Chatham County, Georgia, the two seamen had kidnapped him. In any event, the Brothers Sagur obtained a boat of their own, and began a chase at sea. The Susan put on canvas and outran them back to Maine.

When finally the well-winded Georgians reached Maine and obtained a warrant for Atticus' recovery, the Negro had disappeared. Not until they offered a reward was the slave found, concealed in a barn in Thomaston. Attempting to take him into custody, the Sagurs encountered a crowd of abolitionists; they were "pelted by the populace, and . . . with difficulty escaped from the fury of the mob." However, they did manage to get Atticus back to Savannah.(163)

The Sagurs' next step was to swear out a warrant, in Georgia, charging Philbrook and Kelleran with kidnapping. In June of 1837, Georgia's Governor William Schley formally requested their extradition, but Maine's Governor Robert P. Dunlop, a long-jawed fellow with a deceptively placid look about him, declined on a number of technical and legalistic grounds. In the fall, Georgia met these objections, but Dunlop still declined to return the two men for trial. In December, Georgia's Legislature wrathfully adopted a resolution denouncing Dunlop for failing to perform "the sacred duties which are imposed upon him" by the Constitution, and especially for resisting Georgia's constitutional request "at a time when the minds of the people of the South are justly excited, and their feelings most wantonly outraged, by the machinations of certain fanatics in the North."

In Maine, the portly, white-haired Edward Kent succeeded Dunlop as Governor, but proved equally deaf to Georgia's protestations. Late in 1838, the Georgia Legislature met again, and a special committee pondered what might be done about the situation. One recommendation was that Georgia close all her ports to vessels from Maine, but on mature reflection, it was agreed that under the Constitution this was impossible. A committee member offered a second proposal: To seize upon visitors from Maine and hold them hostage until the felons were returned. But while that might not be unconstitutional, "it would be unjust." A third possibility, solemnly, if briefly considered, was for Georgia to declare war on Maine—but Heaven forfend! "Long, long may it be before the States of this Union shall be involved in civil conflict!" What, then, was to be done? The frustrated committee, "although strongly disposed to recommend the passage of a law imposing quarantine upon all vessels coming into our waters from Maine," ultimately settled merely for further, and stronger, resolutions directed toward Maine. If these failed, a State convention should be called "to devise the course for her future policy."

These resolutions failed. Kent continued to ignore Georgia's resolutions, and perhaps for an understandable reason: Maine had troubles closer at hand, in what almost became a shooting war with Great Britain on her northern boundary. The dispute dated from the period immediately following the War of 1812, when the British claimed the whole of the upper part of the valley of St. John, above the 46th parallel. Maine claimed the same territory under the Treaty of 1783. The residents of Madawacka, evidently regarding themselves as citizens of Maine, sent representatives to the State Legislature, and otherwise identified themselves with Maine. But to New Brunswick authorities, the Madawackans were British citizens.

These claims and counter-claims led to a series of border incidents, climaxed in the summer of 1837 when a congressional agent, sent to the town to take a census in order to distribute the famed Federal surplus of 1836, was summarily arrested by a British constable and clapped in jail. Governor Dunlop, declaring that Maine's soil had been invaded by a foreign power, prepared for the State to go to war against England on its own—as the State, lest it be forgotten, constitutionally had (and still would have) a right to do. (164) The British backed down before Dunlop's bellicose preparations, released the agent, and arranged for an arbitration. Unhappily, the arbitrator, William, King of the Netherlands, accepted neither the boundary line urged by the British, nor the line contended for by Maine: He drew a line of his own, which satisfied no one. Maine was further aggrieved when Van Buren's pussyfooting administration proposed to give Maine 1,000,000 acres of land, to be taken from what now is Michigan, in exchange for the territory Maine would lose under the arbitration award. Maine declined.

Soon afterwards, as border incidents became more aggravated and Van Buren seemed disposed to do nothing more, Governor Kent brought matters to a head. The State's sovereignty had been outraged; her appeals to Washington had proved fruitless. Now Kent was prepared to recommend that Maine "throw herself entirely upon her own resources, and maintain, unaided and alone, her just rights, in the determined spirit of free men." The indignant Legislature backed him by appropriating $800,000, and Kent promptly ordered 10,000 militiamen called out. Within a week they were on their way to Aroostook County, under the command of General George W.

Bachelder. At this, Congress hastily came to life, added its own appropriation of $10,000,000 and the President sent General Winfield Scott and his staff packing off to Augusta. Scott fortunately proved to be an able peacemaker; both sides withdrew their troops and released their prisoners, and the bloodless Aroostook War finally was settled in 1842 by the Webster-Ashburton Treaty. In time, of course, Maine's dispute with Georgia also was settled, but hostility against Maine did not subside in Savannah for generations.(165)

Much resentment also arose over the hotly contested question of annexing Texas—not only as a slave State, but as a previously independent Republic. Connecticut branded the proposal "an alarming encroachment upon the rights of free men."(166) Maryland termed it "a flagrant violation of the Constitution."(167) Ohio, pointing out that the Constitution contained no provision "for incorporating foreign nations," protested hotly.(168) Vermont demanded that Texas be barred unless every State in the Union consented to the annexation, and declared that for her own part, she would never assent to so "flagrant a violation of the national compact."(169)Michigan, Illinois, and Maine, also interposed objections in 1845, but perhaps the most violent opposition to the admission of Texas came from Massachusetts: "Under no circumstances whatever can the people of Massachusetts regard the proposition to admit Texas into the Union in any other light than as dangerous to its continuance in peace, prosperity, and in the enjoyment of those blessings which it is the object of free government to secure."(170) And significantly, Massachusetts subsequently vowed that "such an act of admission *would have nobinding force whatever* on the people of Massachusetts."(171) (Emphasis supplied.)

Texas was admitted, of course, in December of 1845, but the broader controversy roared on. Throughout the 1840's, Northern States continued to encourage the escape of Negro slaves, and to harass the slave-owners in every attempt to recover them. In Ohio, Indiana, and Illinois, armed mobs forcibly took slaves from their Southern masters, evidently with the tacit approval of local law enforcement officers. Occasionally these measures encountered a frown from the Supreme Court; in Pennsylvania, one Prigg, attempting to return a Negro woman, Margaret Morgan, to her owner in Maryland, was indicted for violation of Pennsylvania's personal liberty law, but on Prigg's appeal to the Supreme Court Justice Story resoundingly held the State law unconstitutional.(172)

The only result, however, was that Pennsylvania in 1847 passed a new Personal Liberty Law, as ingenious as the one before. Massachusetts, fourteen months after Story's decision, contemptuously adopted a law providing that "No judge of any court of record in this Commonwealth . . . shall take cognizance or grant a certificate in cases that may arise under the third section" of the Fugitive Slave Law of 1793. (173) Sheriffs and constables were prohibited by the Massachusetts Legislature from detaining fugitive slaves, under penalty of a fine of up to

$1,000. Rhode Island, Connecticut, Vermont, and Michigan followed this example. It was as if Story and the Court had never spoken.

There was little enough the protesting Southern States could do about it. In one outburst of annoyance, in 1855, the Arkansas Legislature proposed, in effect, to sever diplomatic relations with Ohio: It was proposed that "all social and commercial" intercourse be halted. Kentucky also tangled bitterly with Ohio. The Constitution explicitly provided, said Kentucky, that "a person charged in any State with treason, felony, or other crime," i.e., a slave charged with the felonious crime of escaping, "*shall* on demand of the executive authority of the State from which he fled, be delivered up." The Constitution also provided explicitly that no fugitive slave, escaping into another State, "shall, in consequence of any law or regulation therein, be discharged from such service or labour, but shall be delivered up." Yet when Governor Dennison of Ohio adamantly refused to obey this mandate, the aged Chief Justice Taney, speaking for the Court, was compelled to admit that neither the Constitution nor the fugitive slave laws provided "any means to compel the execution of this duty." And the Court thought it clear

that the Federal government, under the Constitution, has no power to impose on a State officer, as such, any duty whatever, and compel him to perform it. (174)

The case that provoked the greatest uproar, of course, was the Dred Scott case. It arose in this fashion: Scott was born in Virginia, the son of slave parents, and taken by his master to Missouri about 1827. In 1835, Scott was sold to Dr. John Emerson, an army surgeon, who took him the following year to Rock Island, in Illinois, and a year or so later to Fort Snelling, in what is now Minnesota. In 1838 Dr. Emerson returned to St. Louis, bringing with him Scott, Scott's wife (a slave woman, Harriet, whom he had married at Fort Snelling), and the slave couple's daughter Eliza, who had been born aboard the steamboat en route back to Jefferson Barracks.

Within the next few years, Dr. Emerson died, willing his slaves to his wife. Then, in July, 1847, Scott brought suit in the Missouri State courts against Mrs. Emerson, seeking his freedom. His contention was that having been taken from slave territory into free territory, he had gained the status of a free Negro and could not thereafter be returned to slavery. One jury trial resulted in a verdict against him, but on retrial he was successful. The Emerson estate appealed, and the Missouri Supreme Court reversed the trial court and declared Scott still a slave.

At some point in this period, Mrs. Emerson remarried. Her new husband was Dr. C. C. Chaffee, a Republican abolitionist from Massachusetts, who represented his State in Congress. In one sense, his wife's slave property might have been embarrassing to him; but in a more useful sense, the Negroes offered the opportunity for a *cause célèbre*. Thus, a dummy sale was arranged, by which the Scott slaves (there was another daughter by this time, Lizzie, born in Missouri) were conveyed to Mrs. Emerson-Chaffee's brother, John F. A. Sandford (or Sanford) of New York.(175) And in 1853, a fresh proceeding was filed in the Scotts' behalf, this time in the Federal Circuit Court at St. Louis. A jury found against Scott, and the case went up to the Supreme Court of the United States.

On March 6, 1857, Chief Justice Taney handed down the Court's 7-2 decision. The Court first tackled the jurisdictional question. Federal courts had authority to hear suits brought by "citizens of different States." Was Scott a "citizen" within the meaning of the Constitution? The Court's ruling —and its legal correctness has not been effectively challenged—was that Scott was not a citizen. It is impossible to quarrel with this finding: Under the Constitution of the United States, and under the laws and constitutions of a dozen other States both North and South, Negroes at that time were not, politically, persons at all; they were property. Scott himself, born in Virginia of slave parents, had no right to sue in a Federal court.

Having decided that question, the Court might have stopped, routinely affirmed the Circuit Court, and dismissed the case. But in one of the greatest judicial blunders in the Court's history, the judges pushed on to other hotly controversial questions. Thus they examined the plaintiff's claim to freedom by reason of Scott's travels with Dr. Emerson in 1837 and 1838; this led them to a consideration of the power in Congress to prohibit slavery in territories. Finding that no such power was vested in Congress by the Constitution, the Court gratuitously held the Missouri Compromise of 1820 (which meanwhile had been repealed by the Kansas-Nebraska Act of 1854) to have been unconstitutional.

Some able students of the Dred Scott case have argued persuasively that it was, in fact, necessary for Taney and his associates to consider these questions—not as to Scott, but as to the child, Eliza. She had been born on the steamboat *Gypsie,* in the Mississippi River north of Missouri. The law of Illinois extended to the middle of the channel; the law of the territory held sway on the other. Which applied? Or did it matter?(176) Yet the almost unwavering tradition of the Court is to avoid large constitutional questions when they are not absolutely essential to a decision, and the weight of criticism holds that the Court needlessly expanded its opinion. In the judgment of Edward S. Corwin, the decision was a grave "abuse of trust" on the Court's part.(177) Charles Warren, perhaps the ablest Court historian this country has produced, agrees that a serious "loss of confidence" in the Court was caused by the decision.(178)

Overnight, the eighty-year-old Taney and his brothers encountered an outpouring of abuse and vilification unmatched by anything voiced in any Southern State in our more effete times.(179)Nor was this hurricane of protest confined to newspaper columns or to the chambers of Congress. The purpose of this essay is to treat the formal and official interposition of States against what they have regarded as Federal usurpation. Thus attention may be directed to the action of respectable and law-abiding Vermont: Its Legislature resolved, in November of 1857, that the Court's opinions "upon questions not contained in the record in the Dred Scott Case, are extra judicial and political, *possessing no color of authority or binding force,* and that such views and opinions are wholly repudiated by the people of Vermont." And to buttress this assertion, Vermont declared anew, the following October, that the doctrines laid down by the Court "are a dangerous usurpation of power, *and have no binding authority upon Vermont, or the people of the United States."*(180)

We may look, also, to the respectable State of Maine. One month after the decision came down, the Legislature of Maine solemnly declared the Court's opinion "extra-judicial," and"*not binding,* in law or in conscience, upon the government or citizens of the United States." The right of each State to determine the political rights of her citizens "is clear and indisputable, and is to be exercised without question by any other State."(181)

So, too, in Massachusetts. Perhaps her citizens of today will find interest in this declaration by their General Court of 1858:

Resolved, that while the people of Massachusetts recognize the rightful judicial authority of the Supreme Court of the United States, in the determination of all questions properly coming before it, they will never consent that their rights shall be impaired, or their liberties invaded, by reason of any usurpations of political power by said tribunal. . . .

Resolved, that no part of the decision of the Supreme Court of the United States, in the case of *Scott vs. Sandford,* is binding, which was not necessary to the determination of that case.(182)

Many other examples might be cited. Ohio, on April 17, 1857, denounced the Court's decision as a "palpable and unwarranted violation" of the Constitution. New York declared the opinion "has impaired the confidence and respect of the people of this State" in the Supreme Court. All told, twenty-two States interposed against the Court, not only with resolutions declaring the opinion void, but with fresh laws effectively to make it so.

For a final note on Northern nullification, we may turn to Wisconsin, and to a night in March of 1854. A fugitive slave, one Joshua Glover, had been taken into custody at Racine by a United States marshal, Ableman, for violation of the Fugitive Slave Act of 1850. A mob of citizens gathered outside the jail where he was confined. Then an intensely anti-slavery editor, Sherman M. Booth of the Wisconsin *Free Democrat,* took leadership of the crowd. In one angry wave, they stormed the jail, and released the slave.

Booth was arrested on March 11, and charged in Federal District Court with violation of Federal law. But he at once applied to the Wisconsin State Supreme Court for a writ of habeas corpus, and Judge A. D. Smith of that court promptly ordered him released. The Fugitive Slave Act, said the full court in affirming his action, was unconstitutional and void.(183)

The persistent Marshal Ableman again arrested Booth, and in January, 1855, succeeded in having him tried and convicted in the Federal court. He was sentenced to one month in prison and fined $1,000; but again, the Wisconsin Supreme Court ordered him discharged on a writ of habeas corpus. This time the United States Supreme Court intervened: Chief Justice Taney issued a writ directing the State Supreme Court to send up a record of the case. The Wisconsin court flatly disregarded the order.

It was not until March of 1857, the month of the Dred Scott decision, that the United States Attorney was able to procure a clerk's copy of the record in the Booth case; and it was not until December, 1858, nearly four years after the storming of the jail at Racine, that the Supreme Court overruled the Wisconsin State court and ordered Booth returned to Federal custody. (184) But once more, the Wisconsin court refused to comply with the Supreme Court's decree. The State Legislature warmly supported the court's resistance, and to make this plain, passed a new and more defiant Personal Liberty Law. It also, in March of 1859, more than half a century after Jefferson and Madison had brought forth the Kentucky and Virginia Resolutions, adopted a resolution that vigorously approved the old Doctrine of '98. The Supreme Court's action in the Booth case, said the Wisconsin Legislature was "an arbitrary act of power, unauthorized by the Constitution . . . *without authority, void, and of no force.*"[Emphasis supplied.] And we may especially note the paragraphs that followed. Gentlemen, this is Wisconsin speaking, as recently as 1859:

Resolved, That the government formed by the Constitution of the United States was not the exclusive or final judge of the extent of the powers delegated to itself; but that, as in all other cases of compact among parties having no common judge, each party has an equal right to judge for itself, as well of infractions as of the mode and measure of redress.

Resolved, that the principle and construction contended for by the party which now rules in the councils of the nation, that the general government is the exclusive judge of the extent of the powers delegated to it, stop nothing short of despotism, since the *discretion* of those who administer the government, and not the *Constitution,* would be the measure of their powers; that the several States which formed that instrument, being sovereign and independent, have the unquestionable right to judge of its infractions; and that a *positive defiance* of those sovereignties, of all unauthorized acts done or attempted to be done under color of that instrument, is the rightful remedy.(185)

Now, it is not the intention of the author of these few notes to erect a large sign, saying "moral," at the end of every section. This is no fable for children, of goose and gander. It is perhaps sufficient to say, by way of summary, that over a period of nearly forty years, in issues relating to the slavery question, States both South and North effectively nullified the Federal Constitution, and acts of Congress, and the decrees of the Supreme Court. In the South, as in South Carolina and Florida, this interposition took the form of State laws prohibiting the ingress of free Negro citizens, State laws preventing the delivery of United States mail termed "incendiary," and State laws (as in Georgia and Virginia) hampering seagoing trade with other States.

Far more serious, because it was more systematically and vigorously pursued, was the interposition of Northern States through their Personal Liberty Laws. In absolute defiance of both Court and Constitution, they contrived to nullify the fundamental law. Yet their contention, vehemently expressed throughout this period, was that they were proceeding in full accord with the Constitution. They took the view, as in New Jersey in 1852, that "the Constitution was a compact between the several States." They insisted, as in Massachusetts in 1855, that the Federal Fugitive Slave Law was a "direct violation" of the Tenth Amendment. And they repeatedly avowed their right to resist laws and decrees which they viewed as palpably unconstitutional.

This point alone will be renewed: If Maine, Vermont, Massachusetts, Ohio, Wisconsin, and their neighbors were wrong then, it may be supposed that Virginia, South Carolina, and Georgia, in resisting the Supreme Court's school decree, are wrong now. But if the Northern States were right then, in resisting and opposing *what they regarded as encroachments upon sovereign rights,* then it equally may be supposed that the South is right today.

Notes

Go to top.

14

The Obligation of Contracts

THE SLAVERY issue, and the hotly contested questions of personal liberty laws, were not the only constitutional issues in the ante bellum period to be involved in conflicts between State and Federal authority. Controversies arising out of a provision in Article I, Section 10 of the Constitution ("No State shall pass any law impairing the obligation of contracts") persistently saw the States and the Supreme Court at loggerheads.

This prohibition was among the relatively few direct prohibitions laid upon the States by the original Constitution. It was first asserted by Marshall, in the Yazoo controversy.(186) It was dramatically expounded in Webster's famed Dartmouth College case ("It is a small school, but there are those who love it").(187) It was refined in the States' favor in a Rhode Island case,

(188)and again interpreted—a bit tremulously—in the States' behalf in a suit involving New York's bankruptcy law in 1827.(189) But it was not until the years immediately preceding and following the War of 1861-65 that the provision led to seriously recurring conflicts between State and Federal authority. For the purpose of these notes, which are intended to sketch representative instances of official interposition by the States of their sovereign power, it will suffice to call attention to certain disputes in Ohio, and in the Midwest.

Here we may begin by observing that one of the greatest problems of the expanding American frontier lay in the establishment of a sound banking system. Some of the problems of the Banks of the United States have been described, but the travails of individual State and private banks were equally severe. It was in an effort to stimulate the organization of sound banks that Ohio, in 1845, adopted a law providing, among other things, that a tax would be imposed of only 6 per cent on a bank's earnings; this tax was to be "in lieu of all taxes to which the company, or its stockholders therein, would otherwise be subject." Pursuant to this law, some one hundred fifty banks rapidly came into existence.

But in 1851, a new Legislature undertook to rewrite the act of 1845, in order to place banks on the same footing, taxwise, with other enterprises. This would have meant a substantial increase in their taxes, and understandably, the banks protested. Their contention was that the act of 1845 had created a contract between the State and the banks; the act of 1851 had impaired the obligation of that contract; therefore, the act of 1851 was unconstitutional. The argument was to occupy the United States Supreme Court for more than a dozen years.

The position taken by the State of Ohio was substantially this: The Legislature of 1845 could not have bargained away forever the taxing power of the State. "If they had attempted it, would it not have been treason—treason of the blackest sort?"(190) The constitutional prohibition against impairment of contracts never was intended to embrace the tax laws of a State, or indeed any enactments of a State legislature. John Marshall's rule in the Dartmouth College case was "subversive of the rights of the people, at war with the principles of our government, and fraught with mischief incalculable."(191) It was "an ill-considered and insupportable dictum."(192) No power of sovereignty was more vital than the power to tax, and if this power were irrevocably bartered away by one legislature as to one subject of taxation, future legislatures would abandon the people's rights in other fields, and ultimately all sources of revenue would have been "contracted" away.

The Supreme Court took an exactly opposite view. On May 24, 1854, through Justice McLean, it declared Ohio's act of 1851 unconstitutional. (193) The Legislature of 1845 had been the "exclusive judge" of the privileges to be offered to the Piqua Branch Bank as a condition of its establishment. Having made a bargain, Ohio must stick to it.

This was a 5-4 decision, with the four Southern judges (Taney, Catron, Daniel and Campbell) warmly dissenting. The exemptions granted to expanding corporations by the various State legislatures had become a growing scandal,(194) and Campbell at least was well aware of "the sly and stealthy arts to which State Legislatures are exposed, and the greedy appetites of adventurers for monopolies and immunities from the State right of government."

The opinion in the Piqua Branch case, Warren comments, "produced a sensation." Hostility to the Court, already running high as a result of the slavery issue, reached a new pitch. Nor was this antagonism tempered by the Court's almost simultaneous decision, in a somewhat corollary case, involving the Ohio Life Insurance and Trust Company. Here the facts were that the company had been incorporated in 1834; its existence had not been conditioned upon the legislative "contract" of 1845. When the State sued to collect the higher tax under the law of 1851, the company cited the binding nature of its original charter; this, it was urged, constituted a contract which no legislature could impair. The Ohio Supreme Court rejected this contention, and on appeal, surprisingly enough, the Supreme Court—through Chief Justice Taney—accepted some of the reasoning of the court below. His opinion is cited in these notes because Taney had some things to say that are pertinent to questions in our own time: "It will be admitted on all hands," he remarked, "that with the exception of the powers surrendered by the Constitution of the United States, the people of the several States are absolutely and unconditionally sovereign within their respective territories." In Ohio, the sovereign people had settled questions of corporate charters in their constitution of 1802—such charters granted no exemptions from future tax levies—and in Taney's view the subject was closed. Let us note what he said next:

When the Constitution of a State, for nearly half a century, has received one uniform and unquestioned construction by all the departments of the government, legislative, executive and judicial, I think it must be regarded as the true one. . . . Certainly a construction acted on as undisputed for nearly fifty years by every department of government, and supported by judicial decision, ought to be regarded as sufficient to give to the instrument a fixed and definite meaning.(195)

Certainly it may be suggested that Taney's comment is a sound guide for giving a "fixed and definite meaning" to any constitution—that of Ohio in 1854, or of the United States precisely a century later.

But if Ohioans thought any sort of truce with the Court had been reached in the Ohio Life case, they shortly were disabused. Two years later, the Supreme Court cracked down again on Ohio's "impairment of contracts" in the matter of bank taxes. This time the Court held that even the sovereign people of Ohio themselves, by amending their own State Constitution, could not wipe out the bank law of 1845. "Moral obligations never die," said the Court, and it went on to read Ohio a stiff lecture on the supremacy of the Supreme Court in its role as final arbiter of the Constitution.(196)

Justices Campbell, Catron, and Daniel again dissented, and some of Campbell's observations merit brief quotation:

As to the claim made for the court to be the final arbiter of these questions of political power, I can imagine no pretension more likely to be fatal to the constitution of the court itself. If this court is to have an office so transcendent as to decide finally the powers of the people over persons and things within the State, a much closer connection and a much more direct responsibility of its members to the people is a necessary condition for the safety of popular rights.

Campbell went on to quote a comment by Justice Levi Woodbury in the politics-ridden case of Luther vs. Borden, some seven years before. "If the people," Woodbury had remarked, "in the distribution of powers under the Constitution, should ever think of making judges supreme arbiters in political controversies, when not selected by nor, frequently, amenable to them, nor at liberty to follow such various considerations in their judgment as belong to mere political questions, they will dethrone themselves, and lose one of their own invaluable birthrights; building up in this way—slowly, but surely—a new sovereign power in the Republic, in most respects irresponsible, and unchangeable for life, and one more dangerous, in theory at least, than the worst elective oligarchy in the worst of times."(197)

Unhappily, Campbell's dissenting opinion was of little value to the angry people of Ohio. But for a time, the State Supreme Court went along with the United States Supreme Court.(198)Then, in 1857, the Ohio judges boiled over. Again they insisted that the Legislature of 1845 had "no right to abridge or extinguish the exercise of this [taxing] power by a future legislature." And with all deference to the Supreme Court, "we do not . . . feel at liberty to depart from our own settled convictions." Judge Brinkerhoff, glaring at the Piqua Branch and Woolsey cases, remarked that the Supreme Court's reasoning had failed to satisfy *his* judgment; he thought the high Court should have an opportunity to reconsider the question.(199)

For some reason, that judgment of the Ohio court does not appear to have been appealed; and perhaps emboldened, the Ohio State Supreme Court again in 1859 interposed its sovereign powers and once more rejected the Supreme Court's ruling. Speaking for the Ohio court, Judge Gholson examined the relationship of State appellate tribunals to the U.S. Supreme Court, and had this to say: "As a practical question, as a question of policy, acquiescence is probably the wiser and better course. But the limited and qualified character of the appellate jurisdiction . . . does not countenance the idea . . . that Congress had in view a uniformity of decision upon questions arising under the Constitution and laws of the United States, and that the Supreme Court was the common arbiter for the decision of such questions." Comity, decorum, and respect, said Judge Gholson, are to be regarded, "but justice and right are entitled to a higher consideration."(200)

This time the rebellious decision of the Ohio judges was appealed, and Mr. Justice Wayne slapped it down in the brusque fashion of Father William. We have said it three times, he said for the Court, and that is enough: Your bank act of 1851 is unconstitutional. Judgment reversed.(201)

The same question of contract impairment figured in a long running battle between the Court and a group of Midwestern States in the matter of railway subsidies. Ordinarily, these grants to the on-reaching railways were financed by municipalities, eager to attract the rail lines, through the issuance of municipal bonds. As often as not, the gaudy hopes of the municipalities soon were reduced to ashes: The railroad never came, or it came ten miles away, or something happened, and the bonds were in time repudiated. In case after case, the contention was advanced that the bonds constituted a contract which no State or a sub-division of the State might validly impair, and in case after case the Supreme Court upheld this contention.(202) Yet a peculiar problem was created when the highest judiciary of a State had ruled the bonds not binding. In overruling the State courts, the Supreme Court in effect undertook to legislate for itself; the States fought back, and in time the States won. Iowa was a leader in this fight. When the United States Supreme Court, in *Gelpcke vs. Dubuque,* undertook to prevent the Iowa State court from reversing itself on the propriety of a bond issue, Iowa rebelliously defied the Court's mandate.(203) When the Supreme Court insisted that State courts "are destitute of all power to restrain either the process or proceedings in the national courts," Iowa demonstrated that she was not destitute at all.(204) When the Supreme Court termed the State injunctions mere "nullities," the State courts made them stick; and when the Court declared that neither State nor Federal tribunals "can impede or arrest any action the other may take, within the limits of its jurisdiction," the antagonized Midwestern States made it apparent that they could, and would, impede such Federal mandates when they deemed the writs palpably unconstitutional and wrong.(205) By 1888, the Supreme Court, obviously having had the worst of it, backed down.(206)

Notes

Go to top.

15

After the War

NOW, ONE of the most cherished criticisms advanced against the doctrine of State interposition is that if the theory had any validity prior to 1865, after that it had none. "The victory of the North killed State sovereignty," said Chase, in ripe satisfaction.(207) "The doctrine so long contended for," said a stern-visaged Bradley, "that the Federal Union was a mere compact of States, and that the States, if they chose, might annul or disregard the acts of the national Legislature, or might secede at their pleasure, and that the general government had no power to coerce them into submission to the Constitution, should be regarded as definitely overthrown."(208) And a contemporary critic has commented that "the denial of the right of secession by the unanswerable argument of superior force put an end to the claim that the American States were full-fledged and independent sovereignties."(209)

The unanswerable argument of superior force. . . . Is the argument in fact unanswerable?*The victory of the North. . . .* In a society that rests upon a fundamental written law, is law thus made? Those who espouse the theory that Appomattox put an end to State sovereignty—that Lee surrendered not only his army, but the Tenth Amendment also—must accept two propositions: First, that the victorious Northern States, which dictated the terms of the peace and dominated the Congress thereafter, were incredibly short-sighted and stupid; and second, that our basic law rests not upon a Constitution, but upon the cannon. Actually, there is a third proposition also: That the Supreme Court, no less than the Congress, has engaged since then in ninety years of palpable dumbshow and nonsense.

If the fundamental nature of the United States as a Union of States truly died at Appomattox, surely so prodigious a revolution of constitutional government would have been embedded in the Constitution by the victors. With Lee's surrender in the spring of 1865, the triumphant Northern States had total control of the Constitution in their hands. This was their magnificent opportunity, won in blood on a hundred battlefields, to consolidate their victory in a consolidated—a national—government. This was their chance to wipe out the last vestige of the States as sovereign political entities, or at the very least, to reduce the States to mere dependent satellites of Washington. The steps toward that end should have been clear to a child's eye: To provide for a President, elected by a majority of all the people, wholly removed from State lines; to establish a Congress composed of Representatives from Federal districts according to national (not State) population; to rewrite Article V, in order to make amendment of the Constitution a matter for the majority of the whole people; to skim through the Constitution, changing every plural reference to the United States to the singular; to wipe out the Tenth Amendment, and provide that all legislative and judicial powers, save only those that might be delegated to the States and their sub-divisions, were to be exercised thereafter by the Congress. Then, in fact, a *national* sovereignty would have been achieved, and the States would have been extinguished.

But what did the victors do? None of these things. Three amendments, and three only, were engrafted onto the Constitution in the years following the War. The Thirteenth (December, 1865) put an end to slavery. The Fourteenth

(July, 1868) provided, among other things, that no State could infringe the equal protection of the laws. The Fifteenth (March, 1870), demonstrating that the Fourteenth was not all-inclusive in the field of civil rights, provided that there should be no racial discrimination upon the right to vote.

That was all. Not a line was changed in the provisions dealing with the Presidency or with the Congress. Not a single timber in the fundamental structure of the basic law was removed. To be sure, the Fourteenth Amendment contained transient references to "insurrection or rebellion," but these subordinate provisions dealt with the holding of public office by officials who had served in the Confederate forces, or to the validity of certain debts. The inconsequential nature of these latter sections of the Fourteenth Amendment is attested by the fact that Corwin's massive annotation of the Constitution (1952) accords 207 pages to the first section of the Fourteenth, and seven pages only to all the rest. That the separateness of the States was not affected by the Reconstruction amendments was further demonstrated with ratification of the Seventeenth Amendment in 1913, which provided for the popular election of "two Senators from each State." If State sovereignty had ceased to exist, as nationalists profess to believe, this amendment would make no sense at all: There would no longer be any such thing, in the political sense, as a State.

The followers of Mr. Justice Chase cannot have it both ways—either sovereignty ceased to exist in the States (in which case, the act of extinguishment must be pointed out), or sovereignty remains there still. Sovereign power must lie somewhere. Obviously, it was not vested, after the War, in the Congress: The Congress cannot change the Constitution. Nor was it vested in the Court, as Mr. Justice Frankfurter has recently reminded us. Neither was the sovereign power shifted to the *whole people:* Article V was not touched. Marshall's critical "power to make and unmake" was left, after the war, just where it was before—in the hands of the States.

A society boasting of its enlightened civilization—its "democracy"—could not have it otherwise. The alternative is a law that rests on a guncotton bed. In this theory, we must look not to Philadelphia in 1787, but to Gettysburg in 1863. The Constitution, so conceived, has value only as wadding for a cannon ball. Armed might succeeds written law.

That it was not the intention of the victorious North to extinguish the States as sovereign entities was demonstrated not only by the wording of the Reconstruction amendments; it has been evidenced countless times in holdings of State and Federal courts down through the years. Let the question be asked: Why were the States so active in "interposing" prior to the War, and relatively so passive thereafter? The answer is perfectly plain: In the period immediately following the war, the major trend of the Supreme Court opinions, strange as it may seem, *was in the direction of States' rights.* And when, twenty-five years after the war, this trend began to shift toward a strengthening of the Federal government, *it was generally with the people's consent and approval.* Also, it may be submitted that the States have not been so wholly acquiescent and supine since the War as it is popularly believed.

Let us examine the first of these responses. An objective study will disclose that, far from advancing the cause of national supremacy, the Supreme Court of the United States, in its most significant opinions over the two decades from 1868 to 1888 repeatedly affirmed the sovereign powers of the individual States. This twenty-year period, extending from ratification of the Fourteenth Amendment to the beginning of Melville Fuller's tenure as Chief Justice, completed the swing of the pendulum that began with Marshall's death in 1835 and the advent of Taney as Chief Justice. Under Marshall, there had been a compulsive swing toward nationalism; this swung back to the States under Taney, but under the impetus of the war swung forward again. Then, under Chase and Waite, the pendulum once more swung in the States' favor. About the turn of the century, in the string of opinions that marked expansion of the commerce clause, the swing went back toward nationalism—and it has been swinging pretty much in that direction ever since.

During this period of 1868 to 1888, seventeen judges sat on the Supreme Court. They included judges good, bad, and indifferent —among them several whose names should not have been so thoroughly forgotten. In an uncertain period, sometimes the Court spoke uncertainly; but over the period as a whole, in a day of emotional exhaustion, these judges managed to restore a terribly needed vitality to the Constitution.

There was Samuel Nelson, a former Chief Justice of New York, named to the Court by Tyler in 1845, a man of strong will though scarcely a student of constitutional law. (He wrote only twenty-two opinions for the court on constitutional questions in his twenty-eight years on the bench.) A more colorful judge was Robert C. Grier, whose term ran from his appointment in 1846 to his reluctant resignation in 1870; he had a "soft and rosy nature," the New York *Tribune* once remarked, but actually he had a good deal of stamina also.

Next in line was the strong-willed and stubborn Nathan Clifford of Maine, who served on the Court from 1858 until 1881. A stout believer in States' rights, Judge Clifford was a man of unyielding convictions: He thought that Hayes had usurped the White House, and so thinking, refused to enter the White House while Hayes held office. Clifford was followed to the Court, in 1862, by Noah Haynes Swayne, an obscure Ohio attorney, who served for nearly twenty years; there is some legend that Lincoln had intended to appoint J. R. Swan, and got mixed up, but the story is probably apocryphal.

Another of Lincoln's appointees, only forty-six when he went on the bench, was Samuel Freeman Miller of Iowa, who was to write the famed Slaughterhouse opinion in 1873. The same year that saw Miller named to the

Court also witnessed the appointment of Lincoln's close personal friend, David Davis, a circuit judge in Illinois, who left the Court in 1877 to become United States Senator from Illinois. Davis, like Miller, was built along massive lines—it was once said of him that he had to be "surveyed" for a pair of trousers—but this corpulent body concealed a sharp mind and a trenchant pen.

The year following Davis's appointment saw the confirmation of Stephen J. Field of California, who surely must rank among the more fabulous personalities identified with the Court. If his last years on the Court were pathetic (like Grier, he had to be told to resign, but only after out-serving Marshall), his early career was impressive.

In 1864 came Taney's long expected death—he was eighty-seven—and with it the appointment of Salmon P. Chase of Ohio as Chief Justice. Chase, a former member of the Senate and Lincoln's Secretary of the Treasury, was a surprise appointment: He had not practiced actively for fourteen years, and generally was regarded (by himself, among others) as an aspirant for the Presidency; but he served, on the whole, quite notably.

Grant's two appointees of 1870—William Strong of Pennsylvania, and Joseph P. Bradley of New Jersey—are little remembered, and justifiably so. The former served for ten years, the latter for twenty-two; both were strong Union men, though Bradley occasionally took a narrow construction of the Fourteenth Amendment. Neither is there much to recall of Ward Hunt of New York, named to the court in 1873. He served actively for only four years, but then, the victim of a paralytic stroke, languished on the Court for five more years until Judge Davis, now a member of the Senate, sponsored a special retirement bill for him.

With the death of Chase in 1873, Morrison R. Waite, white-bearded, black-browed, succeeded to the office of Chief Justice. An Ohioan with no previous judicial experience and little reputation as a lawyer, he was hotly assailed then and has been coolly criticized by centralist historians ever since. But it was largely Waite's remarkably firm hand that kept northern abolitionists from having their own way with the Fourteenth Amendment, and in time he was to write the Court's opinion in the Granger cases, sustaining—for a while—the States' police power in the field of rate-fixing on public-service corporations. Waite deserves better treatment than Court criticism has accorded him.

Waite was followed on the Court, in 1877, by John Marshall Harlan of Kentucky. He, too, had no previous judicial experience, but in his thirty-four years on the bench, he set a notable record. Then came William B. Woods of Georgia, in 1880, first Southerner on the Court since Campbell in 1852, but actually a transplanted Yankee: Like the abolitionist Stanley Matthews, whose nomination to the Court was barely confirmed in 1881, he had served in the Union army as an officer from Ohio. Then came Horace Gray, succeeding Clifford in 1881, long a member of the Supreme Judicial Court of Massachusetts, a stern martinet of a man, six feet four inches tall, "strict and punctilious," a believer in strong national government.(210)

Last of the judges of 1868-88 were Samuel Blatchford of New York, who came on the bench in 1882 with fifteen years' experience behind him as a Federal judge specializing in maritime and patent law,(211) and the black-bearded Mississippian with the lovely rolling name of Lucius Quintus Cincinnatus Lamar.

These seventeen men sat on the bench in a period in which State sovereignty was supposed to have been killed off. But was a *national* supremacy broadly asserted by the Court or conceded by the States? Precisely the reverse was true.

It is notable, in this regard, that in the period of sixty-four years, from Marshall's ruling in *McCulloch vs. Maryland* in 1803 [see note], to the Court's opinion in *Ex Parte Garland* in 1867, only four acts of Congress were held unconstitutional.(212) But in the brief span of four years, 1870-73, no fewer than six acts of Congress were voided. These blows at *national* power began with the first Legal Tender case. This arose in Kentucky in 1860, when a Mrs. Hepburn borrowed $11,250 from one Henry Griswold. At the time the loan was made, only gold and silver were legal tender for payment of private debts, but in 1862, Congress authorized the issuance of $150,000,000 in United States Notes. When Mrs. Hepburn subsequently attempted to pay off her loan in the new Treasury notes, Griswold refused to accept them and suit resulted. To the immense chagrin of President Grant, Chase and three associates (there were two vacancies on the Court) held that Congress had no authority, under the Constitution, to enlarge its power to coin money into a power to make paper currency legal tender.(213) Scarcely had the Court stunned Congress on this major law before it slapped down the Congress on a minor statute: In 1870, the Court voided an act of 1867 which oddly made it a misdemeanor (unrelated to revenue laws) for any person to sell a combination of naphtha and illuminating oil.(214) This was swiftly followed by a ruling in a New York case, in which the Supreme Court justices upheld New York State judges in refusing to approve the removal of a certain case from State to Federal jurisdiction, pursuant to an act of 1863.(215)

The following year came another severe blow against national authority: Between 1864 and 1867, Congress had adopted several laws levying an income tax.(216) In Massachusetts, a county probate judge, J. M. Day, paid his tax under protest, and then sued for its recovery. His contention was that Congress had no power to impose a tax upon State officials. When the case reached the Supreme Court, a solid majority of the Court agreed. Six years after State sovereignty was said to have been extinguished at Appomattox, Judge Nelson said this for the Court:

It is a familiar rule of construction of the Constitution of the Union, that the sovereign powers vested in the State governments by their respective constitutions remained unaltered and unimpaired, except so far as they were granted to the government of the United States. . . . The government of the United States claims no powers which are not granted to it by the Constitution, and the powers actually granted must be such as are expressly given, or given by necessary implication. . . .(217)

The two governments, said the Court, are "on an equality," and if the States could not tax Federal officials, which had been already decided,(218) neither could the Federal government tax State officials.(219) The States, within the limits of their reserved powers, said Nelson, "are as independent of the general government as that government within its sphere is independent of the States."

Just one year later, in 1872, the Court again acted summarily upon an act of Congress. A vengeful law, aimed at confiscation of property owned by Southerners during the War, was ruled unconstitutional.(220)

Finally, completing this group of half-a-dozen blows against nationalist expansion, the Court in 1873 refused to sanction a Federal tax that was imposed, in effect, upon the city of Baltimore. "Of all the burdens imposed upon mankind," said Judge Hunt, "that of grinding taxation is the most cruel." And more than fifty years after a Federalist Court under Marshall had chastised Maryland in a tax case, a States' rights Court under Chase came to Maryland's rescue.

This is not to say, of course, that every major decision in the postwar period went in the States' favor. Of course not. There was, notably, a case from Wisconsin that arose when an eighteen-year-old boy, Edward Tarble, falsified his age and his name and enlisted in the army. His father obtained a writ of habeas corpus from a State commissioner, who directed that the youth be released. On appeal to the State Supreme Court, this judgment was affirmed. The recruiting officer then appealed to the United States Supreme Court, and Judge Field delivered himself of some remarks to the very State court that twelve years earlier, in the Booth case, had defied the Federal tribunal:

There are within the territorial limits of each State two governments, restricted in their spheres of action, but independent of each other, and supreme within their respective spheres. Each has its separate departments; each has its distinct laws, and each has its own tribunals for their enforcement. . . . The two governments in each State stand in their respective spheres of action in the same independent relation to each other, except in one particular, that they would if their authority embraced distinct territories. That particular consists in the supremacy of the authority of the United States when any conflict arises between the two governments.(221)

Notably, Chief Justice Chase dissented from his brothers' view. In his opinion, there was no doubt that State courts had a right to issue writs of habeas corpus for inquiry into the jurisdiction of a Federal court over a prisoner. And he was still more convinced, if possible, that State courts had a right to inquire, through habeas corpus, into the detention of a citizen held merely by a Federal official, without the sentence of a court. To deny such powers to a State court, he said, "is to deny the right to protect the citizen by habeas corpus against arbitrary imprisonment in a large class of cases."

But the majority's holding in Tarble's case was the exception in this period, not the rule. Time after time, in major cases, States' rights prevailed. In *Thomson vs. Union Pacific,* the Court upheld the right of States to tax a railroad built with Federal funds.(222) In *Osborne vs. Mobile,* the Court approved a State license tax on express companies doing business partly outside a State.(223) When a woman in Illinois contended that she had a right, under the Fourteenth Amendment, to practice law in State courts, the Supreme Court affirmed the power of Illinois to legislate on such matters for itself.(224) When a murderer in California was sentenced to death on proceedings that stemmed from an information instead of an indictment, the Court held this was the exclusive business of California.(225) Similarly, Pennsylvania was upheld in a law suppressing the manufacture of oleomargarine;(226) Iowa and Kansas were upheld in State liquor laws, (227) and Mississippi was affirmed in a State act creating a railroad commission.(228) Why should the States have interposed? Their high place was repeatedly affirmed.

Notes

Go to top.

16

The Reconstruction Cases

BUT THE most significant cases in this period, of course, were those in which the Supreme Court construed the newly imposed Reconstruction Amendments. And of these, the most vital to the cause of States' rights was the Court's ruling of 1873 in the famed Slaughterhouse cases.(229) Warren has written of this decision that it "profoundly affected the course of the future history of the country."(230) It was "one of the glorious landmarks of American law."(231) The case arose when a corrupt, carpet-bag legislature of Louisiana awarded a twenty-five-year monopoly on the operation of a slaughterhouse in New Orleans to a single company. Independent butchers protested that a thousand men had thus been deprived of their right to engage in business; they had been denied, in the language of the new amendment, "equal protection of the laws"; their privileges as United States citizens had been abridged, and their property had been taken from them without due process of law.

But in April, 1873, nearly five years after the Fourteenth Amendment had been declared ratified, the Court ringingly held that the amendment was not intended "to destroy the main features of the general system" of constitutional government. The amendment was not designed to bring within the jurisdiction of the Court "the entire domain of civil rights heretofore belonging to the States." To thus enlarge the scope of the Fourteenth Amendment would be to make the Court itself "a perpetual censor upon all legislation of the States, on the civil rights of their own citizens, with authority to nullify such as it did not approve as consistent with these rights." This responsibility the Court was not prepared to accept.

The "great source of power in this country," said Miller for the Court, lies in "the *people of the States.*" They have reserved unto themselves, he said, in their respective States, broad police powers; and upon the preservation of these powers, in State hands, "depends the security of social order" and "the enjoyment of private and social life." To seize these powers away from the States would be to "fetter and degrade" the State governments, and "radically to change the whole theory of the relations of the State and Federal governments to each other, and of both these governments to the people."

Within a period of a few years followed five other cases in which the Supreme Court continued to uphold and defend the rights of the States under the Reconstruction amendments. The opinions are important to us today for the strong light they shed on what the amendments meant then, when they were freshly adopted and their intended effect on State and Federal relationships was clear.

In the first of these, the Court voided parts of the Civil Rights Enforcement Act of 1870; the judges saw it as their duty to "annul [the act's] encroachments upon the reserved powers of the States and the people."(232) In the second, the Court took a level-headed look at the indictment of a group of white men who had been charged with conspiring to prevent two Negroes from voting in Louisiana. The right to vote, said the Court, is a right that comes from the State; it is not a right subject to regulation as a right of "citizens of the United States."(233) In *United States vs. Harris,* the Court threw out the first anti-lynch law to come from Congress. The so-called Ku Klux Act of 1871 was not warranted by the Reconstruction Amendments: Congress could pass laws to inhibit abridgments of privileges and immunities *by a State,* but it could not constitutionally legislate against ordinary crimes of violence.(234) In the Civil Rights cases, decided in October of 1883, the entire Civil Rights Act of 1875 was thrown out. This act had undertaken to provide a fine of $500 to $1,000, or a jail sentence of thirty days to one year, on any person convicted of refusing a Negro equal access to a public inn, conveyance, theater, or other place of public amusement. The cases originated in Kansas, California,

Missouri; and Tennessee. But the rules laid down by a theater owner for his audience, or by an inn keeper for his guests, are his own personal business, said the Court. Congress cannot validly encroach upon this reserved domain.

Finally, attention may be directed to *Barbier vs. Connolly,* in 1885, in which the Court upheld a municipal ordinance in San Francisco which prohibited laundry work at night. The ordinance was palpably directed at Chinese laundry operators. But the Court held that in its guarantee of civil rights, the Fourteenth Amendment aimed only at such civil rights as these—the right of all men to equal access to the courts, to enforcement of their contracts, to equal protection of their property, and equal punishment for crime. The amendment was not designed, said the Court,

to interfere with the power of the State, sometimes termed its "police power," to prescribe regulations to promote the health, peace, morals, education, and good order of the people.(235)

In refusing thus to intervene in California's local affairs, the Court was not making new law. It was adhering to what was, for a time at least, solidly established policy. Forty years earlier, in upholding a port inspection law adopted by New York, the Court had assumed a position it was pleased to call "impregnable":

That a State has the same undeniable and unlimited jurisdiction over all persons and things, within its territorial limits, as any foreign nation, where that jurisdiction is not surrendered or restrained by the Constitution of the United States.(236)

The internal police powers of a State, never having been surrendered or delegated, therefore could not be restrained by Federal authority; in these fields, the authority of the State was "complete, unqualified, and exclusive." Taney had said the same thing, at about the same time, in the famed Charles River Bridge case: "We cannot . . . by legal intendments and mere technical reasoning, take away from [the States] any portion of that power over their own internal police and improvement, which is so necessary to their well-being and prosperity."(237)

But in time, of course, the Court was to take the power away. Taney was dead then, God rest him.

Notes

Go to top.

17

The Commerce Clause (Commenced)

THESE WELL-FOUNDED doctrines of State power were upheld for a time not only as to "civil rights" cases growing out of the Reconstruction Amendments, but also in a wide variety of other actions in which, long after the War, States both North and South asserted their sovereign authority. Notable among these were the Granger cases, in which the Court approved State laws in Illinois, Wisconsin, Minnesota, and Iowa fixing freight and passenger rates on railroads and fees at grain elevators.(238) Some of Marshall's old rules upon impairment of contracts tumbled in cases from Massachusetts and Mississippi.(239)

But in the final decade of the nineteenth century the judicial trend that had been swinging toward the States began to turn back toward an expansion of Federal powers. State immigration statutes toppled; sweeping new authority was vested in Congress as to the issuance of currency and the construction of internal improvements; in a series of opinions in the 1880's, the Supreme Court sharply curtailed the effectiveness of the Eleventh Amendment, by sanctioning suits against States for enforcement of obligations under bond issues.(240)

In no field, however, was this swing of the pendulum more significant than in the construction given by the Court to the "commerce clause." The story is too well known, perhaps, to justify very extended review, yet no account of State and Federal conflicts, or of the growth of judicial supremacy over the States, would be complete without some chronicle of the melancholy tale. Congress and the Court, working in beautiful harmony, together snatched from the States and the people almost the last vestige of local control over local affairs. And they did it under the guise of that brief clause in Article I of the Constitution, vesting Congress with power "to regulate commerce . . . among the several States."

It was an insidious process, conducted with the care of the cat that stalks her prey—now creeping forward, now pausing to sniff the air; now advancing, now lying still as the bird takes alarm; then edging forward again, and so, step by inexorable step, moving to the ultimate seizure. Probably it is too late now for the States to do much about it. But perhaps a backward look might even yet save them from ending up like Prokofieff's duck, quacking feebly from inside the wolf.

In the beginning, it was thought that "commerce" meant simply *the act of transporting goods.* Commerce began when the thing transported moved to a carrier for transportation.(241)The power to regulate such commerce among the States, in this uncomplicated era, was viewed primarily as a power vested in Congress to see to it that no hindrance was placed in the way of such transportation.

But in time, a second gateway opened up: The original doctrine grew into a concept that the clause applied not only to transportation, *but also to regulation of the thing transported.* If these things had, in themselves, "some harmful or deleterious property," Congress could exercise its power to regulate as a power to prohibit.(242)

The second gateway gave way to a third: Congress had power to regulate not only commerce, and the commodity in commerce, but also to regulate *the conditions under which the commodity or thing were manufactured*—and the conditions under which the commodity could be bought and sold.

In recent years, even that concept has proved inadequate to the aggrandizement of centralist power. The theory now is that should "the wells of commerce go dry," as Hughes once observed, the Congress has broad power to fill them up again—that is, to encourage, stimulate, and foster commerce among the States.(243) Let us trace some of the more significant milestones on this road to nationalist power.

As early as 1876, the Court began to modify some of the stout assertions it had made in the Miln case (1837) in behalf of State inspection laws.(244) The brave powers given to the States in the Granger cases were abridged within a decade after their promulgation.(245) Then, in 1890, came what one critic termed "the most crushing blow against the rights of States which has ever been dealt by that tribunal"—the Court's ruling that States could not exercise their reserved powers against the importation and sale of goods in their "original package."(246) What this meant, in immediate application, was that prohibition States could not prevent the importation and sale of liquor, but the doctrine opened a wide doorway for other laws to follow.

These major strides toward national authority were accompanied, to be sure, by an occasional backward step and a bow to the States. Thus, certain aspects of mining and manufacture were held—temporarily—to be not a part of interstate commerce.(247) In the first major case under the Sherman Act, the Court held, 5-4, that sugar interests were not subject to the law's restraint. The Court, indeed, was a little shocked that this should even be suggested: "Slight reflection will show that if the national power extends to all contracts and combinations in manufacture, agriculture, mining, and other productive industries, whose ultimate results may affect external commerce, comparatively little of business operations and affairs would be left for State control."(248) The Court, as events were to prove, was to give this apprehension very "slight reflection" indeed.

Yet for a time, the eagle's wings were clipped. Most astonishing of all the decisions in this period, unfavorable to national authority, was the Court's stunning decision in 1895, by which it invalidated the whole of an income tax law adopted by the Cleveland administration.(249) Actually, it is a little unfair to say that "the Court" voided the law: One man, Justice George Shiras, shaped the Constitution by changing his not very brilliant mind. The result was that the century-old precedent of *Hylton vs. United States* (1796) (250) vanished in a twinkling, and the shocked country won a clear view of the vagaries of judicial legislation. Justice White, dissenting, offered the interesting argument—and it is quite pertinent to the point of this essay—that the failure of the people to amend their Constitution in this hundred-year period, in order to overthrow the Hylton decision and prohibit an income tax"—was practically a ratification of that policy, and an acquiescence in the settled rule of interpretation theretofore adopted." William Jennings Bryan noted furiously that "the income tax was not unconstitutional when it was passed; it was not unconstitutional when it went before the Supreme Court for the first time; it did not become unconstitutional until one judge changed his mind, and we cannot be expected to know when a judge will change his mind."(251) But though scores of Congressmen and jurists protested strenuously, it took the Sixteenth Amendment to undo the opinion.

The same session of 1895 that brought invalidation of the income tax saw many a States' Righter outraged by the Court's ruling in the Debs case, in which the Court approved the use of both Federal troops and Federal injunctions to put down a major strike.(252) The months just preceding the Debs case also had seen the States offended by opinions outlawing statutes from Texas and Maryland relating to rate regulation of railroads.(253) These rulings were so drastic in their implications that Field protested the Court was palpably invading the reserved authority of the States. Other observers thought so, too: The Democratic National Convention of 1896 adopted a plank denouncing this "new and highly dangerous form of oppression by which Federal judges, in contempt of the law of the States and rights of citizens, become at once legislators, judges and executioners." In Oregon, Governor Sylvester Pernoyer condemned a system of government "by the plausible sophistries of John Marshall" as a government in which "a judicial oligarchy has supplanted the Constitution."

For the States there was worse to come. In 1896, the Court took another big step toward nationalism, when it sanctioned Federal condemnation of the Gettysburg Battlefield for a national cemetery as a necessary and proper action under the general welfare clause.(254)

Then a riptide of opinions began to wash away State powers. Congress helped. Following the basic Interstate Commerce Act of 1887, the Congress had piled onto the statute books the Safety Appliance Act of 1893. Now it added the Automatic Coupler Act of 1903, the Hours of Service Acts of 1907 and 1916, the Employers Liability Acts of 1905 and 1908, the Hepburn Act of 1906 (which superseded all State laws limiting recovery for loss of goods intransportation), the Boiler Inspection Acts of 1911 and 1915, the Plant Quarantine Act of 1912, and ultimately the Adamson Act of 1916, which undertook to fix wages and hours for railway employees.

With the single exception of the Employers Liability Act (the so-called "Yellow Dog Act"),(255) each of these bold ventures into the "regulation of commerce" won the Court's approval. Thus, with the Court's blessing, the second gateway of the commerce clause swung wide: Congress no longer found itself limited to regulating mere transportation—it was invited to regulate the *things* transported. In swift succession, the Supreme Court approved laws that banned the interstate shipment of such evils as lottery tickets,(256) impure food,(257) narcotics,(258) prostitutes,(259) and an infinite variety of other goods held to be inherently evil—diseased nursery stock, moths and plant lice; stolen autos, prize-fight films, and game birds taken in violation of State law.

This deliberate widening of Federal authority was accompanied, in another field of law, by a corresponding restriction of State powers: In a series of cases, the Supreme Court sustained suits brought against State officials to restrain them from enforcing State laws alleged to be unconstitutional. Oregon was estopped from enforcing an act governing the sale of land; North Carolina, Missouri, Texas, and Nebraska ran into Federal injunctions on their railroad laws; South Carolina was snubbed on a dispensary statute; Michigan and Indiana saw their tax-assessment statutes effectively nullified. These cases came to an angry boil in March of 1908, when the Supreme Court upheld the punishment imposed by a Federal court upon Edward T. Young, Attorney General of Minnesota, for his temerity in attempting to test a State rate law against a railroad.(260) The Federal Circuit Court had ordered Young (and in effect, had ordered Minnesota) not to bring such a suit, but Young persisted and it cost him a $100 fine. He refused to pay, and was taken in custody by a United States marshal. Then a writ of habeas corpus, issued by the Supreme Court itself, brought the matter up for review. A majority of theCourt, through Justice Peckham, held that Minnesota's rate law was "unconstitutional on its face," and therefore, that Young's action in bringing suit was void. Justice Harlan interposed a thirty-five-page dissenting opinion, in which he commented that the majority's view, if long sustained, "would inaugurate a new era in the American judicial system, and in the relations of the national and State governments."(261) It would enable subordinate Federal courts, said Harlan, "to supervise and control the official action of the States as if they were 'dependencies' or provinces," and it would leave the States of the Union "in a condition of inferiority never dreamed of when the Constitution was adopted or when the Eleventh Amendment was made a part of the supreme law of the land."

Many of the States quite agreed with Justice Harlan. The Nebraska Legislature adopted a strong resolution demanding that Congress pass remedial legislation to curb the Court's mandates. And Congress, in 1910, complied.

But the Court was unmoved. In 1914, in the Shreveport case, it cracked down again on State regulation of railroads with a decision so drastic that the Attorneys General of forty-two States intervened—futilely—against the encroachment.(262) The Court opened the vast Pandora's box of public power, when it authorized Federal sale of excess electric power resulting from navigation projects.(263) It started upon the trail of Federal regulation of natural gas.(264)

Then—gently at first, but irresistibly—Court and Congress opened still a third gateway in the Commerce Clause: Having established the power of Congress to regulate transportation and the things transported, the judges turned to regulation of the terms and conditions by which commodities are manufactured. It was not an easy turning. When a test of the first Child Labor Law came along, the Court held, a little uneasily—perhaps a little guiltily—that it had gone far enough.(265) In this case, the father of two teen-aged boys, employed in a mill in Charlotte, N.C., brought suit to prevent enforcement of the Federal act of 1916 prohibiting child labor. A Federal District Court held the act unconstitutional, and on appeal, the Supreme Court agreed. It was one thing, said the Court, to prohibit interstate shipment of things that were evils in themselves—diseased plants, prostitutes, lottery tickets, and the like—but cotton goods were not inherently evil: The Congress had gone too far; it had over-reached its authority. And the Court, through Justice Day, observed:

In interpreting the Constitution, it must never be forgotten that the Nation is made up of States to which are entrusted the powers of local government. And to them and to the people, the powers not expressly delegated to the national government are reserved. . . .The far-reaching result of upholding the act cannot be more plainly indicated than by pointing out that if Congress can thus regulate matters entrusted to local authority by prohibition of the movement of commodities in interstate commerce, all freedom of commerce will be at an end, and the powers of the States over local matters may be eliminated, and thus our system of government be practically destroyed.

Justice Holmes (joined by McKenna, Brandeis, and Clarke) filed a ringing dissent. "I should have thought," said he, "that if we were to introduce our own moral conceptions where in my opinion they do not belong, this was preeminently a case for upholding the exercise of all its powers by the United States." But the Court, Holmes asserted, had no right to intrude its judgment upon questions of policy or morals. That was the prerogative of Congress. And if the Congress chose to regard child labor as an evil, Holmes did not see how a Court that had sanctioned a ban against strong drink could rule against "the product of ruined lives."

In time, to be sure, Holmes' views were to prevail. But in 1918, Federal prohibition of child labor was more than a majority of the Court would accept. Yet the Packers and Stockyards Act of 1921 met the Court's approval,(266) and the Grain Futures Act of 1922 seemed clearly within the powers of Congress.(267)

Notes

Go to top.

18
Interlude in a Speakeasy

IF THE flow of the commerce doctrine may be left in a literary bayou for a few pages, attention may be directed abruptly toward an entirely separate issue that resulted in sharp conflict between State and Federal authority in the period under consideration. This was, of course, the matter of national prohibition.

It is an everlasting testimony to the sincerity, the optimism, and the blind idiocy of man that no fewer than forty-six of the forty-eight sovereign States ratified the Eighteenth Amendment as proposed, late in 1917, by the Sixty-fifth Congress. Only Connecticut and Rhode Island kept their heads. The other States, losing theirs, agreed that after January of 1920, "the manufacture, sale, or transportation of intoxicating liquors," was to be prohibited.

But scarcely had the long dark night begun before a thirsty people, suddenly appalled, began to resist the amendment just adopted. Twenty thousand persons, spurred on by the late Mr. Mencken, paraded through the streets of Baltimore; another ten thousand participated in a protest before the Capitol in Washington.(268) Bootleggers and rumrunners came forward, dutifully, to perform those patriotic services for which Nature had fitted them. In New York, an Association Against the Prohibition Amendment was chartered, with an announced purpose "to make the Eighteenth Amendment forever inoperative." Rhode Island made the mistake of testing the Amendment, only to be told that no State could undertake "to defeat or thwart" its provisions. (269) Eminent attorneys urged Connecticut to take a still bolder position— that not even forty-six ratifying States and the Supreme Court could take from sovereign Connecticut the power reserved inalienably by her people to engage, intrastate, in the distillation and sale of whiskey.(270) The late Owen Brewster, then Governor of Maine, encouraged the opposition: "Centralization and usurpation have been the keynote of American government in the decade that is just passed."(271) So, too, did New Jersey's Governor A. Harry Moore in his inaugural address of 1926: "'An indissoluble Union of indestructible States,'" he said, quoting Chase in *Texas vs. White,* "is rapidly becoming an indissoluble Union of impotent States. . . . Let 'restoration of States' rights' be our watch-word."(272)

The amendment had given Congress and the States concurrent power to enforce prohibition. New York in 1923 exercised her sovereign powers by a form of nullification in reverse: New York repealed her State prohibition enforcement act, and blandly left Federal authorities to carry on as best they could. The United States Attorney for the Southern District of New York termed this unkind action "the hardest blow the enforcement of the Eighteenth Amendment has received." And so uninterested was New York in enforcing the plain language of the United States Constitution, that speakeasies multiplied as assiduously as rabbits. By 1929, Manhattan police matter-of-factly reported they had counted 32,000 speakeasies, but "might have missed a few."

Throughout this period, as Alfred E. Smith was to remark later, the citizens who continued to fight prohibition were "referred to as Nullificationists, as enemies of the Constitution, as people that wanted to destroy organized and properly constituted government." But in actual fact, in the view of Senator Herbert Lehman, who was then Governor of New York, these foes of prohibition were in reality "devoted and patriotic men and women [who carried on a fifteen-year struggle] against sumptuary legislation which at no time represented the uncontrolled sentiment of a majority of the people of this country." The amendment's ultimate repeal in 1933, said Mr. Lehman, showed "the force of intelligent, well-considered public opinion, aroused by the abuses and failures of a statute that never commended itself to the reasoned judgment of the people." Repeal, to Mr. Lehman, represented victory in a fight "to regain that balance between State and Nation which is guaranteed by the Constitution of the United States, and to substitute temperance for hypocritical and unenforceable prohibition."

Noting Mr. Lehman's words, Virginia's Senator A. Willis Robertson, summed up the point here sought to be made: "Will the gentleman not recognize that the decree demanding that instead of providing separate but equal schools for the races, the Southern States must mix them all together, is in our eyes 'sumptuary' legislation of the worst sort, and that such action does not commend itself to the reasoned judgment of the people in our States?"

And it may also be suggested that some of the South's critics, now most articulate in denouncing resistance to a ruling of the Court, were themselves most active thirty years ago in vigorously resisting not merely the Court's interpretation of the Constitution, but the Constitution itself. In their eyes, then, national prohibition was an unwarranted and wrongful encroachment upon individual liberties. It is perhaps needless to pursue the parallel.

Notes

Go to top.

19

The Commerce Clause (Continued)

DURING the 1920's, the Supreme Court under Taft moved first forward, now slightly to the rear, and then forward again, in sanctioning gradual enlargement of the powers of Congress under the commerce clause. But it was not until about the time that Taft died, in 1930, and Hughes returned to the Court as Chief Justice, that the death struggle began between the State and Federal authority.

For a few years, the tide of battle flowed to the States. The first major test of Roosevelt's depression measures came with the National Industrial Recovery Act of June, 1933, which set up some seven-hundred codes of fair competition by which hours, wages, customer relations, and collective bargaining would become subject to Federal control. Under one of these codes—the Live Poultry Code for New York City—a small slaughterhouse in Brooklyn fell into the hands of Federal authority. Its sin, among others, was that the Messrs. Schechter had sold "an unfit chicken" to a customer.

Hughes himself spoke for a unanimous Court. True enough, he said, times were desperately bad—but "extraordinary conditions do not create or enlarge constitutional power."(273) In the Court's view, the act went far beyond the limits set down by the Tenth Amendment; the act not only usurped a power not delegated to Congress—it also undertook to delegate that power to private hands. It was "delegation running riot," as Cardozo remarked in a concurring opinion.(274) Plainly, in the Court's view, the power to regulate commerce extended only to actions that affected the current of commerce; and in the case of Schechter's chickens, in Brooklyn, "the flow in interstate commerce had ceased." Hughes went on to cite what he called "the necessary and well-established distinction between direct and indirect effects" on interstate commerce; and where an effect is "merely indirect," such transactions "remain within the domain of State power." If this were not so, he said reflectively, "the Federal authority would embrace practically all the activities of the people, and the authority of the State over its domestic concerns would exist only by sufferance of the Federal government." So saying, the Court gazed upon Mr. Schechter's chickens and slew the Blue Eagle. It was a memorable decision.

Shortly thereafter came a second major test of the New Deal program. In 1933, Congress had passed the Agricultural Adjustment Act, which undertook, among other things, to levy a tax upon cotton processing for the benefit of cotton farmers who would plow under their surplus crops. When the receivers for the Hoosac Mills declined to pay the tax, and contested the act's constitutionality, the Supreme Court in 1936 held the law void. (275) The act, said Roberts for the Court, was no more than an attempt to take money from processors and bestow it upon the farmers; it was an attempt to regulate production, "a matter beyond the powers delegated to the Federal government," and hence in violation of the Tenth Amendment. To accept Mr. Roosevelt's construction, said the Court, would require that "every provision and every fair implication from [the Constitution] . . . be subverted, the independence of the individual States obliterated, and the United States converted into a central government exercising uncontrolled police power in every State of the Union, superseding all local control or regulation of the affairs or concerns of the States."(276)

It was brave language. But perhaps the States were so pleased by the outcome of the case that they failed to penetrate some dicta that Roberts put forth, foggily but firmly, on the matter of the "general welfare" clause. It was the government's position that the AAA was justified by the power vested in Congress "to lay and collect taxes, . . . to pay the debts and provide for the common defense and general welfare of the United States." What about this clause? Roberts remarked, with a great gentleness, that students of the Constitution for many years had disagreed about the meaning of the welfare clause. Madison had asserted that the clause added nothing—it referred only to the enumerated powers of Congress, and the power to tax did not extend beyond these. Hamilton, on the other hand, had maintained that the general welfare clause conferred a power separate and distinct from the enumerated powers—that Congress was limited in its power to tax and spend only by what Congress deemed to be the general welfare. Justice Story, observed Roberts, had espoused the Hamiltonian position in his *Commentaries,* but until now, the view had not been "authoritatively accepted" by the Court. Taking a breath, he continued in a fateful paragraph:

We shall not review the writings of public men and commentators or discuss the legislative practice. Study of all these leads us to conclude that the reading advocated by Justice Story is the correct one. While, therefore, the power to tax is not unlimited, its confines are set in the clause which confers it, and not in those of Section 8 which bestow and define the legislative powers of the Congress. It results that the power of Congress to authorize expenditure of public moneys for public purposes is not limited by the direct grants of legislative power found in the Constitution.[(277)](#)

Roberts interjected a few tactful qualifiers: The power invoked by Congress must be truly for the general welfare—that is, the national welfare—and could not affect merely local matters. It could not be exercised, he added in a horrified afterthought, "for the destruction of local self-government in the States." Not even Hamilton had suggested that, nor had Story ever countenanced the thought. After all, "it hardly seems necessary to reiterate that ours is a dual form of government," in which the Federal government may exercise only such powers as are expressly conferred upon it.

The qualifiers are forgotten now. In the moment Roberts' opinion came down, constitutional limitations dissolved into the shapeless mass of a sand castle on a beach, slapped by a passing roll of foam.

But just as a tide stays at its peak for a brief hour, so the Court was to hand down one more decision that limited, for a few years, the expanding Federal authority. In 1935, Congress had passed the Bituminous Coal Conservation Act, in which regulation was attempted of the wages and hours of miners, and the price of soft coal. In [Carter vs. Carter Coal Company](#), on May 18, 1936, the Court in a 5-4 decision applied its Schechter doctrine in reverse: Coal at the mine had not yet entered the current of commerce; it was still at rest. Speaking for the majority, Sutherland agreed that the aims of protecting the health of miners and the comfort of the people doubtless were "objects of great worth." But he asked himself, "are they an end, the attainment of which has been committed by the Constitution to the Federal government?" He could not agree that they were. Once more, valiant to the end, the Court majority called attention to "the ruling and firmly established principle"

that the powers which the general government may exercise are only those specifically enumerated in the Constitution, and such implied powers as are necessary and proper to carry into effect the enumerated powers.(278)

And Sutherland went on, arguing publicly with the dictum Roberts had laid down just a few months before, dealing with the welfare clause.

The proposition, often advanced and as often discredited, that the power of the Federal government inherently extends to purposes affecting the Nation as a whole with which the States severally cannot deal or cannot adequately deal, and the related notion that Congress, entirely apart from those powers delegated by the Constitution, may enact laws to promote the general welfare, have never been accepted but always definitely rejected by this court.

In plain truth, this very "notion" had been embraced by Roberts in the AAA case, and the reign of Sutherland's "ruling principle" of the Tenth Amendment was fast ending. Sutherland could add only a valedictory, and he was done: "The States were before the Constitution," he said defiantly. Their legislative powers "antedated the Constitution." In all the powers they had reserved to themselves, "they are supreme."

Every journey to a forbidden end begins with the first step; and the danger of such a step by the Federal government in the direction of taking over the powers of the States is that the end of the journey may find the States so despoiled of their powers, or—what may amount to the same thing—so relieved of their responsibilities which possession of the powers necessarily enjoins, as to reduce them to little more than geographical subdivisions of the national domain.(279)

That was the last of the 5-4 rulings by the conservative majority among the nine old men. "This decision was the high-water mark," Roberts later remarked.(280) Thereafter the tide ebbed. The *Carter* decision came down in May of 1936. In February of 1937, Mr. Roosevelt brought forth his court-packing scheme. He proposed that any judge who had reached the age of seventy, and had served ten years on the court, be retired on full pay—but if any judge failed or refused to retire, a new judge should be appointed, up to a total court of fifteen. It was an invitation to six of the nine judges—all but Roberts, Stone, and Cardozo—to get off the bench. Barely three months elapsed before the Court reached another landmark decision, this time in a series of cases upholding the National Labor Relations Act of 1935. But the Court that had stood 5-4 for States' rights in May of 1936, stood 5-4 for Federal authority in April of 1937. Now the Court jettisoned the doctrines of the *Carter* case. "How can it be maintained," asked Hughes, waggling an indignant beard, "that industrial labor relations constitute a forbidden field that Congress may not enter?" To be sure, the authority of the Federal government "may not be pushed to such an extreme as to destroy the distinction . . . between commerce 'among the several States' and the internal concerns of a State," for the distinction between things national and things local "is vital to the maintenance of our Federal system." But labor relations within a steel company—or within a clothing company or a trailer manufacturing company—did "affect commerce." Labor strife could in fact impose a burden that might obstruct commerce. Hughes did not propose that the Court "shut our eyes to the plainest facts of our national life, and . . . deal with the question of direct and indirect effects in an intellectual vacuum."(281)

McReynolds put in a despairing dissent. Van Devanter, Sutherland, and Butler joined him. The majority's doctrine was subversive of States' rights. It would mean "serious impairment of the very foundations of our federated system." But the Court was shifting its direction. One month later, on May 24, the Court through Cardozo took the greatest step yet toward expansion of Federal powers in approval of the Social Security Act of 1935, The tax thus imposed, said the majority, was imposed for the general welfare—and the general welfare was for Congress to define without the Court's intervention.

Again McReynolds raised his voice: What was it that Chase had said in *Texas vs. White* in 1869? "The Constitution looks to an indestructible Union composed of indestructible States." But what was the effect of the majority's opinion? It "opens the way for practical annihilation of this theory, and no cloud of words or ostentatious parade of irrelevant statistics should be permitted to obscure that fact."(282) Sutherland and Van Devanter also dissented: The majority's ruling would deny to the States "that supremacy and freedom from external interference in respect to [their] affairs which the Constitution contemplates." If the Union were to survive "as the United States, the balance between the powers of the nation and those of the States must be maintained." And prophetically, they remarked:

There is grave danger in permitting it to dip in either direction, danger—if there were no other—in the precedent thereby set for further departures from the equipoise. The threat implicit in the present encroachment upon the administrative functions of the State is that greater encroachments and encroachments upon other functions will follow.(283)

By this time the tide was running out fast. When the Fair Labor Standards Act came along in 1938, the third gateway of the commerce clause swung to its widest point. Here the court asserted for the Federal government the widest possible control of wages and hours, overtime, working conditions, and the like. In *United States vs. Darby*, Stone traced at some length, as if to justify his conscience and the Court's, the growth of the commerce doctrine.

The judges were unanimous: The Tenth Amendment was but a "truism."(284) Any process or occupation necessary or related to the current of interstate commerce henceforth was subject to congressional control. "The motive and purpose of a regulation of interstate commerce are matters for the legislative judgment upon the exercise of which ihe Constitution places no restriction, and over which the courts are given no control." "The effect of sustaining the act," Roberis observed in his lectures at Harvard in 1951, "was to place the whole matter of wages and hours of persons employed throughout the United States, wilh slight exceptions, under a single Federal regulatory scheme and in this way completely to supersede State exercise of the police power in this field."(285)

The rest of the tale is quickly told. The year following the Darby case saw the court approve the Agricultural Marketing Agreement Act of 1937, by which the farmers were delivered into Federal custody: Congress, it was ruled, plainly had authority to fix a minimum price on milk in Chicago, for "the commerce power is not confined in its exercise to the regulation of commerce among the States—it extends to those activities intrastate which so affect interstate commerce, or the exertion of the power of Congress over it, as to make regulation of them appropriate means to the attainment of a legitimate end." And the Court happily cited John Marshall in *McCulloch vs. Maryland* to prove it.(286) Almost immediately thereafter, the Court gave its benediction to the Agricultural Adjustment Act of 1938. This extended Federal controls even to wheat or corn consumed on a farm. The judges saw nothing wrong in this: "It can hardly be denied that a factor of such volume and variability as home-consumed wheat would have a substantial influence on price and market conditions." After all, "the stimulation of commerce is a use of the regulating function."(287) That was the fourth doorway opening there: *The stimulation of commerce.* No great powers of prophecy are required to foresee that in this fourth gateway, new vistas appear of Federal projects under the commerce clause.

> The Constitution looks to an indestructible Union, composed of indestructible States.
>
> —SALMON P. CHASE
> *Texas vs. White*

1
The Southern States

ON MAY 17, 1954, the Supreme Court of the United States handed down its opinion in Brown vs. Board of Education.(1) By this pronouncement, the Court undertook to put an end to racial separation in public schools.

"We conclude," said Mr. Chief Justice Warren, "that in the field of public education the doctrine of 'separate but equal' has no place. Separate educational facilities are inherently unequal. Therefore, we hold that the plaintiffs and others similarly situated for whom the actions have been brought are, by reason of the segregation complained of, deprived of the equal protection of the laws guaranteed by the Fourteenth Amendment."

This conclusion of the Court, this holding, had no basis in law; it had none in history. It was based primarily upon what the Court was pleased to term "intangible considerations." To separate Negro children from white children, said the Court, "generates a feeling of inferiority as to their status in the community that may affect their hearts and minds in a way unlikely ever to be undone." Whatever may have been "the extent of psychological knowledge" in 1896, when the Court approved the "separate but equal" doctrine, it now was clear to the Court that racial separation creates a "sense of inferiority [which] affects the motivation of a child to learn." Citing *The American Dilemma,* by Gunnar Myrdal, as a general authority for its sociological views, the Court turned smoothly to the task of formulating an appropriate decree.

It is plain, now, that the opinion should have been foreseen. There had been rumblings of judicial thunder in preceding years: the Gaines case,(2) the McLaurin case,(3) the Sweatt case.(4)But all these had involved segregation in institutions of higher learning, and none of them had quite turned on the fundamental question: *Is segregation in itself, as a State policy in public institutions,* a violation of the Fourteenth Amendment? This question had been pondered by a few lawyers, a few editors, a few educators. The people themselves, for the most part, had pondered the matter scarcely at all. The earlier admission of a few Negro college students in Missouri, Oklahoma, and Texas was something that had happened to some other fellow in some other place, a long way away. It seemed inconceivable that anything drastic could happen to the neighborhood elementary school or the village high school.

Thus the Court's opinion, that Monday afternoon in May, struck with a stunning shock. At first the reaction was largely one of bewilderment and dismay. Accustomed to obedient acceptance of anything purporting to be law, most Southern spokesmen fumbled to express both opposition and acceptance. There was relief that immediate integration had not been ordered; there was a widespread hope that "something would turn up." Gradually this Micawberish sentiment faded. In its place came resentment, resistance, and at last a grim comprehension of the violence that had been done to the Constitution.

It is this last aspect to which this essay now turns. It is important to understand the constitutional position taken by Southern States in the school case, not only for an appreciation of the great and complex problems that have arisen in the South, but more importantly for what we may learn of the prospect that lies ahead for all States. The opinion of May 17, 1954, it is said, affected the eight States of the Old South and the Deep South most of all. The more accurate statement is that it affected every State equally. For the extinction of one power exercised by a few States creates precedent for the extinction of all powers exercised by all States. Judicial encroachment, like any vice, is habit-forming. And a series of opinions since *Brown vs. Board of Education* offers graphic warning of the swift deterioration of the Constitution now in progress. "Where law ends," Pitt said, "tyranny begins." Neatly bound in recent volumes of the *United States Reports,* it is submitted, is precisely such an ending and beginning.

In presenting their case, States of the South appear before their sister States neither as prisoners at the bar nor as petitioners seeking favors. They stand as members of a *Union of States*. And if a parliamentary analogy may be drawn, they take the floor as fully-qualified members of this federation, appealing a ruling of the chair. The motion they make holds nothing of pride or of defiance either. What they charge is that the chair—the high Court—has gravely erred; the Court in the school cases of May 17, 1954, has taken an action *it was not qualified to take;* and the Southern States ask of the membership as a whole: If the Court's decision be the wish of the States, then the States themselves must so ordain. Not otherwise may the decision validly be imposed upon us.

It ought not to be necessary to preface these observations with a recollection of common burdens shared, and blood spilled equally on foreign soil. Yet so passionate is the animosity now voiced against the South that perhaps a gentle reminder may not be amiss. These States, these Southern States, yield to no States in their devotion to those ideals of liberty and law that are our common glory. Sons of the South have fought and died, equally with men of the North, that this heritage might be preserved. These States have shared equally in the payment of taxes, and in the acceptance of the obligations placed upon all members of the Union. In the immediate matter of their public schools, they have for nearly ninety years worked toward full compliance with the law as the law repeatedly was defined and understood; by this law, believing in the stability of law, they erected their institutions and poured their wealth and affections into them. Their sole request is that, if the law must now be changed, then let it be by lawful process, not by lawless usurpation.

That is not so complicated a position. It asks of the member States of the Union only that they read the Constitution and lay the South's case beside it. Here is no threat to dissolve the Union: Here is rather a plea that the Union be sustained for what it is and always was meant to be, *a Union of separate sovereign States.* Neither does the South's position imply destruction of the Constitution: On the contrary, the despairing cry is that the Constitution be preserved, sacred now and hereafter, the supreme law of the land, not to be corrupted by men, but to be amended, if need be, by States.

Now, the case for the South cannot be set down, complete, in any book or essay: It has to be lived and sensed and felt; it is an amalgam of the smiles, hopes, fears of the Southerner's life, a mosaic of countless fleeting impressions and experiences. The South, it has been wisely said, is a state of mind; but this is to say no more than that the essential South is a metaphysical abstraction, beyond the pathologists of the *New York Times,* certainly beyond the Gunnar Myrdals of a distant Sweden. Its most vital tissues elude a statistician's X-ray. Thus it is not suggested that what follows is "the" case for the South; there is no more a single case for the South than there is a single South—the evidence varies in kind and in degree. Yet certain contentions are shared in common by the protesting States, and it is to these arguments, both on the law and on the merits, that attention is now directed.

Notes

Go to top.

2

Some Notes on the Fourteenth Amendment

THE FIRST proposition is this: The Fourteenth Amendment to the Constitution, never having been validly ratified, cannot provide a valid basis for the mandate the Supreme Court proposes to inflict upon the Southern States. Is this a preposterous contention? It must seem so at first, yet few historians would term it so. Is it too late now to correct an initial wrong? Surely the South's adversaries cannot concede that age must be respected. Is the proposition something conjured upon on the spur of a desperate moment? Not so: The Supreme Court repeatedly was asked to rule on the point in the Reconstruction period, and the Court as repeatedly ducked the issue; the Court has not faced it squarely to this day. Lawyers, jurists, and scholars repeatedly have discussed the point.[5]

The facts are not obscure. The War ended with Lee's surrender on April 9, 1865. Two months earlier, the Thirteenth Amendment, abolishing slavery, had been approved by the Congress; it was even then making the rounds of the States for ratification. In due course, the resolution came before the legislatures of the defeated Southern States; they ratified it, and their ratifications were duly recorded in a count of the three-fourths necessary to engraft it upon the Constitution. Thus, in the summer of '65, the Confederate States formally and officially were counted back in the Union—indeed, it was the North's position that legally they had never left it: Mortal men might rebel; whole States could not secede. That was the North's contention, and not by law, but by the force of superior arms, the North made it stick.

Yet the following December of 1865, when the Thirty-ninth Congress convened, it appeared that ten Southern States were not States after all. Their Senators and Representatives were denied seats in the Congress. As justification, Thaddeus Stevens advanced the argument that under the Constitution, "each House shall be the judge of the elections, returns and qualifications of its own members."(6) No Southerner, in Stevens' view, was "qualified"; therefore, all were rejected. This summary action did palpable violence to two other provisions of the Constitution, each explicit in its language—that no State may be deprived of its equal vote in the Senate without its consent, and that every State shall have at least one Representative in the House. Had the Southern States been represented, the amendment surely would have failed of approval in the Congress: It barely won a two-thirds majority in the Senate—33-11—even with the South excluded.

Yet if the Southern States were not officially States for purposes of proposing the amendment, it appeared at first they would be counted as States for purposes of ratification. In June of 1866, the amendment went forth to the thirty-seven States to be considered. In the South, the amendment came before the very legislatures that so recently had been counted in ratification of the Thirteenth Amendment. They promptly rejected it. The three border States of Kentucky, Delaware, and Maryland also refused to ratify; California took no action. The result was that the requisite twenty-eight States required for ratification could not be found.

Stevens was not dissuaded. In his view, "the conquered rebels were at the mercy of the conquerors."(7) Thus, if the Southern States would not ratify the amendment voluntarily, they would be compelled to ratify as the price of readmission to the Congress. In March of 1867, the Radicals wrote into law (over Johnson's veto) the Reconstruction Act, which opened with a recital that "no legal State government" existed in the Southern States, and continued with provisions for government by military rule. Federal registrars were put in charge of voting lists, and puppet legislatures were set up throughout the South. In time, these paper parliaments duly said "ja"—there was nothing else they could say—and their "consent" was solemnly recorded in Washington. Meanwhile, Ohio and New Jersey, *while the amendment was still pending and before a sufficient number of ratifications had been obtained,* adopted resolutions rescinding their earlier resolutions of approval. In Oregon, as Joseph B. James has pointed out, a favorable vote of 25-22 in one house included the ayes of two men illegally elected; when they were replaced, and a count of 24-23 against the amendment resulted, a rescinding resolution was declared too late to be effective. It was Oregon's Legislature that voiced the first formal protest, perhaps, against the invalidity of counting coerced ratifications from the Southern States.

Efforts were made, of course, to challenge this ruthless process of writing fundamental law. Had not President Johnson himself described the Reconstruction Act as a "bill of attainder"? Yet the high Court weakly evaded every opportunity to come to grips with the question. The issue, said the Court, was political, not justiciable.(8) And again, in the famed McCardle case, the Court permitted Congress to amend the Reconstruction Act, in the very middle of a judicial proceeding, in order to prevent a determination of the law's constitutionality.(9) The following year, in July of 1868, the Fourteenth Amendment was proclaimed "adopted." In the bitterness of defeat, the South offered no further contest. And though in recent years, the Court has again indicated that it would not look into "the political departments of the government,"(10) the fact still remains that it was only by virtue of a palpably unconstitutional series of actions that the Fourteenth Amendment ever was ratified at all. The amendment certainly was not ratified by the voluntary act of free men under a republican form of government. This was puppet-law, sanctioned by States, as Professor Joseph B. James has said, that "were States in name only." And nothing could be clearer than the line of reasoning which holds that if the amendment were void at the outset, it remains void to this day, whether one thousand or ten thousand cases have been decided pursuant to its terms.

This objection on the South's part, to be sure, is not pressed with great earnestness. Freely elected legislatures, since Reconstruction days, have tacitly acquiesced in the amendment's existence. It is doubtless futile to revive now the denunciation voiced then: Too much water has poured over the damn.

The objection the South relies most firmly on is this: (1) Under the Tenth Amendment, all powers not delegated to the United States nor prohibited *by the Constitution* to the States are reserved to the States respectively or to the people; (2) the power to operate racially separate schools never was prohibited to the States by the Fourteenth Amendment or by any other provision of the Constitution, but on the contrary was clearly understood to be reserved to them; (3) therefore, that power remains vested in the States respectively to this day, and can be prohibited to them only by the Constitution itself, and not by any judicial construction.

South Carolina put it this way, in her resolution of February 14, 1956:

The right of each of the States to maintain at its own expense racially separate public schools for the children of its citizens and other racially separate public facilities is not forbidden or limited by the language or intent of the Fourteenth Amendment.

Virginia, in her resolution of Interposition (February 1, 1956) declared this:

That the State of Virginia did not agree, in ratifying the Fourteenth Amendment, nor did other States ratifying the Fourteenth Amendment agree, that the power to operate racially separate schools was to be prohibited to them thereby. . . .

These are not frivolous contentions. They go to the heart of our Constitutional process. Implicitly, they raise this question: Is it right—morally or constitutionally right—for the States solemnly and honorably to agree to Proposition "A", only to have Proposition "Not-A" put upon them by judicial fiat? Is there any boundary at which "interpretation" stops, and effective amendment begins? Surely there must be some such boundary, or the amendatory process becomes mere dumbshow, and the act of ratification the gauziest stage-setting. Article V of the Constitution must have some meaning, and its plain meaning is no more than this: That amendments proposed to the Constitution cannot become a part of the Constitution *unless they are acceptable to not fewer than three-fourths of the States.* But when it is said that an amendment must be acceptable, what is meant is that the *meaning and intention* of the amendment must be acceptable; the end sought must be acceptable; the object to be served by the amendment must be an object acceptable to three-fourths of the States. If in time, it is proposed that different intentions, ends, and objects be engrafted upon the Constitution, then it is clearly reasonable to urge that these new aims must also be acceptable to three-fourths of the States.

If Constitutional government is to be preserved, if government is to be one of laws instead of men, these new aims must be spelled out in words of plain meaning. Ponder the definition of Constitutionalism set forth—not by a Southern legislator during the heated summer of 1956—but by a Yale University professor two decades ago:

Constitutionalism is the name given to the trust which men repose in the power of words engrossed on parchment to keep a government in order. The writing down of fundamental law, beyond peradventure and against misunderstanding, is an important political invention. It offers exact and enduring language as a test for official conduct. . . .(11)

Unless the exercise of a power by government is authorized by words engrossed on parchment, and unless those words are exact and enduring, the test for official conduct vanishes—and along with it the trust of men, upon which in the long run government itself depends.

With that in mind, let us examine the meaning, the object, the intention, and the end sought to be served by the Fourteenth Amendment at the time of its ratification. Was it intended that the Fourteenth Amendment, in itself, should prohibit the States from maintaining racially separate public institutions? What, in *terms of public schools,* was meant by "the privileges and immunities of citizens of the United States" and "the equal protection of the laws"?

The questions can be answered; they can be answered clearly and decisively. It should be remembered that 1868, after all, was not so terribly long ago. Records of the period are conveniently available. No vital evidence is lost or missing. No reason exists for uncertainty.

And what the evidence shows is this: *Neither the Congress that proposed the Fourteenth*

Amendment, nor a single one of the thirty-seven States that considered it, understood that the amendment, of and by itself, outlawed segregation by race in the public schools.

Three amendments were added to the Constitution in the five years that followed Appomattox. The first of these, the Thirteenth Amendment, became effective in December, 1865; it put an end to slavery. The last of these, the Fifteenth, became effective in March of 1870; it declared that the right to vote could not be abridged by reason of race or previous servitude. In between these came the Fourteenth, proposed in June of 1866, declared ratified in July of 1868.

The Fourteenth Amendment grew out of the Civil Rights Act of 1866 and gave constitutional sanction to that law. An important point to keep in mind, in considering the Civil Rights Act, is that the act was to apply to all States; its provisions were not to affect, as was true of the Freedmen's Bureau Bill, only the States that had seceded. Thus when the Civil Rights Bill, as introduced by Senator Trumbull of Illinois, undertook to lay down a sweeping commandment that

There shall be no discrimination in the civil rights or immunities among the inhabitants of any State . . . on account of race, color, or previous condition of slavery [emphasis supplied]

the meaning of "civil rights or immunities" became a matter of immediate concern to spokesmen of Northern States. Trumbull attempted to allay these apprehensions:

The first section of the bill defines what I understand to be civil rights: The right to make and enforce contracts, to sue and be sued, and to give evidence, to inherit, purchase, sell, lease, hold and convey real and personal property.[12]

Others were doubtful. Senator Edgar Cowan of Pennsylvania, a Republican, feared this "monstrous" bill[13] might mean the end of segregated schools in his State. Others thought it might ban miscegenation laws. But Senator Trumbull repeated that the bill dealt with civil rights only, as he had defined them, and had "nothing to do with the political rights or status of parties."[14]

On the House side, in March of 1866, the Trumbull bill encountered further objections. What was meant by the provision guaranteeing to all inhabitants "full and equal benefit of all laws"? How could "civil rights or immunities" be defined? Wilson of Iowa, chairman of the Judiciary Committee to which the bill had been committed, had a clear and precise response:

What do these terms mean? Do they mean that in all things civil, social, political, all citizens, without distinction of race or color, shall be equal? By no means can they be so construed. . . . *Nor do they mean that . . . their children shall attend the same schools. These are not civil rights or immunities.* [15] [Emphasis supplied.]

But in view of the objections, going chiefly to the doubtful constitutionality of the bill as an encroachment upon reserved powers of the States, the Civil Rights Bill went back to committee. On March 13, it emerged with the reference to "civil rights or immunities" eliminated as such, but with the meaning of the bill pinned down:

> Citizens of every race and color, without regard to any previous condition of slavery or involuntary servitude . . . shall have the same right to make and enforce contracts, to sue, be parties, and give evidence, to inherit, purchase, lease, sell, hold and convey real and personal property and to full and equal benefit of all laws and proceedings tor the security of persons and property as is enjoyed by white citizens. . . .

In this form the bill passed. It was vetoed by President Johnson on the constitutional objection that Congress was attempting to invade the vast field of State jurisdiction covered by the reserved powers, but in April it was adopted over his veto. What may be learned from this brief chronology is, first, that the patrons of the act did not intend "civil rights" to have any application to segregated schools; and secondly, that the Congress as a whole was unwilling that there should be misunderstanding on the point. The phrase, "full and equal benefit of all laws," to the men most intimately concerned in the long debate, had no application to segregated schools.

Now, the resolution that led to the Fourteenth Amendment was simultaneously before the 39th Congress. It was the work of a committee of six Senators and nine Representatives, headed by Thaddeus Stevens of Pennsylvania. The version they proposed went to a Committee on Reconstruction, which on February 10, 1866, sent to the floor a proposed amendment as follows:

> The Congress shall have power to make all laws which shall be necessary and proper to secure to the citizens of each State all privileges and immunities of citizens in the several States; and to all persons in the several States equal protection in the rights of life, liberty and property.(16)

At once the question arose that concerns us in this review: Rogers of New Jersey thought the language might authorize Congressional power to compel amalgamated schools. Proponents swiftly moved to quiet this objection: The aim, they said, was not to confer any new power upon Congress, but only to permit Congress to enforce the provisions of the Constitution already in existence. The "privileges and immunities" covered in the proposed amendment were only those of Article IV, Section 2. (The citizens of each State shall be entitled to all privileges and immunities of citizens in the several States.) But his version of the Amendment was sidetracked, and it was not until April 21 that a new proposal, much closer to the final form of the Amendment, came to the floor of the Senate.

On April 25, the key sentence was written into Section 1 of the proposed amendment, exactly as it appears today:

> No State shall make or enforce any law which shall abridge the privileges or immunities of citizens of the United States; nor shall any State deprive any person of life, liberty, or property without due process of law, nor deny to any person within its jurisdiction the equal protection of the laws.

It is significant that in neither the majority nor minority reports accompanying this draft of the amendment was there the slightest reference to public schools. Can it be argued persuasively that this omission is because "everyone understood" the language would prohibit the States from operating separate schools? Plainly not. For this very question had been raised in debate on the Civil Rights Act, and the intention of the sponsoring members of Congress had been spelled out. It was Stevens' aim to nail into the Constitution what was attempted to be secured by the Civil Rights Act: A mere law could be repealed by a majority of Congress; an amendment to the Constitution was something else. Others joined Stevens in this point of view. Boyer of Pennsylvania, who opposed the whole resolution, thought "the first section embodies the principles of the civil rights bill."(17) Broomall, who favored it, agreed: The pending measure already had been considered "in another shape, in the civil rights bill." Senator Raymond, publisher of the *New York Times,* saw the amendment as embracing the same matter of the Civil Rights Bill. Eliot of Massachusetts concurred. So did Rogers of New Jersey, who opposed the measure: It was "no more nor less than an attempt to embody in the Constitution of the United States that outrageous and miserable civil rights bill."

From all of this—and the available evidence is, of course, far more voluminous—it is evident that the House of Representatives regarded the proposed Fourteenth Amendment as a constitutional restatement and validation of the Civil Rights Act simultaneously under debate. And it is clear that the House understood that neither the act nor the proposed amendment related to segregated schools.

The story was repeated in the Senate debate. In all the prolonged argument over the effect of the proposed resolution on the States, it never once was suggested by a proponent that the amendment was intended to outlaw racially separate schools. The whole history of the amendment, as Professor James has made abundantly clear in his meticulous monograph, rested (1) in political considerations of Negro suffrage, and (2) in a possibly humane desire to accord certain "civil rights" to the recently freed Negro. On the first point, many of the Midwestern and Northern States shared a concern almost equal to that which might be felt in the South: Ohio at the time denied the vote to Negroes; so did Indiana (indeed, Indiana by her Constitution, explicitly forbade Negroes to immigrate to or settle in that State). More importantly, it was recognized that if the vote were given with a free hand to the former Negro slaves, on a straight population basis, the just-defeated South would gain enormously in congressional representation. Thus, what was to become the second section of the Fourteenth Amendment for a long period of time received far greater consideration than was given to the first section. In the eyes of Thaddeus Stevens, this was "the most important in the article."(18)

The debates during the first half of 1866, in terms of "equal protection" and "privileges and immunities," scarcely can be misunderstood. Henry Ward Beecher, the abolitionist, had no doubts on this score: The aim was to protect the Negro's right to work, and further to make him "the equal of all other men *before the courts and in the eyes of the law.* He should be just as much qualified to be a witness as the man who assaults him."(19) Nor did Justin Morrill of Vermont, who was to be a member of the joint committee that framed the amendment: The object was to preserve for the Negro a right "to hold property, be a party and witness in . . .(court)."(20) The amendment was designed to backstop the Civil Rights Act.(21) It was intended to make sure that the black man was not to be hanged "for a crime for which the white man is not to be hanged."

These were the only considerations and intentions that Congress would agree to. The radicals recognized this. Kelley of Pennsylvania, Schenck of Ohio, Eckley of Ohio, Thad Stevens himself confessed that the amendment, in its final form, fell short of their vengeful desires.(22) The amendment, said Stevens, covered only civil rights — it "does not touch social or political rights."(23) And when the resolution finally was approved, on June 13, could it be said the radicals had won? Obviously not: "Why, we defeated every radical proposition in it," remarked John Sherman of Ohio.(24) It was not what the radicals wanted, says Professor James: "It was the best that they could get."(25)

It was the best they could get, for obvious reasons: Laws restricting the Negro, in one way or another, obtained in 1866 not only in the vanquished South, *but also in the victorious North.* Had the Fourteenth Amendment been intended to prohibit segregated schools, or to abolish State laws against inter-racial marriage, the amendment would have been rejected *by the North* regardless of what the South might have done about it. This consideration was so plain that it did not warrant discussion.

The Congress itself, it is clear, did not regard racial separation as inherently evil: It separated white and Negro in the congressional galleries. More importantly, on May 8, 1866, barely a month before both houses approved the Fourteenth Amendment, the Senate passed a bill (it became law in July) that established segregated schools in Washington and Georgetown "for the sole use of . . . colored children."(26) It is utterly incomprehensible that a Congress, if it intended the Fourteenth Amendment to prohibit racially separate public schools, simultaneously would have provided for such schools. Yet that is precisely what the 39th Congress did. That is what the Congress, for more than eighty years thereafter, was to provide in Washington.

Nor did the ratifying States have the slightest doubt on this point. In Maine, New Hampshire, Vermont, Oregon, and Wisconsin, Negro populations were so infinitesimally small that the question did not arise. This same thing was essentially true of Connecticut, Iowa, Massachusetts, Michigan, Minnesota, Nebraska, and Rhode Island, where segregated schools either had been prohibited before the Fourteenth Amendment came along, or were prohibited contemporaneously with its adoption. But witness the roll call of States *in which the same legislatures that ratified the Fourteenth Amendment also provided for segregated schools:* Alabama, Arkansas, Georgia, Kansas, Kentucky, Mississippi, Nevada, North Carolina, Tennessee, Texas, Virginia, and West Virginia. We may also note seven States in which segregated schools existed both before *and after* their ratification of the amendment: California, Illinois, Missouri, New Jersey, New York, Ohio, and Pennsylvania. Let it also be observed that within two years *after* the amendment had been proclaimed, while it still was fresh in everyone's mind, Indiana and Maryland joined the other segregation States in establishing racially separate schools.

Can it be argued, seriously, that all the States were thus in immediate violation of the constitutional amendment they had just adopted? The question refutes itself. Forget the Southern States. Is it conceivable that Ohio, Indiana, and Pennsylvania would have "prohibited" separate schools by a constitutional amendment *and then instantly sanctioned them by State law?* No. The evidence is overwhelming that the States, North and South, which ratified the Fourteenth Amendment plainly understood that it never was intended to prohibit the establishment and operation of racially separate schools, provided only that the schools were substantially equal.

Indeed, the evidence is plain that many States outside the South fully shared the South's approval of segregated schools. Was it a Southern governor who recommended, in June of 1867, that white and colored children "not be placed together in the same schools," since this would "create a dissatisfaction and conflict, and impair the usefulness of the schools"? That was Governor Morton of Indiana.(27) Was it in a Southern State Legislature that the House voted 72-1 for a law authorizing local school boards "to organize and maintain separate schools for the education of white and colored children"? That was Kansas, in 1868.(28) At the time the amendment was under consideration in Ohio, where it first was ratified in 1867 and then rejected in 1868, some ten thousand Negro pupils were in segregated schools in fifty-two of Ohio's eighty-eight counties.(29) New York City had segregated schools. So did Pennsylvania, for a period of thirteen years after ratification of the amendment. In West Virginia, the Legislature that ratified the amendment on January 16, 1867, on February 27, 1867, adopted a statute providing that "white and colored persons shall not be taught in the same schools." Consider any State then in the Union or, if you please, out of the Union: In every case, without a single exception, the understanding of the amendment's effect on public education was perfectly accepted: It was not intended to prohibit the establishment and maintenance of racially separate schools.

This plain, unequivocal agreement was comprehended not only by the Congress and by the State legislatures, but by both State and Federal judges also. In case after case, in the highest State courts, the propriety of separate schools repeatedly was upheld. When the question first reached the Supreme Court of the United States, the Court thought it too plain for argument. This was the case of Plessy vs. Ferguson, involving racially separate facilities in rail transportation. In upholding a Louisiana statute, the Court held that such laws

have been generally, if not universally, recognized as within the competency of the State legislatures in the exercise of their police power.

And the Court added, matter-of-factly:

The most common instance of this is connected with the establishment of separate schools for white and colored children, which has been held to be a valid exercise of the legislative power even by courts of States where the political rights of the colored race have been longest and most earnestly enforced.

(30)

This same opinion was reiterated by a unanimous Court in 1899,(31) and again was upheld by a unanimous Court as recently as 1927. In Gong Lum vs. Rice, Chief Justice Taft spoke for a Court that included such luminous minds as those of Brandeis, Holmes, and Stone. "Were this a new question," said the Court, and let that qualification be noted carefully: *Were this a new question,* "it would call for very full argument and consideration. . . ." But it was not a new question:

we think that it is the same question which has been many times decided to be within the constitutional power of the State Legislature to settle without intervention of the Federal courts under the Federal Constitution.(32)

The power of the States to operate separate schools for Negroes and whites, said the Court, "does not conflict with the Fourteenth Amendment."

Now, the position taken by the Southern States today once was summed up clearly by Sutherland. He agreed, in one of his dissenting opinions, that the Constitution is not static—that it is absurd to pretend an absolute rule of *stare decisis* should be applied to constitutional constructions. The Constitution, he said, of course "is made up of living words that apply to every new condition." Then he added:

But to say, if that be intended, that the words of the Constitution mean today what they did not mean when written—that is, that they do not apply now to a *situation to which they would have applied then* —is to rob that instrument of the essential element which continues it in force as the people have made it until they, and not their official agents, have made it otherwise.(33) [Emphasis supplied.]

This was exactly what Hughes had in mind in the Carter case when he asserted, on a question of labor relations, that if the people wanted to vest such power in the Congress, they could do so "in the appropriate manner," but "it is not for the court to amend the Constitution by judicial decree."(34) This was what Washington had in mind, in his farewell address: "But let there be no change by usurpation; for, though this, in one instance, may be the instrument of good, it is the customary weapon by which free governments are destroyed." So, too, with Madison, in his Virginia Report of 1799. So, too, with Jefferson: Should grave question arise, he said, of whether a governmental power had been delegated or reserved, it is not for the Supreme Court to decide: "A convention of the States must be called to ascribe the doubtful power to that department which they may think best."(35)

It is idle to pretend in the matter under review that some new or different problem is involved in the operation of public schools, as of 1954, that was not involved in the public schools as of 1868. There were public schools then; there are public schools now. There were Negro pupils then; there are Negro pupils now. To be sure, it is popularly believed that the schools are better now: They teach band, basketweaving, and traffic safety. It is urged that the Negro is vastly different now—more cultured, more cultivated. But assuming all this to be true, the plain fact remains that if schools and society have changed, *the Constitution has not changed by an applicable comma.* And it is the Constitution, not the lamentations of Gunnar Myrdal, that remains *the supreme law of the land.* If it be the will of three-fourths of the States to amend the Constitution so as to prohibit the operation of separate schools, then let the States, so desiring, get on with the job of constitutional amendment. But only the States can amend the Constitution—the Court cannot.

The proposition can be challenged only by those centralists who are prepared to scrap the Constitution altogether—to brush aside Article V and the Tenth Amendment as if these provisions simply did not exist. They must interpolate into Article VI some new language that would make it read, "The Constitution *as interpreted, modified and revised by decrees of the Supreme Court,* and the laws of the United States which shall be made in pursuance thereof," etc., shall be the supreme law of the land. But the Constitution does not say this. The Constitution, in Article VI, does not mention the Supreme Court. What is to be the supreme law of the land? The Constitution itself, the laws made in pursuance thereof, and the treaties made under Federal authority. That is all. The Court's sole authority is to decide cases in *law and equity* arising under the Constitution; and in deciding them, it cannot validly go beyond the plain boundaries of the Constitution. When it steps beyond the limits of interpretation, and crosses over into substantive amendment, it has usurped a power never delegated to the Federal judiciary.

The charge of judicial encroachment is no thesis new to Southerners, vintage 1954. One of the great liberal members of the Court, the first Justice Harlan, remarked long ago:

When the American people come to the conclusion that the judiciary of this land is usurping to itself the functions of the legislative department of the government, and by judicial construction only is declaring what should be the public policy of the United States, we will find trouble. Ninety millions of people—all sorts of people—are not going to submit to the usurpation by the judiciary of the functions of other departments of the government.(36)

Nor have the apprehensions voiced by Harlan been confined to liberals of the turn of the century. It was Mr. Justice Holmes, dissenting in 1930 in Baldwin vs. Missouri, who criticized his brethren for "evoking a constitutional prohibition from the void of 'due process of law.'" Looking at the declining status of State rights then, Holmes remarked that he could see "hardly any limit but the sky to the invalidating of those rights if they happen to strike a majority of this court as for any reason undesirable." And he added:

I cannot believe that the Amendment was intended to give us carte blanche to embody our economic or moral beliefs in its prohibitions.(37)

So, too, Mr. Justice Black, who a decade ago was inclined to insist upon a strict adherence to the Constitution. He denounced the theory that the Supreme Court has some boundless power under "natural law," by which the Court periodically may "expand and contract constitutional standards to conform to the Court's conception of what at a particular time constitutes 'civilized decency' and 'fundamental liberty and justice.'" Any such theory, he said, tends to degrade Constitutional safeguards and simultaneously to appropriate to the Court "a broad power which we are not authorized by the Constitution to exercise." It is not for the Court, he concluded ringingly, "to roam at large in the broad expanses of policy and morals and to trespass, all too freely, on the legislative domain of the States as well as the Federal Government."(38)

Chief Justice Vinson made the same point in *Barrows vs. Jackson:* "Since we must rest our decision on the Constitution alone, we must set aside predilections on social policy and adhere to the settled rules which restrict the exercise of our power to judicial review. . . ."(39) And even Mr. Justice Douglas, of all people, once also recognized the dangers described by Harlan and Black and Vinson. He said this:

From age to age the problem of constitutional adjudication is the same. It is to keep the power of government unrestrained by the social or economic theories that one set of judges may entertain. It is to keep one age unfettered by the fears and limited vision of another. There is in that connection one tenet of faith which has crystallized more and more as a result of our long experience as a nation. It is this: If the social and economic problems of State and Nation can be kept under political management of the people, there is likely to be long-run stability. *It is when a judiciary with life tenure seeks to write its social and economic creed into the Charter that instability is created.* For then the nation lacks the adaptability to master the sudden storms of an era. It must be remembered that the process of constitutional amendment is a long and slow one.(40) [Emphasis supplied.]

Mr. Justice Douglas, of course, tends to forget his own sage advice in the promotion of his own odd concepts of sociology and economics. He is not the first to do so, nor the first to corrupt the Constitution in the process. It was neither a Talmadge nor an Eastland that said of the Court:

The judiciary of the United States is the subtle corps of sappers and miners constantly working underground to undermine the foundations of our confederated fabric. They are construing our Constitution from coordination of a general and special government to a general and supreme one alone. This will lay all things at their feet.(41)

That was Thomas Jefferson, late in his life. It was Jefferson who saw the Supreme Court "advancing with a noiseless and steady pace to the great object of consolidation." It was Jefferson who warned most clearly, that "You will have a . . . difficult task in curbing the Judiciary in their enterprises on the Constitution."

Granted that the task is difficult, let the question be raised once more that has been posed from time to time throughout this essay: *How is the judiciary to be checked and brought to an accounting?* Or is the high Court alone, of all agencies of government, to go unchecked—never challenged effectively, never subjected to the direct approval of the people? If it be conceded that the Court has the power to take one reserved right from the States or the people, then what restrains it from seizing all rights? Can it be true, as Stone remarked in the Butler case, that "the only check upon our own exercise of power is our own sense of self-restraint"? If this be true, then a judicial oligarchy has been substituted for a republican government, and a divine right of judges has replaced the divine right of kings. Five men—a majority of one on a Court of nine—may effectively arrogate unto themselves the sovereign powers of not fewer than three-fourths of the States.

It cannot be imagined that a free people have thus abandoned the effective control of their fundamental law. Judges are not divine; they are most pathetically mortal: In the brief span of Sixteen years, between 1937 and 1953, the Court reversed itself not fewer than thirty-two times on questions of constitutional law. It was no Southern editor, but a member of the Court, Mr. Justice Roberts, who remarked despairingly in 1944 that the stream of reversals

<blockquote>indicates an intolerance for what those who have composed this court in the past have conscientiously and deliberately concluded, and involves an assumption that knowledge and wisdom reside in us which was denied to our predecessors. . . . [It] tends to bring adjudications of this tribunal into the same class as a restricted railroad ticket, good for this day and train only.(42)</blockquote>

The fundamental law of this Union cannot be maintained on any basis so "flexible" or "dynamic" as this. What the South says, in the matter of school segregation, is that the Court settled the question nearly sixty years ago. The Southern States thereafter had every right of law, and every guarantee of honor and fair dealing, to believe that they were proceeding constitutionally in erecting and maintaining a system of racially separate schools. Had there not been such assurance—had there ever been a question of their reserved powers—this system would not have been established. The schools would not have been built, or would have been differently built.

It was Trumbull of Illinois, certainly no Southern sympathizer, who declared in 1872 that "the right to go to school is not a civil right and never was."(43) The "right" of United States citizens, preserved from State abridgment by the Fourteenth Amendment, is a right to substantially equal schools, *not to the same or identical schools.* And it is the earnest contention of the South today that however imperfect its efforts may have been in a poverty-stricken past to provide equal facilities for the children of both races, it approaches that constitutional objective now. The sole function of the courts, in the eyes of a South pleading for stability in our basic law, is to see to it that the intention of the law is fulfilled while the powers of the States over essentially domestic affairs are left unimpaired.

Notes

Go to top.

3

Some Notes on Police Power

NOW, THE greatest of the State powers over essentially domestic affairs is the State's "police power." It is the power the people themselves exercise when they prohibit beer in Kansas and authorize casinos in Las Vegas; it covers the whole fabric of community relations, provides for public order, and undertakes to establish "for the intercourse of citizen with citizen, those rules of good manners and good neighborhood which are calculated to prevent a conflict of rights."(44)

In the States of the Old South and the Deep South, legislative bodies over a long period of years—with the complete sanction of Federal courts—have exercised their reserved police power to require a separation of white and Negro races in certain areas of public life. Outside the South, the South's requirements for racial separation often are regarded as capricious and arbitrary, based upon mere bigotry or blind prejudice. There is a feeling on the part of our critics that police power is being abused.

It is not the primary purpose of this essay to defend school segregation, or to dwell at any length upon the conditions by which the practice may be justified in the South today. To paraphrase Mr. Chief Justice Marshall, it is a Constitution that is being here expounded. Yet some of the considerations that are uppermost in the minds of the South may well be sketched briefly, if only to emphasize the wisdom of the constitutional reservation to the States of control over essentially domestic affairs.

It was William Alexander Percy (and the Southern Negro had no truer friend) who once commented that white and black in the South, however, strongly they may exchange affections, understand each other not at all. Between them, he said, is "a barrier of glass: you can't see it, you only strike it." An understanding of this glass wall of separation is basic to any understanding of the American South, yet nothing is more difficult for the visitor, intent upon diagnosing our social ills, to recognize or to comprehend. We of the South live, by necessity and perhaps by instinct, in a dual society. Though white and Negro may stand patiently in queues together, side by side in supermarkets and country stores; though we sleep at night a few hundred feet or a few acres apart, white and Negro dwell in essentially separate worlds. On this basic separation, the whole structure of Southern society is erected. Remove these pillars, tamper with them, undermine them, and the structure falls.

There are reasons for this separation. The experience of generations has demonstrated that in the South (whatever may be true of the Negro in urban areas of the North and West) the Negro race, as a race, has palpably different social, moral, and behavioral standards from those which obtain among the white race. After generations of rising income, better housing, expanded education, improved communications—after years of exposure to the amenities of civilization from which the Negro might profit by example —one out of every five Negro children in the South today is the product of illicit sexual union. The rate of Negro illegitimacy, indeed, is not improving: It grows worse. That necessary program of the professional welfare worker, styled "aid to dependent children," is very largely aid to Negro bastardy. When mention is made of these facts, the South's critics are wont to make two answers, one irrelevant, the other immaterial. The first is that "white slaveowners had Negro mistresses in Civil War days," which has nothing to do with the illegitimate offspring of Negro men and Negro women today. The second is that "low income and poor living conditions" account for it all, which is no answer to the palpable fact that an illicit pregnancy results not from a low paycheck. That such promiscuity must result in widespread venereal disease is as predictable as the case histories are demonstrable. In areas where Negroes make up less than one-third of the population, colored patients account for 90 per cent of all reported syphilis and gonorrhea.

The undisciplined passions which find one outlet in sex find another in crime. There were in Richmond in one recent year thirty-four homicide cases; of these, twenty-eight were killings of Negroes by Negroes. It was a wholly typical year. The evidence in these cases follows a constant and elemental pattern: The unfaithful woman, the triflin' man; a fancied wrong, a bloody vengeance. Yet as often as not, the evidence discloses no reason —no white man's reason—that conceivably might justify murder: A quarrel, not even a serious quarrel, and suddenly a razor flashes or a gun explodes. Monday morning in a Southern police court is a strange recital of Saturday nights in Jackson Ward. What was the fight about? The defendant is mystified. "Me and Willie," he says winningly, "we's friends, judge." And where is Willie? He lies in St. Philip Hospital, with forty-two stitches in his side.

Out of this milieu come Negro children—and often one's heart goes out to them—pathetically ill-equipped to compete with whites in public school education. As the experience of every Southern State has made vividly clear, Negro pupils as a group are woefully less educable than white pupils as a group. In reading, in reasoning, in educational aptitudes, in all the standardized tests that produce an "I.Q.," the median Negro at the eighth grade level customarily is found nearly three school years behind the median white. Is this deficiency to be blamed upon the quality of the South's Negro schools? Basically, the same findings have turned up in the District of Columbia, where a bounteous Congress in times past provided the finest Negro schools on earth.

These are harsh truths to set down. They are truths that Negro leaders seldom bring themselves to face. The figures, says Roy Wilkins of the NAACP, shrugging his well-groomed shoulders, are only "statistics." Yet these and many other considerations go far to explain the insistence—the determination—of white parents in the South to maintain separate schools. They feel, and with some reason, that when the white people of a community have provided 95 per cent of the funds for a Negro school, the white people have done all that should be required of them. To be told that not only their taxes, but their sons and daughters also, must be subrogated to the Negro—this is to ask of them something they ought not to be compelled to surrender.

What is it that the Court, in effect, has commanded the South to give up? It is no less than this: The basis of the South's society, the vitality of her culture. The Southern States are ordered, subject to drastic penalties, either to abandon their schools or to breach the immutable law by which the South's character has been preserved. And the law is this: That white and black cannot come together, as equals, in any relationship that is *intimate, personal and prolonged.* And when to these guides are added further considerations of sex, and of compulsion, the barrier is complete.

Now, the only place—*the only place*—in which this line is threatened, and the law put in jeopardy, is in the field of public education. On buses, in elevators, in crowded stores, in arenas and ballparks, the races may be brought intimately together as equals, but the relation is not personal and it is not prolonged. On inter-racial boards and commissions, the relationship is of equals, it may be personal, it often is prolonged; but it is not intimate.

Public schools are something else entirely. Here the relationship is keenly intimate—as intimate as two desks touching, as two toilets in a washroom. It is personal—the social mingling of boys and girls in the same school activities. It is prolonged over the twelve-year period of elementary and secondary education. In the formative years of adolescence, the element of sex arises in its most dangerous and experimental form. And whether school attendance is required by law, or dictated by society, the element of compulsion exists. To integrate the schools of the Southern States thus is to demand a relationship forbidden by the mores of the people; and it is to risk, twenty or thirty years hence, a widespread racial amalgamation and a debasement of the society as a whole. This the Southern States are determined to resist. They will resist for a long, long time.

One thing more should be said: The South does not regard itself, in maintaining school separation, as "indicting a whole race." Every informed Southerner acknowledges—*of course*he acknowledges—that there are first-class Negro communities and hosts of decent, respectable, law-abiding Negro teachers, bankers, students, artisans, and servants. *The South knows this better than any other region.* For in no other part of the country has the industrious Negro advanced further, or progressed more rapidly, or been more rewarded for individual merit than in the Southern States. The pity is that the industrious are relatively so few.

It is objected, to be sure, that the South's system of segregated education imposes unfairly upon the individual Negro student of unusual brilliance and capacity; it is urged that constitutional rights are individual, that they attain to each citizen in his own right, and not as part of any group. The objection would have validity only if constitutional rights were absolute rights, to be exercised by each person at his unfettered will. But no right is an absolute right. The right of free exercise of religion does not sanction the handling of rattlesnakes at a Faith Healers' public meeting. The right of free speech, as Holmes once observed, gives no man the right to cry "fire!" in a crowded theater. The right to bear arms embraces no right to conceal a pistol. Rights are individual and "absolute" only as their exercise may act upon others.

So far as the Negro student's "right" is concerned in the matter at bar, he holds no *right* to an education at public expense. No one does. The maintenance of public schools is a State and local function, to be continued or abandoned as the people choose. In the field of education, all that is required is that, if public education be provided, substantially equal opportunities shall be made available to all. The Fourteenth Amendment, to quote Thomas Cooley, never was intended to require "that every person in the land shall possess the same rights and privileges as every other person." The amendment, he said, "contemplates classes of person, and the protection given by the law is to be deemed equal, if all persons in the same classes are treated alike under like circumstances and conditions both as to privileges conferred and liabilities imposed."(45)

In following Cooley's maxim in the establishment of separate schools, the Southern States do not comprehend that they are doing anything more than is done in countless other fields. Automobile liability rates, for one example, commonly are fixed by public bodies at a higher level for drivers under twenty-five than for drivers over that age. Does this imply that *all* drivers under twenty-five are unusual accident risks? Of course not. Thousands of responsible teen-agers are better drivers than their fathers. What the rates reflect is the demonstrably higher incidence of accidents among younger drivers *as a class*. Is there at Harvard or Chicago some precocious lad, a Phi Beta Kappa and still in his teens? And is he denied the "right to vote," though his intellectual qualifications are infinitely superior to those of the ward boss? It is because those under twenty-one, *as a class,* are treated differently from their elders in matters of franchise. The whole structure of our income tax, for another example, rests upon class legislation. The class of individuals earning $100,000 a year fares far differently from the class earning $3,000, yet it is not contended that "equal protection" is violated in tax rates that vary from 20 per cent to 90 per cent.

Finally, it may be recalled that in Minnesota, whence cometh Senator Humphrey and other strong advocates of integration, there once was a law which prohibited the sale of alcohol to Indians. Was this an unconstitutional imposition upon the red man? Not so, said the Supreme Court of Minnesota:

> The statute is a police regulation. It was enacted in view of the well-known social condition, habits and tendencies of Indians as a race. While there are doubtless notable individual exceptions to the rule, yet it is a well-known fact that Indians as a race are not as highly civilized as white; that they are less subject to moral restraint; more liable to acquire an inordinate appetite for intoxicating liquors, and also more liable to be dangerous to themselves and others when intoxicated.(46)

And Minnesota's Chief Justice Rudkin added that the law was in no way "arbitrary class legislation." The difference in conditions between "Indians as a race and the white race," he said, "constitutes a sufficient basis of classification."

Perhaps Senator Humphrey would insist that Minnesota was wrong then (this was 50 years ago), in legislating as to Indians and liquor, and declare the Southern States equally wrong today, in legislating as to Negroes and schools. Perhaps he would and perhaps some would agree. Yet is it not equally conceivable that the people of Minnesota, in their wisdom, were right then, and that the South is equally right today? Is it not possible that in each generation, in each society, the people who compose it and give their character to its institutions are themselves the best judges of the prudent exercise of the regulatory powers with which they invest their government? Surely that has been the rule of "police power" through our history. It is a good rule now.

Notes

4

The Transcendent Issue

ONE WAY or another, for good or ill, the South will live through the problems created by the Court's opinion of May 17, 1954. As this is written, a sort of lull has come upon us. What began as a sudden and violent storm in the summer of 1954 has settled down in the late autumn of 1956 to slow and steady rain. Now and then, as in Sturgis and Clinton, lightning flashes; but over most of the South, the people have closed their shutters. From time to time we even talk of other things. Many of us had begun to think we never would. Compulsory race-mixing is progressing gradually through the border States, but the movement has not advanced to the point that a permanent pattern has emerged. Here and there in the cities, as in Washington, it seems evident that integration in schools in time will result in greater segregation of neighborhoods. In most urban areas, the prospect is that the court's sociological objective will be effectively frustrated simply by the unwillingness of a free people to be coerced into a pattern of living unacceptable to them. It is far more difficult to venture predictions as to rural areas, especially in the Deep South. Here the melancholy prospect is that, driven to a hard choice of bitter alternatives, many counties will abandon public education altogether. Compelled finally to choose between mixed schools and no schools, they will take no schools—that is to say, no public schools, for white parents, at least, may be expected to form private educational corporations and educate their children without tax support.

What happens to the Negro children in these rural areas? God knows. The question troubles the thoughtful Southerner far more than it appears to trouble either the Supreme Court or the NAACP. For the Southerner, accustomed to looking after the Negro, cannot adjust easily to the idea of leaving the Negro to fend for himself. Neither can he adjust, at all, to the idea of an intimate social relationship with individuals of a different race. He is apprehensive for what the future holds; the tradition of defeat lies within him. Yet he is patient, and he feels that time is on his side; one Reconstruction ended when his foes wore out, and he is possessed of that tradition too.

Probably it is fruitless to speculate too much on the road ahead. The South sees itself, in all this, as a child of Atreus. Endlessly it travels down the corridors of time, pursued like Orestes by fates it could not have prevented and cannot possibly deter. The essence of Greek tragedy, Richmond Lattimore once wrote, is not that it pits right against wrong, but that it pits right against right. This is the core of the South's tragedy also, for the white Southerner, enmeshed in the web of a dual society, is not insensitive to the aspirations and desires of the Negro people with whom he dwells in so intimate a remoteness. He recognizes a certain rightness in Negro demands; and until the school crisis arose, the white South had been moving in a score of areas toward relief of grievances: In the hiring of Negro police and Negro firemen, in the election of Negroes to public office, in the gradual relinquishment of Jim Crow laws in places of public assembly, in the opening of new job opportunities to Negroes equally with whites—in these and in other fields, without the compulsion of court proceedings, perceptible changes were taking place. Many other changes, not involving the intimate, personal, and prolonged relationship of equals, could have been foreseen.

Now, with the Negro's threat to the white South's schools, the customs that had been yielding have stiffened again. Until May of 1954, Southern cities were building public swimming pools, white and Negro, with public funds; that work has stopped. The increasing pattern, in both urban areas and in rural communities, is one of private recreational corporations, financed by individual families for their own use only. In one Virginia community, which had for years operated a municipal golf course with certain days set aside for Negro use, Negroes sued for completely integrated operation. The suit never even came to trial. The course simply was sold the next day, in fee simple, to a fraternal lodge; and the sign at the front gate now reads, For Members and Guests only.

A fair presumption is that the future holds a great deal more of this; and the two societies, black and white, instead of coming closer together in the South, will go more rigidly apart. If private school operation is found to work successfully in rural communities where public schools are abandoned, a number of fair-sized cities may also switch to a private operation. The South's determination to preserve its essential institutions, and to stave off what is seen as the catastrophe of racial amalgamation, grows daily more resolute.

Yet the fate of the schools, or the fate of the resisting Southern States, is not the most vital issue here at bar. Far transcending any question of race or instruction, is the greater conflict over the stability of the Constitution. The nature of education in the South is primarily the South's concern; but the nature of the Union—the relationship of the States to their Federal government—vitally concerns the American republic as a whole.

The decision in the school segregation cases was not the first major usurpation of power by the Supreme Court in the postwar period. It was merely the most flagrant. It is keenly important to understand that the trend put newly in motion under Vinson's Court continues, at increasing speed, under Warren's administration. If States outside the South are to comprehend the peril before them, they would do well to look beyond the frontal fight of *Brown vs. Board of Education* to the flanking decisions in which State powers also are being steadily destroyed.

Half a dozen such mileposts will suffice to mark the way. They involve drillers for oil off California and the Gulf; a small trucker in Pennsylvania; a railwayman named Hanson; a Communist, Steve Nelson; a professor of German, Harry Slochower; a thief named Griffin. Their cases are all a part of the ending and beginning.

Let us go back, then, to June 23, 1947. That was the day the Court, by a 6-2 decision, undertook on its own fiat to seize for the United States government "the lands, minerals and other things of value" underlying the Pacific Ocean along the coast of California for a distance three miles seaward from the ordinary low water mark. This was the first "Tidelands" case.(47)

As Justice Black defined the issues, four principal questions were presented. On each of these, the majority of the Court ruled flatly against the position taken by California.

California first raised an entirely proper question of jurisdiction. Under the Constitution, the Supreme Court has original jurisdiction "in all cases . . . in which a State shall be Party." It was California's contention, and an entirely sound one, that this was no "case" in the plain and commonly understood meaning of the word. This was not a legal proceeding in which one State, or two States or three States, had filed suit against the State of California. It was, in brief, a proceeding in which the national government was suing a State; but if it ever crossed the minds of Justice Black that the Supreme Court, as the judicial branch of the national government, was not the proper forum in which to hear the national government's claim against a State, no such concern may be found in his opinion. He was satisfied that the "conflicting claims of governmental powers," which is to say, conflicting claims of Federal and State officials, should be disposed of by the Federal Court.

California contended, secondly, that if one State were to be sued by all the States collectively, then some such authorization for the proceeding should be shown. Had Congress authorized the suit? Plainly, Congress had not. Indeed, Congress twice had refused to grant such authority to the Attorney General (in 1937 and 1939), and in 1946 had approved a joint resolution (vetoed by the President), in which the States were given quitclaim to the three-mile belt. The majority of the Court ruled that the Attorney General, whether or not Congress approved, had sufficient authority vested in his office to bring the action anyhow.

The third contention went directly to the merits. California marshaled impressive testimony to show that the original thirteen States, as an attribute of sovereign power, held title to a three-mile belt of land underlying the Atlantic Ocean on their borders. As a State admitted on an equal basis, California properly claimed an equal sovereign privilege. Further, California was able to show that this ownership of coastal areas had been plainly acknowledged by the Congress at the time California was admitted to the Union; by definition nailed into her State Constitution, California had fixed her boundaries three English miles from shore. All this made no impression on Mr. Justice Black. He expounded the right and responsibility of the United States Government "as a member of the family of nations" to maintain national security in coastal waters. (Not one living soul ever had challenged this right or responsibility). Mr. Justice Black waxed eloquent on the conduct of foreign relations. (No one had questioned the conduct of foreign relations). And then in a complete *non sequitur,* Mr. Justice Black concluded that the only question to be decided was "whether the State or the Federal government has the paramount right and power to determine in the first instance when, how, and by what agencies, foreign or domestic, the oil and other resources of the soil of the marginal sea, known or hereafter discovered, may be exploited." His conclusion, of course, was that "California is not the owner of the three-mile marginal belt along its coast, and that the Federal government rather than the State has paramount rights in and power over that belt, an incident to which is full dominion over the resources of the soil under that water area, including oil."

Finally, the Court majority swept aside California's defense that over a long period of years, agents and agencies of the Federal government repeatedly had acknowledged California's dominion over the off-shore properties. The Federal government, indeed, had acquired title to some of this land *by deed from the State;* the Department of the Interior had denied coastal leases on the ground that California owned the lands. Perhaps officials of the government *had* been negligent, Mr. Justice Black agreed. It did not matter. Federal ownership was not to be denied "by the ordinary court rules" of civil cases. Mr. Justice Black would make up new rules. The majority ordered an appropriate decree prepared.

Two members of the Court dissented. It is important to note what they said. Mr. Justice Reed faced the issue squarely. When the Union was formed, he said, "*the original States were sovereignties in their own right,* possessed of so much land underneath the adjacent seas as was generally recognized to be under their jurisdiction." (Emphasis supplied.) Thus, he said, "the original States owned the lands under the seas to the three-mile limit." And because California entered the Union on an equal basis, California "had the same rights bordering its littoral." Then he pointed out what Black had been unable to see:

This ownership in California would not interfere in any way with the needs or rights of the United States in war or peace. The power of the United States is plenary over these undersea lands precisely as it is over every river, farm, mine, and factory of the nation.(48)

Mr. Justice Frankfurter, as is his custom, approached the matter obliquely. He laid down the view, in his dissenting opinion, that *no one* owned the land: It was simply "unclaimed land." He said this:

Of course the United States has "paramount rights" in the sea belt of California—the rights that are implied by the power to regulate interstate and foreign commerce, the power of condemnation, the treaty-making power, the war power. We have not before us the validity of the exercise of any of these paramount rights. Rights of ownership are here asserted—and rights of ownership are something else. Ownership implies acquisition in the various ways in which land is acquired—by conquest, by discovery, and claim, by cession, by prescription, by purchase, by condemnation. When and how did the United States acquire this land?"(49)

The answer, Mr. Justice Frankfurter implied on the following page, was that his colleagues had acquired it just now. They had undertaken to establish a federal interest "by sliding from absence of ownership by California to ownership by the United States."

Three years later, on June 7, 1950, the Supreme Court continued its slide. Louisiana had resisted the Court's usurpation of her property, just as California had resisted. The Court paid as little attention. Louisiana raised the same jurisdictional objection; this time the Court did not even discuss the point. Louisiana had conceded, willingly, that the Federal government had "paramount rights" in the property "to the extent of all governmental powers existing under the Constitution, laws and treaties of the United States." But the Court majority, speaking this time through Mr. Justice Douglas, was not interested in rights acquired pursuant to the Constitution, laws and treaties. The Court was busy forging new law of its own. Thus, "the claim to our three-mile belt was first asserted by the national government" (this, in the teeth of overwhelming evidence to the contrary), and "the marginal sea is a national, not a State concern." Louisiana had not denied it. But "concern" is one thing, Louisiana argued, and ownership quite another. Mr. Justice Douglas could not see the distinction. The California case, he held, was controlling.(50)

On the same day, again speaking through Douglas, the Court brushed aside a solid case established by the State of Texas for continued ownership of her own offshore land. Texas had an even better case than California and Louisiana could offer, for there was no question—rather, it was thought there was no question—of the terms and conditions under which the independent Republic of Texas had been annexed to the United States a century before. Mr. Justice Douglas handsomely agreed that prior to admission, Texas was an independent nation which possessed "not only full sovereignty over the marginal sea but ownership of it, of the land underlying it, and of all the riches which it held." But when Texas became a State, by his reasoning, the "equal status" doctrine came to apply in reverse: Texas did not gain what other States had claimed; it lost what it clearly had.

Justices Reed and Minton balked at this decision, and Mr. Justice Frankfurter demurred. (Because Jackson and Clark took no part, several billion dollars in property thus were wrested from Texas by four men alone—Vinson, Black, Douglas, and Burton.) Reed emphasized that the doctrine of "equal footing," as he saw it, always had been held to embrace only political rights. The majority, he said, was interpreting the doctrine so as "to take away from a newly admitted State property that it had theretofore owned." Mr. Justice Reed, joined by Mr. Justice Minton, could see "no constitutional requirement that this be done." The needs of defense and foreign affairs, Reed observed, cannot transfer title to an ocean bed "any more than they could transfer iron ore under uplands from State to federal ownership."

In his own separate dissent, Mr. Justice Frankfurter remarked briefly, with a strange deference to *stare decisis*—a deference not to be visible four years later—that "time has not made the reasoning of *United States vs. California* . . . more persuasive, but the issue there decided is no longer open for me." In the Texas case, he was satisfied that the lands in controversy "were part of the domain of Texas when she was on her own." And he added: "The court now decides that when Texas entered the Union she lost what she had and the United States acquired it. How that shift came to pass remains for me a puzzle."(51)

There was no puzzle here. The United States never acquired the contested coastal lands by any valid process. A majority of the Supreme Court simply seized them. And it took a subsequent act of Congress to put them back again.

The Court has not been content to claim fields of oil; in the steady move toward aggrandizement of the Federal government, it has claimed whole fields of law also. This is the process of "preemption," by which the Court holds that where Congress has occupied one area of government regulation, the States may not be there too: Congress has "preempted" the field as a whole.

Cases from Pennsylvania, Illinois, and Texas may illustrate the point. In December, 1953, the Court decided the case of *Garner, et al, trading as Central Transfer Co. vs. the Teamsters Union.*(52) Here the facts were that four of Garner's twenty-four employees belonged to the Teamsters Union. His was a small operation; he had no objection if all the workers joined—it was a matter for the workers themselves to decide. This attitude of indifference was not the sort of cooperation the union thought sufficient, so the union began picketing Garner's terminal. There was no controversy, no labor dispute, no strike —but the effect of the picketing was to destroy Garner's business. His volume of freight declined by 95 per cent as shippers' unionized drivers refused to cross the picket line. In desperation, he obtained an injunction from a State court under the Pennsylvania Labor Relations Act, to put an end to the picketing. The Pennsylvania State Supreme Court, by a divided ruling, reversed the trial court and ordered the injunction dissolved. It was the appellate court's view that Garner's grievance fell within the purview of the National Labor Relations Board, and hence that a State remedy was precluded.

With this viewpoint, the United States Supreme Court agreed. It affirmed the Pennsylvania Supreme Court. Clearly, said Mr. Justice Jackson, Congress had vested the NLRB with power to hear such complaints. The only question was whether a State, through its own courts, could extend its own form of relief also. He thought not. Congress had confided primary interpretation of "unfair labor practices" to a specific and specially constituted tribunal of the Federal government. "Congress evidently considered that centralized administration of specially designed procedures was necessary to obtain uniform application of the substantive rules and to avoid diversities and conflicts likely to result from a variety of local procedures and attitudes toward labor controversies." That is a long and misty sentence, but the meaning emerges on examination: In the eyes of the Court, uniformity is the thing; conformity is to be revered; diversity and variety (which is to say, locally administered law to deal with local problems) must be deplored. Mr. Garner's plea in this case was that a local Pennsylvania court could act promptly—it could provide a timely remedy which might mean something; a petition to the NLRB might languish for months while his business declined to nothing at all. Mr. Garner's small problem moved the Court not at all. "A multiplicity of tribunals and a diversity of procedures are quite as apt to produce incompatible or conflicting adjudications as are different rules of substantive law." This doubtless was a great solace to the plaintiff.

Attention also may be directed to another opinion affecting the trucking industry, just one year later. In this case,(53) Attorney General Latham Castle of Illinois argued vehemently in behalf of an Illinois statute which permitted the State itself to crack down effectively on willful violators of the State's load limit law. It was shown that a truck line repeatedly had ignored the State's limits on gross weight and axle weight. When all else failed, the State sought to prohibit the trucker from using State highways for a period of 90 days. But the trucking company contended—successfully—that the State of Illinois could not thus deny him the use of Illinois highways. When he operated in interstate commerce, said the trucker, he operated under the protecting wings of the Interstate Commerce Commission and the Federal Motor Carrier Act.

Quite true, said Mr. Justice Black for a unanimous Court. When Congress adopted a "comprehensive plan" for regulating the trucking industry in interstate commerce, the "former power of States over interstate motor carriers was greatly reduced." No power at all, said the Court, was left in the States to determine what carriers could or could not operate on their highways in interstate commerce. The carriers might violate every law on the books of the State; they might ruin highways with excessive gross loads; they might weaken bridges by repeated strain upon them. And what could the States do? The States could rely upon "the conventional forms of punishment"; the States could plead with the ICC; but the one punishment that would mean the most—to deny a carrier the use of State roads until he behaved—that punishment the States could not impose. Only an agency of the Federal government could do that.

One of the most startling encroachments by the Court upon State powers occurred on April 2, 1956, when the Court, by a 6-3 decision, dismissed Pennsylvania's prosecution against Steve Nelson, an admitted Communist.(54) Here the issue, again, was one of Federal preemption—or as Mr. Chief Justice Warren termed it, the "supercession" of State laws. Nelson had been convicted in the trial courts of Pennsylvania for violation of a State anti-sedition act. There he had been sentenced to prison for twenty years, and fined $10,000 plus court costs of $13,000. The State Supreme Court had reversed the conviction on the single, helpless ground that the United States government had so preempted the field of sedition law that Pennsylvania's State law, covering the same offenses, lacked validity.

Mr. Chief Justice Warren and his colleagues upheld this view. Surveying all the acts passed by Congress against sedition, the Court majority found the conclusion "inescapable that Congress has intended to occupy the field of sedition." Taken as a whole, said Warren, the several Federal acts "evince a congressional plan which makes it reasonable to determine that no room has been left for the States to supplement it." And among other things, in the majority's view, to permit State prosecution of sedition would be to present "serious danger of conflict with the administration of the Federal program." Quoting from the Garner case, Warren found it exceedingly unwise to permit the States "to exercise a concurrent jurisdiction in this area." The States, he feared, might get in the way: That would never do. Therefore, "since we find that Congress has occupied the field to the exclusion of parallel State legislation, that the dominant interest of the Federal government precludes State intervention, and that administration of State acts would conflict with the operation of the federal plan, we are convinced that the decision of the Supreme Court of Pennsylvania is unassailable."

Three members of the Court—Reed, Burton, and Minton— dissented strongly. The effect of the majority opinion, they noted, was to void the anti-sedition laws of forty-two states, Alaska, and Hawaii. Reed pointed out the flat and obvious fact (immediately attested by an outraged Howard Smith of Virginia) that Mr. Smith's act never had "specifically barred the exercise of State power to punish the same acts under State law." On the contrary, the act had been inserted routinely in Title 18 of the United States Code, which begins with an encompassing recital that "Nothing in this title shall be held to take away or impair the jurisdiction of the courts of the several States under the laws thereof."

But in the minority's view, there was something more important than this: "We are citizens of the United States and of the State wherein we reside, and are dependent upon the strength *of both* to preserve our rights and liberties." (Emphasis supplied.) Both State and Federal legislative bodies, said the minority, may enact laws for mutual protection unless Congress has otherwise provided. In the instant case, there was not a scintilla of evidence to suggest that State anti-sedition acts had hampered or embarassed the Department of Justice. On the contrary, the Department of Justice itself had avowed that "the administration of the various State laws has not, in the course of the fifteen years that the Federal and State sedition laws have existed side by side, in fact interfered with, embarrassed or impeded the enforcement of the Smith Act." No better disclaimer could be suggested.

Nevertheless, the decision of the majority, of course, prevailed. And in one contemptuous sweep of the pen, the concept of a *union of States* was further degraded. The States were left, gratuitously, with a meaningless power to punish acts calculated to overthrow a State government, but they were denied (in the language of the dissenting opinion) their plain right "to punish local acts of sedition, nominally directed against the United States."

It may be argued, perhaps, that the importance of the Nelson case has been over-inflated. Few of the forty-two States with anti-sedition acts ever had launched so much as a single prosecution under their laws. Yet from a broader standpoint, the importance of the majority opinion in the Nelson case scarcely can be overemphasized. In the very act of adopting their anti-sedition acts, the States had exercised some of the old and far-off prerogatives of *sovereign* States. The significance of the Nelson opinion is to be found in the fact that the Court recognized these stirrings of sovereign spirit, and set about to quash them. In the eyes of the Court majority, for the States to punish sedition would be for States to behave as States. And this, above all things, the States must never be permitted to do.

Just three weeks after the Nelson opinion came down, the cause of States' rights was even more seriously crippled by the court's ruling in *Griffin vs. Illinois*.(55) Curiously, this far-reaching 5-4 decision of the Court claimed little attention. A more damaging blow against the concept of State sovereignty seldom has been struck.

Here the facts were that two men, Griffin and Crenshaw, had been convicted in Illinois of armed robbery. Immediately after their conviction, they had filed a motion in the trial court demanding that a stenographic transcript of the record be furnished them without cost. The State law on the subject limited such free transcripts to pauper defendants placed under sentence of death; in all other cases, State law permitted appeals to be taken simply on a narrative record of alleged errors in the trial, plus a complete bill of exceptions. The petitioners argued that lack of a stenographic transcript would prevent them from the "equal protection of the law" that might be enjoyed by wealthy defendants in the same position.

The court majority, speaking through Mr. Justice Black, sympathetically agreed. For the purposes of their decision, the majority assumed that the two felons, if only they had a transcript, could point to reversible error in the trial court proceedings. This was unthinkable: "In criminal trials a State can no more discriminate on account of poverty than on account of religion, race or color. . . . There is no meaningful distinction between a rule which would deny the poor the right to defend themselves in a trial court and one which effectively denies the poor an adequate appellate review accorded to all who have money enough to pay the costs in advance. . . . There can be no equal justice where the kind of trial a man gets depends on the amount of money he has."

Four members of the Court concurred in that opinion, and Mr. Justice Frankfurter uneasily concurred in the result. It is a frequent device of Mr. Justice Frankfurter to join what he deems to be the right side, but for his own reasons. Here he pointed out that obviously, the State of Illinois could not be held responsible for the varying economic conditions of defendants in criminal trials. And "of course," he said, a State in providing for appellate review, "need not equalize economic conditions." After all, said Mr. Justice Frankfurter, thoughtlessly demolishing the whole spurious structure of his four colleagues' opinion, "a man of means may be able to afford the retention of an expensive, able counsel not within reach of a poor man's purse." These are contingencies of life "which are hardly within the power, let alone the duty, of a State to correct or cushion."

Four members of the Court, to judge by the tone of their dissenting opinions, were sorely concerned at the majority's palpable intrusion upon long-established prerogatives of the States. In a beautifully reasoned dissenting opinion, Mr. Justice Harlan pointed out, gravely, that the effect of the majority's opinion would be to create "a host of problems affecting the status of an unknown multitude of indigent convicts." The record, he insisted, was too obscure possibly to justify a decision of so sweeping an impact. Apart from this, he sharply attacked the majority's plea that "the poor" and "the rich" must fare equally. This declaration, he said wryly, "hardly sheds light on the true character of the problem confronting us here." What was the true character? Let Mr. Justice Harlan speak at length. What he has to say bears on many other constitutional problems under review in these notes:

. . . no economic burden attendant upon the exercise of a privilege bears equally upon all, and in other circumstances the resulting differentiation is not treated as an invidious classification by the State, even though discrimination against "indigents" by name would be unconstitutional. Thus, while the exclusion of "indigents" from a free State university would deny them equal protection, requiring the payment of tuition fees surely would not, despite the resulting exclusion of those who could not afford to pay the fees. And if imposing a condition of payment is not the equivalent of a classification by the State in one case, I fail to see why it should be so regarded in another.

Thus, said Mr. Justice Harlan, the crucial point was not whether the State had created legal disabilities on the basis of a reasonable classification, but rather—and this is vital—whether the State possibly could be condemned as unreasonable for failing "*to remove natural disabilities."* (Emphasis supplied.) For his own part, Mr. Justice Harlan was not ready to label this "discrimination" on the part of Illinois.

Mr. Justice Harlan concluded by commenting that the legal matter at issue was primarily a question of the criminal procedure provided by Illinois in her own State courts. "Whatever might be said were this a question of procedure in the Federal courts," he added, "regard for our system of federalism requires that matters such as this be left to the States." He thought it beyond the province of the Court to tell Illinois that it must provide the procedures thought desirable by the majority.

Harlan then joined three other members of the Court (Burton, Minton, and Reed) in a separate dissenting opinion emphasizing further objections to the opinion of the majority. The four agreed that free stenographic transcripts in criminal proceedings may constitute "a desirable social policy," but—let this be noted carefully—

what may be good legislative policy is not necessarily required by the Constitution of the United States. Persons charged with crimes stand before the law with varying degrees of economic and social advantage. Some can afford better lawyers and better investigations of their cases. Some can afford bail, some cannot. Why fix bail at any reasonable sum if a poor man can't make it?

The Constitution requires the equal protection of the laws, but it does not require the States to provide equal financial means for all defendants to avail themselves of such laws.

Mr. Justice Black's opinion . . . *is an interference with State power for what may be a desirable result, but which we believe to be within the field of local option.* [Emphasis supplied.]

Is it necessary, really, to add anything to this final sentence?

Brief review of two or three more cases will suffice to suggest the trend against the States. We may study with profit the Phillips case, decided June 7, 1954.(56) Here a majority of the Court seized from the Southwestern States the State control of natural-gas production and gathering which historically they had exercised. As Justices Clark and Burton emphasized pointedly in a dissenting opinion, the Natural Gas Act specifically provided that the act was not to apply to the production or gathering of natural gas. "Language could not express a clearer command," they remarked, yet the majority had rendered the language "almost entirely nugatory." And they added:

By today's decision, the Court restricts the phrase "production and gathering" to "the physical activities, facilities, and properties" used in production and gathering. Such a gloss strips the words of their substance. If the Congress so intended, then it left for State regulation only a mass of empty pipe, vacant processing plants and thousands of hollow wells with scarecrow derricks, monuments to this new extension of Federal power. It was not so understood.

Rather, said the dissenting justices, the legislative history of the act, the demonstrable interpretation placed upon the act by the Federal Power Commission, and the obvious prospect that Federal regulation would seriously interfere with State conservation practices—all these considerations established a clear intent on the part of Congress that production and gathering of gas should be exempt from Federal control. "Observance of good faith with the States," said the minority, "requires that we interpret this Act as it was represented at the time they urged its enactment, as its terms read, and as we have, until today, declared it, viz., to supplement but not to supplant State regulation."

It is a long jump from the natural gas fields of Texas and Oklahoma to the academic groves of Brooklyn College, New York City, but let us take it. On September 24, 1952, the Internal Security Subcommittee of the Senate Committee on the Judiciary held hearings in New York. One of the witnesses was Dr. Harry Slochower, associate professor of German. He had been identified by another witness as a member of the Communist party, prior to 1941. Dr. Slochower was asked about this. And Dr. Slochower declined to answer. He took the Fifth Amendment. He lost his job. He sued to regain it.

To understand the legal point at issue, it is necessary to look much farther back, to the time of the Samuel Seabury Report of 1932. That was an investigation into graft and corruption in the municipal government of New York City. During the course of that investigation, a number of city employees were summoned, only to assert before the frustrated Mr. Seabury that a truthful answer to the questions he propounded them might tend to incriminate them, and therefore they declined to answer. In his final report, Mr. Seabury recommended an ordinance that in 1938 became Section 903 of the Charter of the City of New York. It provided that whenever an employee of the city utilized the privilege against self-incrimination in order to avoid answering questions relating to his official conduct, "his term or tenure of office or employment shall terminate and such office or employment shall be vacant." As the highest courts of New York were to interpret the provision, any employee who invoked the FifthAmendment was to be deemed, as of that moment, to have tendered his resignation.

Thus when Dr. Slochower, in September of 1952, declined to answer questions concerning his membership in the Communist party in 1940 and 1941, Section 903 came into play. He had been twenty-seven years at Brooklyn College. Abruptly, his tenure terminated. It was the professor's contention that this summary dismissal (for he did not agree that he had "resigned") was an infringement upon his guarantee of due process of law. By a 5-4 division, the Supreme Court of the United States accepted his contention. In the eyes of Mr. Justice Clark and his colleagues on the majority, New York City's Section 903 was a perversion of a constitutional right. The charter section, as they saw it, served to impute "a sinister meaning" to the exercise of the Fifth Amendment; it was as if New York City regarded this privilege "as equivalent either to a confession of guilt or a conclusive presumption of perjury." Appalled at this thought, the majority denounced "the heavy hand" of New York's arbitrary statute, and ordered the lower court reversed.(57)

Reed, Burton, and Minton dissented in vigorous terms. They commented that the majority's opinion "strikes deep into the authority of New York to protect its local government institutions from influences of officials whose conduct does not meet the declared State standards for employment." Then they made clear what the majority had been strangely unable to see—that New York's Section 903 established not a judgment of disloyalty, but a standard of propriety. The city "does have reasonable ground to require its employees either to give evidence regarding facts of official conduct within their knowledge or to give up the positions they hold." An employee who lacks candour, in the eyes of New York, is "a person unfit to hold certain official positions." New York had decided "it did not want that kind of public employees," and the dissenting three added: "We think New York had that right."

Mr. Justice Harlan, dissenting separately, boiled the bone of contention down still further: "In effect, what New York has done is to say that it will not employ teachers who refuse to cooperate with public authorities when asked questions relating to official conduct. . . . I think that a State may justifiably consider that teachers who refuse to answers questions concerning their official conduct are no longer qualified for public school teaching, on the ground that their refusal to answer jeopardizes the confidence that the public should have in the school system."

But, again, the majority prevailed. As this is written, the supreme law of the land (which is to say, the Constitution, which is to say, the Constitution rewritten by the Supreme Court of the United States) thus limits a State in fixing the standards of propriety a State may demand of its own public servants in matters of their official conduct.

For a final case (and especially because of some things Mr. Justice Douglas had to say), we may consider the Court's unanimous action in ordering Robert L. Hanson, Horace A. Cameron, Harold J. Grau, and others, to join an AFL railway union in order to hold their jobs on the Union Pacific Railroad. Messrs. Hanson, Cameron, and Grau did not want to join the union. They regarded themselves not only as citizens of the United States, but also as citizens of Nebraska, and they pinned their faith in a provision of the Nebraska Constitution: "No person shall be denied employment because of . . . nonmembership in a labor organization." But the Union Pacific entered into a union shop contract, and the objecting employees were ordered to join the union within sixty days or lose their jobs, their seniority, their pensions, and their other rights. The Nebraska Supreme Court held that they could not be forced into a labor organization against their will—that they had a right to work, under the Nebraska Constitution, which could not be denied them.

But the Supreme Court of the United States held otherwise. Speaking through Mr. Justice Douglas, the Court declared that Congress had acted within its powers in 1951, when it wrote a sanction for union shop contracts into the Railway Labor Act. The Court was careful to point out that its decision was directed to one narrow issue: If the objecting workers found their political freedom infringed, or other personal liberties denied them by union coercion, they might return to the courts for redress. But the union shop clause was an "allowable" provision for facilitating interstate commerce, and the court would not interfere.

Why would the Court not interfere? Let us pay close heed:

The question is one of policy with which the judiciary has no concern. . . . Congress, acting within its constitutional powers, has the final say on policy issues. *If it acts unwisely, the electorate can make a change.* The task of the judiciary ends once it appears that the legislative measure adopted is relevant or appropriate to the constitutional power which Congress exercises. The ingredients of industrial peace and stabilized labor-management relations are numerous and complex. They may well vary from age to age and from industry to industry. What would be needful one decade might be anathema the next. *The decision rests with the policy makers, not with the judiciary.*(58) [Emphasis supplied.]

A citizen of Virginia may perhaps be forgiven some bitterness, as he reads over this pious dictum from the Supreme Court of the United States. "The question is one of policy with which the judiciary has no concern." For nearly ninety years, it has been universally understood that the maintenance of racially separated public schools was a matter of State policy; that the ingredients of this problem were "numerous and complex"; that they varied from age to age and from State to State; that what a State regarded as necessary in one decade it might abandon in the next. And all such decisions had been held to rest with the policy makers, not with the judiciary. For if the policy makers acted unwisely, *the electorate could make a change.* But the electorate cannot touch a supreme judiciary appointed for life.

"We have come full circle," said Mr. Justice Frankfurter, concurring in the Hanson case. He was reflecting that in the Adair case (1908), the Court had upheld the "right" of railway companies to deny work to a union man. Now, in 1956, they had upheld the right of unions to deny work to a non-union man. From sanctioning the "yellow dog" contracts of the turn of the century, the Court had come to bless the union shop contracts of our own time. The former were now universally condemned. But the latter? The latter had become "allowable." And no State could be permitted to say otherwise.

These cases (and countless others could be cited) define a trend: The deification of the Federal government, and the steady stultification of the States. They point to a problem, a great and difficult constitutional problem. It certainly is not a new one. It existed in Jefferson's day, and in Calhoun's, and for that matter, in Teddy Roosevelt's also. It is to preserve unto the States, for good or ill, that which is rightfully the States', and to guard with equal jealousy that which is the proper function of the Federal government. Yet to an ominous degree, the problem now is far more acute than it has ever been before. When Jefferson and Calhoun were protesting most furiously, enormous areas of public administration remained to the States; even at the turn of the century, States' rights still held some meaning. Now, month by passing month, the States steadily are being stripped of the last of their sovereign powers—not by their own wish, as expressed through constitutional amendment—but by judicial usurpation. Those who had conceived the Constitution itself to be the supreme law of the land are now told, imperiously, that today's opinions of the Court, however palpably in violation of the Constitution these mandates may be, are supreme above all things. We are told to bow and fawn before a judicial oligarchy which has asserted unto itself powers as arrogant as those of any tyrant: "This is compassionate," says the Court, "*therefore* it is constitutional." This, in the Court's view, is socially desirable; therefore the Court will make it the law. And to resist, as in Clinton, is to travel in handcuffs to Knoxville, there to face prosecution for contempt.

The end of this process is the corruption of a constitutional Union, by judicial fiat, into a consolidated government in which the States are mere political dependencies. The end is a centralization of all meaningful powers in the hands of Federal authority. And so long as the constructions placed by the Court upon the Constitution are agreeable to one-third of the House of Representatives, plus one, timely remedy cannot even be found in constitutional amendment.

The remedy lies—it must lie—in drastic resistance by the States, *as States,* to Federal encroachment. "If those who voluntarily created the system cannot be trusted to preserve it," asked Calhoun, "who can?" The checking and controlling influence of the people, exerted as of old, through their States, can indeed preserve the constitutional structure. The right to interpose the will of the sovereign people, in order that the evils of encroachment may be arrested, once more can be exerted toward the preservation of a Union and the dignity of States.

A long time ago, a great Virginian had this to say: "So far as our [Federal] government is concerned, I venture to predict that it will become absolute and irresponsible, precisely in proportion as the rights of the States shall cease to be respected and their authority to interpose for the correction of Federal abuses shall be denied and overthrown."(59)

Abel Parker Upshur's prediction of 1840 has been grimly fulfilled. The American people have lost sight of the old concept that the States, as such, form the balance wheel—in Upshur's term, "the only effectual check upon Federal encroachments." We have lived to see the truth of his prophecy, that the danger to constitutional separation of powers is "not that the States will interpose too often, but that they will rather submit to Federal usurpations, than incur the risk of embarrassing the government, by any attempts to check and control it."

The States have submitted too long to Federal usurpations. At their grave peril, they can submit no longer. Through every device of interposition they can bring to bear—political, legislative, judicial—once more they must invoke their sovereign powers to insist that Federal encroachments be restrained. Thankfully, half-a-dozen Southern States—Alabama, Georgia, Mississippi, North Carolina, South Carolina, Virginia—have spoken through their legislatures against the Court. The people of Texas and Arkansas, by referendum, have approved the doctrine of interposition. Southerners in Congress have made their position clear in a ringing Manifesto, denouncing judicial legislation. The Supreme Court of Georgia has not hesitated to rebuke the Supreme Court in Washington: "We will not supinely surrender sovereign powers of this State."(60) This awakening of State sovereignty, met at first with mockery and ridicule, will be met next with all the hostility and force that centralists can bring to bear. If this force is to be overcome, the conservatives of this Republic—those who believe in limited government and in individual responsibility—must be prepared to risk those sacrifices which the hour demands. Others have risked them before—a Matthew Lyon in Vermont, a Michael Bright in Pennsylvania, a Troup in Georgia, a Calhoun in South Carolina, a Booth in Wisconsin, a Sullivan in Ohio, a Young in Minnesota. These and many others, strong in their convictions, have dared to hold their ground when lesser men surrendered.

Yet there is one thing more that also must be done. The States, for their own preservation, must insist upon shouldering those proper responsibilities they too often have abandoned by default. The people will not let the States sink into the insignificance of mere administrative suburbs if the great value and wisdom of local government can be impressed upon them.

"The people's highest interest," said Upshur, "is at home; their palladium is their own State governments. They ought to know that they can look nowhere else with perfect assurance of safety and protection. Let them then maintain those governments, not only in their rights, but in their dignity and influence. Make it the interest of their people to serve them: an interest strong enough to resist all the temptations of Federal office and patronage. Then alone will the voice [of the States] be heard with respect at Washington; then alone will their interposition avail to protect their own people against the usurpations of the great central power. It is vain to hope that the federative principle of our government can be preserved, or that any thing can prevent it from running into the absolutism of consolidation, if we suffer the rights of the States to be filched away, and their dignity and influence to be lost, through our carelessness or neglect."

Thus Abel Parker Upshur ended his essay in 1840. And thus, well over a century later, this one ends also.

NOTES

Part 1. The Sovereign States
Section 1. *The Beginnings*

1. Jonathan Elliot (ed.), *The Debates in the Several State Conventions on the Adoption of the Federal Constitution* (Washington, 1836), III, 301.
2. Capitalization, punctuation, and spelling have been followed in this section as in Charles E. Tansill (ed.), *Documents Illustrating the Formation of the Union* Washington, 1927).
3. Paul Leicester Ford (ed.), *The Writings of Thomas Jefferson* (New York, 1882-99), V, 461.
4. *Ware v. Hylton*, 3 Dallas 199 (1796).
5. *McIlvaine vs. Coxe's Lessee*, 4 Cranch 209, 212 (1808).
6. *Sturges vs. Crowninshield*, 4 Wheaton 122 (1819).
7. *Graves, et al, vs. New York, ex rel O'Keefe*, 306 U.S. 466, 488 (1939).
8. James Brown Scott, *Sovereign States and Suits Before Arbitral Tribunals and Courts of Justice* (New York, 1925), pp. 37ff.

Section 2. *The State*

9. *Texas vs. White*, 7 Wallace 700 (1869).
10. *Cherokee Nation vs. Georgia*, 5 Peters 1 (1831).
11. Scott, *Sovereign States*, p. 18.
12. John Taylor, *New Views on the Constitution* (Washington, 1823), Section VIII.
13. See *Cohens vs. Virginia;* 6 Wheaton 264, "The people made the Constitution, and the people can unmake it. It is a creature of their will and lives only by their will." Then Marshall fell into obvious error when he continued: "But this supreme and irresistible power to make or to unmake resides only in the whole body of the people, not in any subdivision of them." The fallacy in this statement is made apparent by the merest reading of Article V. The power to make or unmake does not lie in 51 per cent of the people, or in any fraction of the whole body of the people. It lies in not fewer than three-fourths of the States.
14. William Blackstone, *Commentaries on the Laws of England* (Philadelphia, 1825) I, 33-56.

Section 3. *The Articles of Confederation*

15. *Penhallow vs. Doane*, 3 Dallas 54, at 92-93 (1795).
16. The text here is from Tansill (ed.), *Documents on the Formation of the Union,* pp. 27-37.
17. Interestingly enough, the Articles contained a clause that many a Postmaster General, laboring against his postal deficit, must often wish had been retained in the Constitution itself: The Congress was to exact "such postage on the papers passing through the same as

Flex your rights

"I hereby invoke and refuse to waive all of the following rights and privileges afforded to me by the U.S. Constitution:
-I invoke and refuse to waive my Fifth Amendment right to remain silent. DO NOT ASK ME ANY QUESTIONS.
-I invoke and refuse to waive my Sixth Amendment right to an attorney of my choice. DO NOT ASK ME ANY QUESTIONS WITHOUT MY ATTORNEY PRESENT.
-I invoke and refuse to waive all privileges and right pursuant to the case Miranda v. Arizona. DO NOT ASK ME ANY QUESTIONS OR MAKE ANY COMMENT TO ME ABOUT THIS DECISION.
-I invoke and refuse to waive my Fourth Amendment right to be free from unreasonable searches and seizures. I DO NOT CONSENT TO ANY SEARCH OR SEIZURE OF MYSELF, MY HOME, OR OF ANY PROPERTY IN MY POSSESSION. Do not ask me about my ownership interest in any property. I DO NOT CONSENT TO THIS CONTACT WITH YOU. If I am not presently under arrest or under investigatory detention, please ALLOW ME TO LEAVE.
-Any statement I make, or alleged consent I give, in response to your questions is hereby UNDER PROTEST AND UNDER DURESS and in submission to your claim of lawful authority to force me to provide you with the information.
-If you have no Probable cause or RAS and you continue to hold me against my will, you have now opened the door for a Chapter 42 US Code 1983 Civil Rights Law Suit.

am I free to go"?

www.ingramcontent.com/pod-product-compliance
Lightning Source LLC
Chambersburg PA
CBHW071756200526
45167CB00017B/318